Wandering WebWood

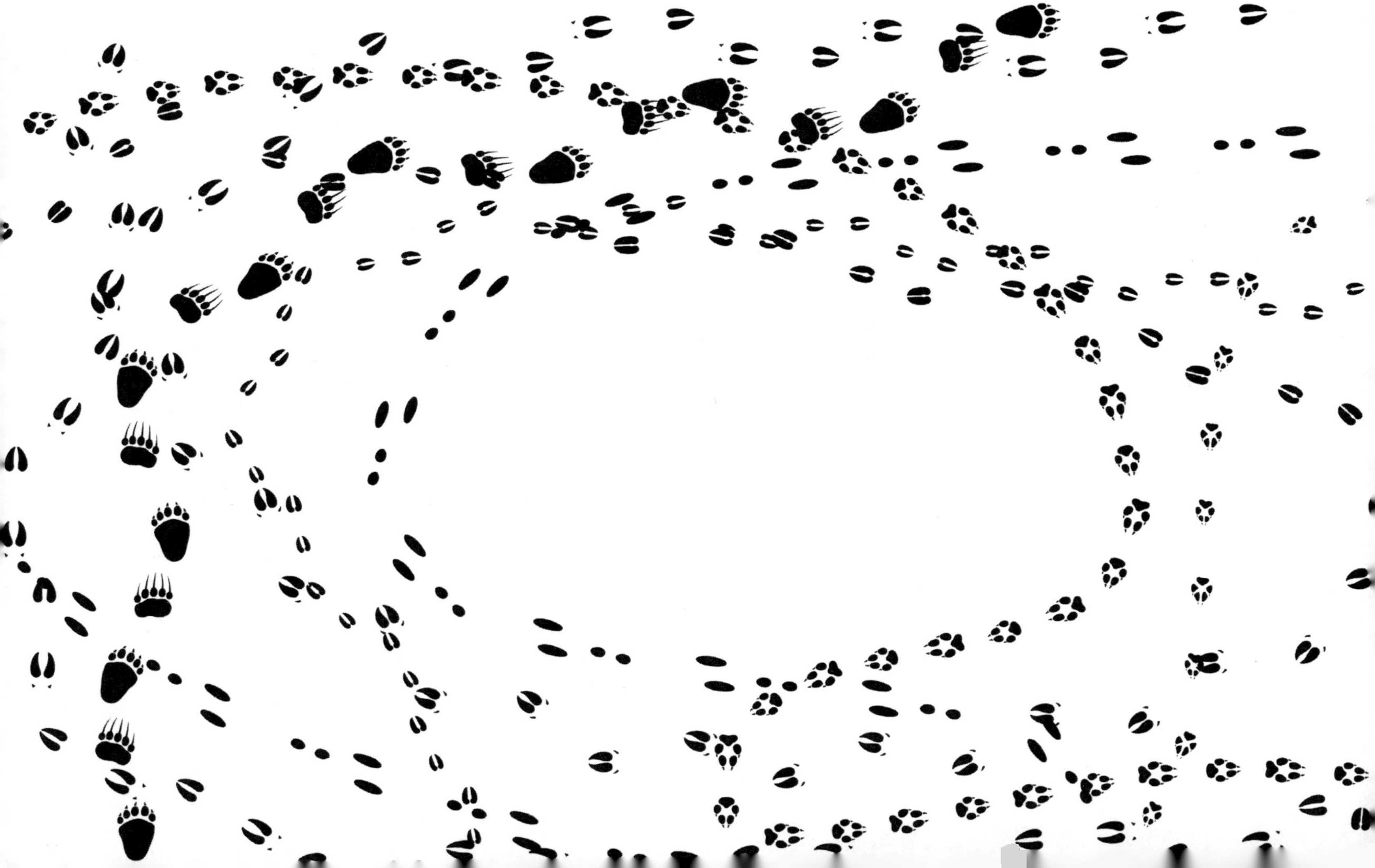

Also by Larry Weber:

Minnesota Phenology

Webwood

Butterflies of the North Woods

Spiders of the North Woods

Fascinating Fungi of the North Woods

Teaching Phenology-Based Science

A Guide to Web-Watching

Awesome AutWin

In a Patch of Goldenrods

Backyard Almanac

365 Days of Northern Nature

Through the Year with Northland Nature

Wandering WebWood

Stay-At-Home Nature During the Pandemic

Larry A. Weber

North Star Press of St. Cloud
www.northstarpress.com
Since 1969

North Star Press of St. Cloud Inc.
www.NorthStarPress.com

ISBN: 978-1-68201-158-4

First Edition

Printed in the United States of America

Titles set in Fredericka the Greatest and American Typewriter, Text set in Times New Roman

Photography by Larry Weber, except for for a few done by Mark Sparky Stensaas.

Dedication:

To my companion for life, Frannie; taking many of the walks with me. And to all the critters of WebWood; making life here so interesting. And to the many medical workers who helped all of us to cope with the COVID pandemic.

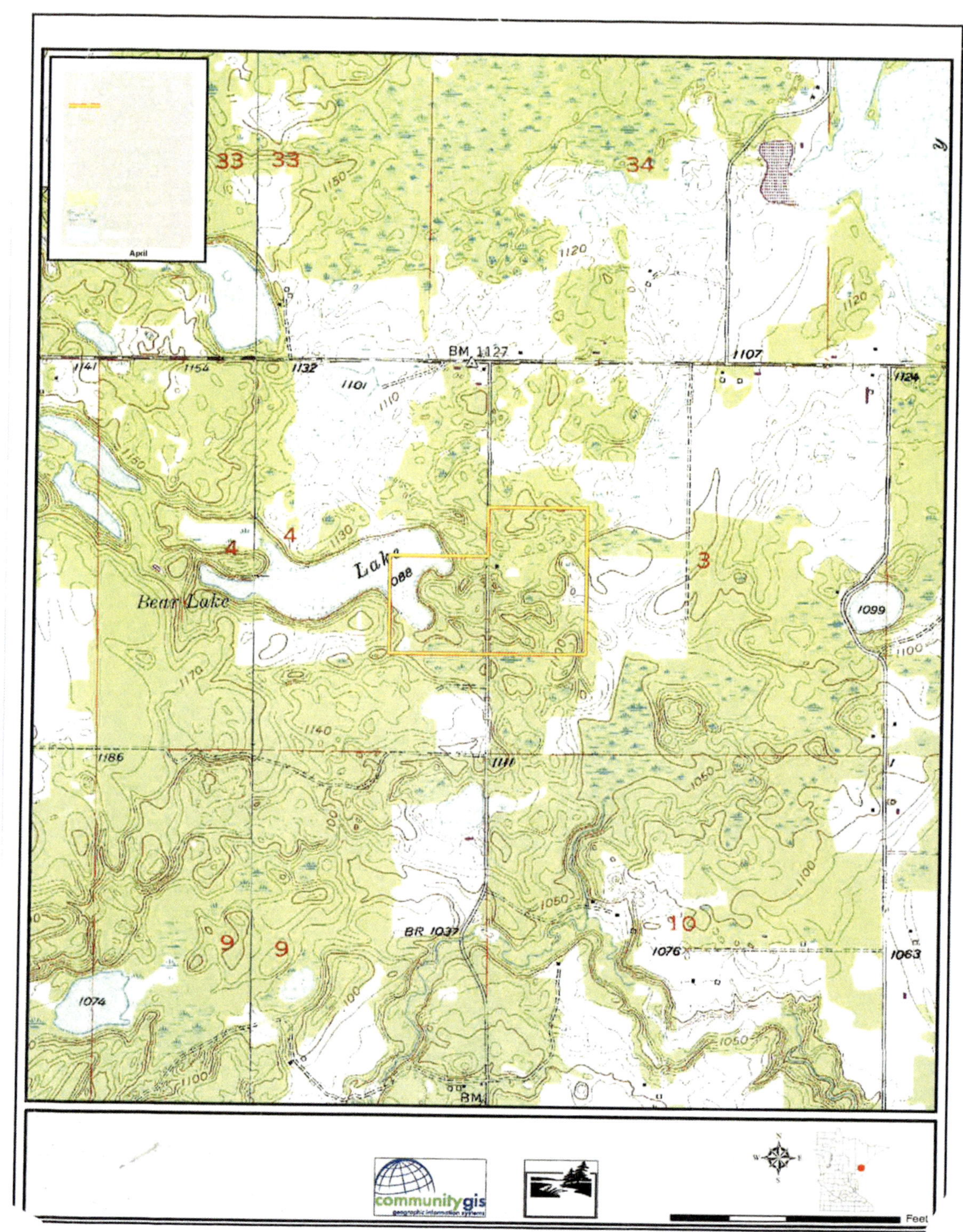

A topographic map showing WebWood and a two-mile radius of the surrounding areas.

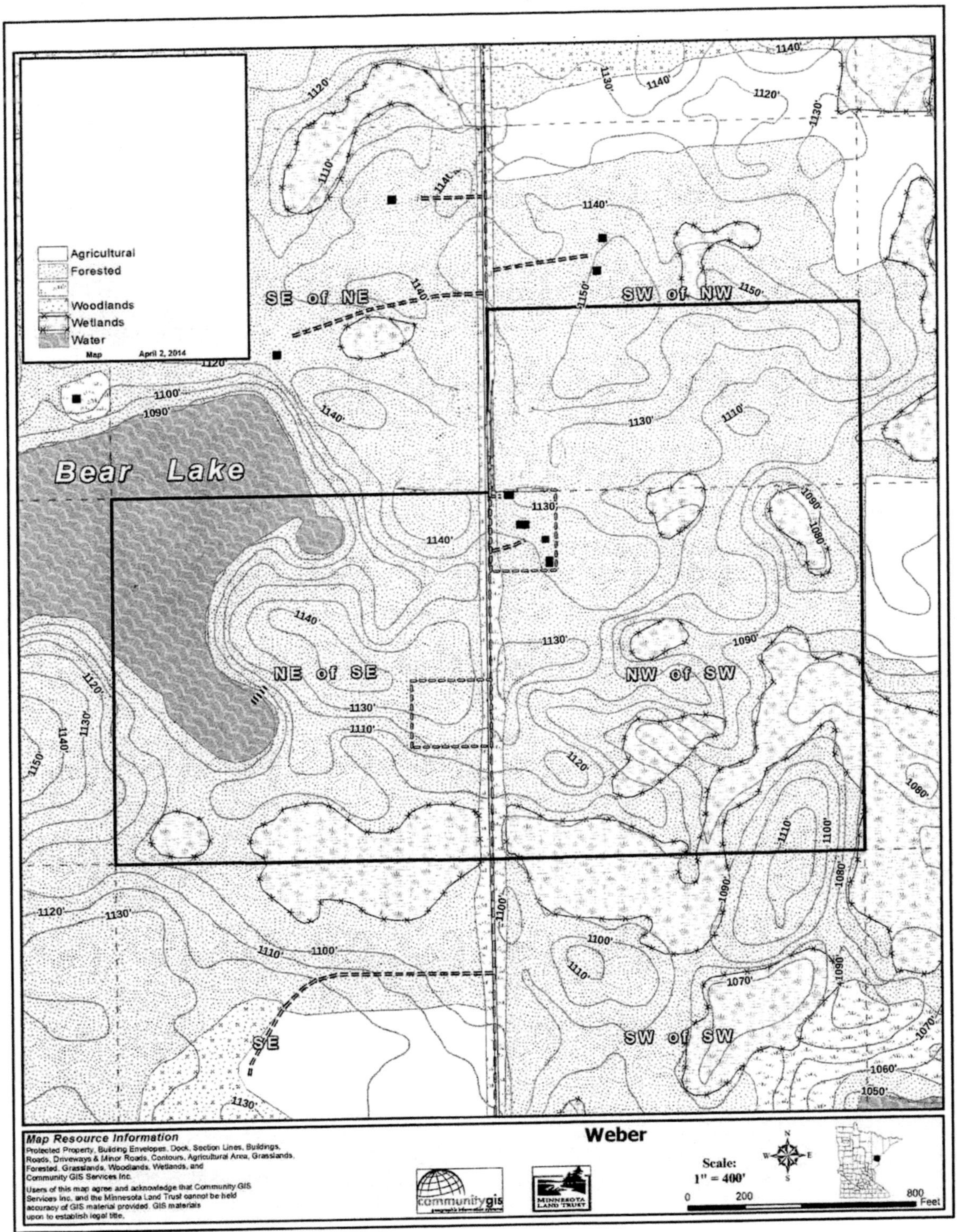

A closer look at WebWood: 40 acres to the west (left) of the road, and 60 acres to the east (right).

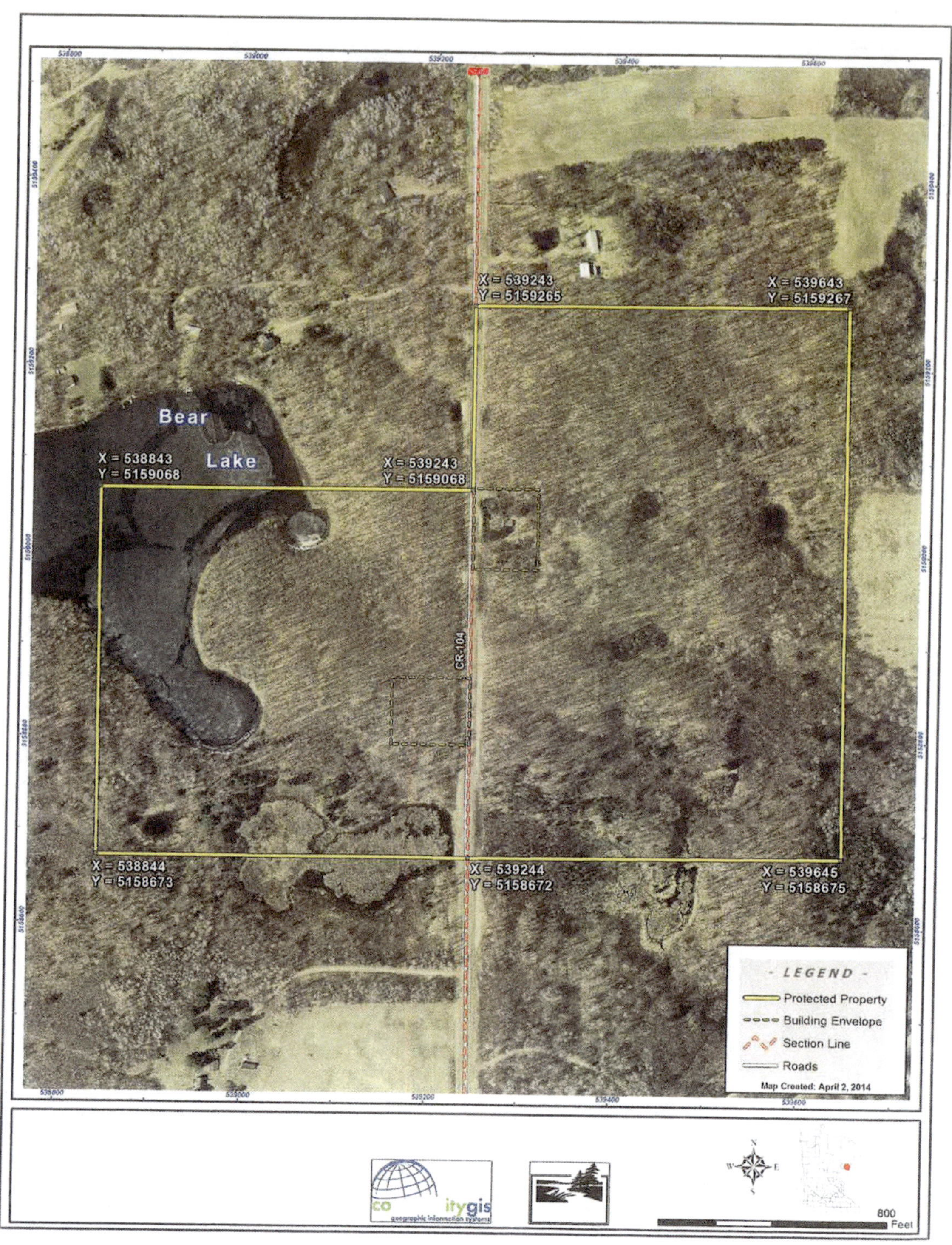

Aerial Photo of WebWood taken in early spring.
Note the ice on the lake and green foliage on trees has not yet grown.

Introduction

Like many others, when word spread of the COVID-19 outbreak that morphed into a pandemic, our lives were suddenly more restricted. We shopped fewer times; more done from home. We learned to communicate via zoom, stayed at home more, and wore masks when going anywhere. What followed was a couple of years where we seldom left the immediate area; remaining in the routes of a few counties in Minnesota and Wisconsin. Despite the self-imposed isolation, I decided that I could continue to write my weekly Nature column for the Duluth News-Tribune and do a few speaking programs.

Nearly all I wrote about weekly over a period of three years was Nature as seen nearby; following the seasons. Nearby Nature proved to be very interesting and during daily walks, I noticed much; never being without a seasonal topic to write about.

This book is a compilation of 150 columns that I wrote for my newspaper column, Northland Nature, during this pandemic time. The daily walks were filled with discoveries and nearly every column was written as I witnessed these phenological happenings near at hand.

My place of residence during this confined time is the same place that I lived before and after. Home was previously a farm, but has regrown to be as it is now. I call it a "forested former farm" and from the beginning, we have named it WebWood. The original forty acres has grown to become one hundred. Except for constructing a barn, building a dock in the adjacent lake and trails through the woods, we have not altered the forested site. I walk frequently on the trails, but also along the road and often in the open field.

There was always much to see over the three years of "stay-at-home" Nature; 2020-2022. To paraphrase the great naturalist John Burroughs "If you want an interesting walk in Nature, take the same walk that you took yesterday and do so again tomorrow." Nearby Nature can be, and usually is, very interesting. Nature is Here and Now.

Larry A. Weber
January, 2023

WebWood

Normal Annual Temperature: 40.5° F
Normal Annual Precipitation: 31.18 Inches
Normal Annual Snowfall: 90.3 Inches.

Average Temperature: 41.3° F

Highest Temperature (July 2): 93° F

Lowest Temperature (Feb 12): -13° F

Total Precipitation: 21.26 Inches

Total Snowfall: 83.6 Inches

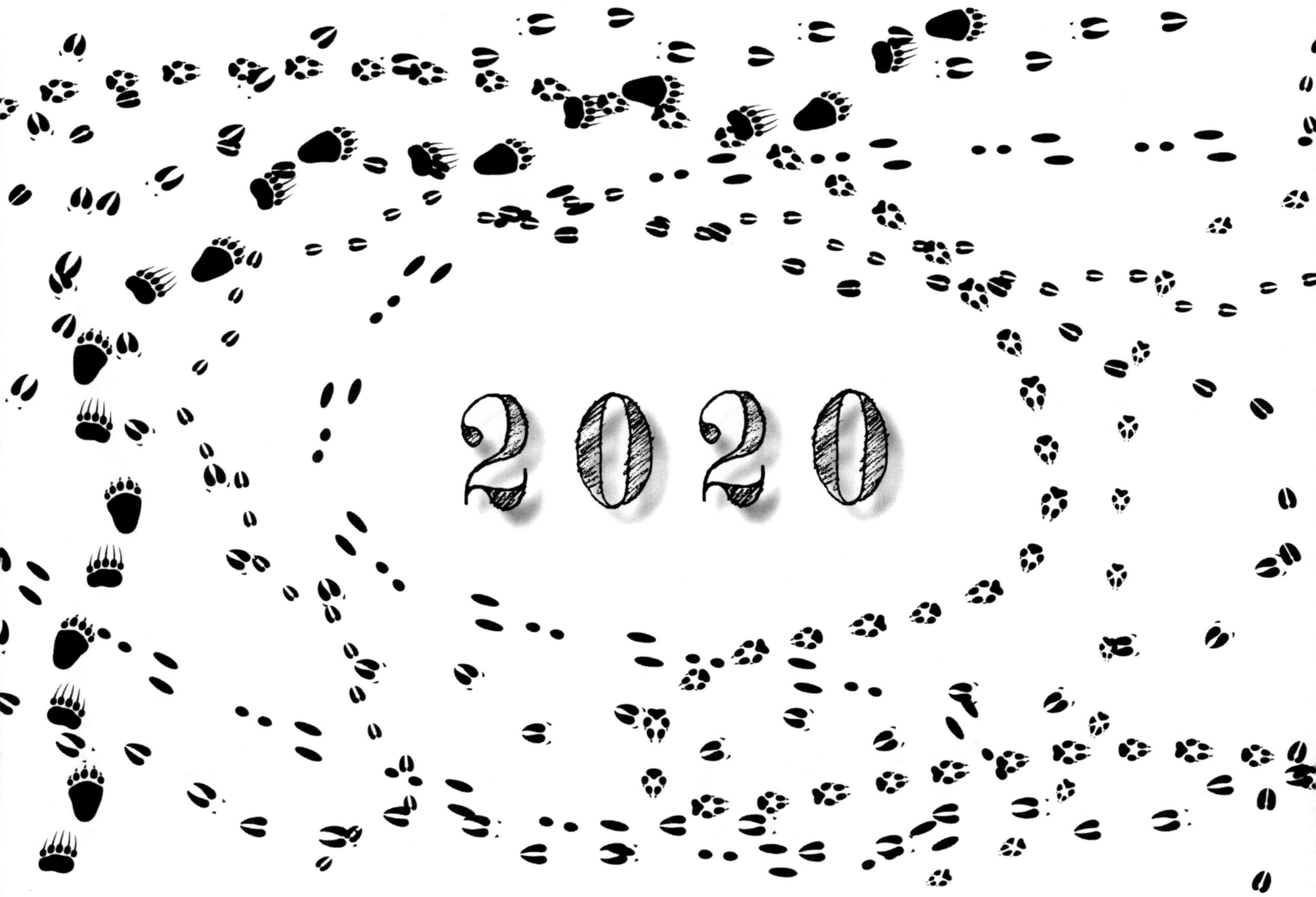
2020

First Quarter

January 5, 2020

Discovering a "Lodge Island"

Each winter, I like to get out to visit a variety of ponds. Like everything else in this January landscape, they are snow covered. The snowpack has settled a bit in recent weeks, but is still ample. Such a snow covering is a good sign for these small ponds. This snowpack coats the ice that formed here weeks ago and serves as a good preparation for the coming spring. We are a long way from April, but this winter scene will provide for moisture when melting time comes. The subsequent vernal ponds are vital for the growth and development of myriads of aquatic critters that have some or all of their lives here. And so, I like to see if winter is being good for these ponds and swamps.

Whether walking, snowshoeing or skiing, I try to go to about ten ponds. Some have water only intermittently; drying in the warmth of summer. Others retain their water from melting and rains of spring. As much as I can, I'll go onto these bodies of water. On the surface of the snow along the way, I see that a few persistent leaves have fallen and many birch seeds are scattered on the snow. At the base of some trees, I see chips of wood that tell of the work of pileated woodpeckers in the trunks above. And a red squirrel has left a pile of middens; mostly spruce cones, where it had arboreal meals.

I walk onto an old beaver pond. The years-old dam is still able to retain the present water level. Earlier in the season, I found tracks here of fox, coyote, raccoon, weasel and vole. Now the deep snowpack hides their movements beneath or discourages travel above.

This beaver pond is larger than the other ponds that I visit. I cross the ice to explore more of this scene. In the center of the pond is the old beaver lodge. It has been a few years since the aquatic rodents were living here and now it appears to be a snow-covered mound. But when I take a closer look, I see that there is more here.

With no beavers to maintain the lodge, opportunistic plants have taken advantage of this place to live; and I see plenty. Three kinds of trees stand up from the lodge; speckled alder, white birch and a willow. Nearby is a growth of raspberries. Also rising above the snow cover are some plants that flowered last summer and fall and now hold seeds. I find plants of goldenrod, aster, joe pye weed, water horehound, curl dock and stinging nettle. Some are more than five feet tall. A couple of aquatic plants have taken advantage of this place to live and I see cattails and rushes (Scirpus). Non-flowering plants that are usually not associated with aquatic sites, ferns of several species, are present as well. I locate lady fern, wood fern, sensitive fern and marsh fern.

In just the short time that I stopped to look at this snow-covered lodge, I have noted the presence of more than a dozen kinds of plants that are now using this site for their homes. And I'm sure there are unseen animals here too. The build-up of sticks by beavers a few years ago has provided a place for seeds to fall and be able to grow. The former beaver lodge, no longer a home for the makers, has become a well-populated "lodge island" in this pond. The next step in succession of this aquatic site has begun.

January 12, 2020

Lichens Respond to Winter Rain

Similar to the weather patterns of the last several months, December of 2019 showed quite a difference in the first half and the second half. During the early weeks, we had an average temperature of about thirteen degrees with seven days of subzero. Along with this cold, we received nearly twenty inches of snow. Going through a change in the second half, the temperature was close to ten degrees warmer and about eight inches of snow fell. A reading of nearly forty degrees on December 22 was the high for the month. The ten days following the winter solstice averaged twenty-eight degrees with lots of clouds, mist, wet snow and rain; plenty of precipitation.

Winter is not only our coldest season; it is also our driest. December typically has only about 1.2 inches of precipitation for the whole month. Cold days are dry and snow that falls has little moisture content. But not so during the end of this December. Though warmer with less snow, there was more precipitation. We seldom get rains at this time, but during the two days of December 28 and 29, rains gave as much moisture as we usually get for the whole month. It brought interesting changes. Snow on the ground became wet and sticky. Slush and puddles formed on the roads and moving about was a bit difficult for us and others who live through these conditions.

While walking among the slush and puddles on the road on this wet thirty-degree winter day, I noticed fewer tracks; critters less active. This weather can cause harm for wildlife that live under the snowpack. Here they find shelter in tunnels and homes. Wet snow can ruin this. But as I walked and looked at the woodland trees, I saw that some growths on their bark were taking advantage of this wet time; the lichens.

Lichens are a strange and hardy form of life that abounds in the northland; especially on trunks and branches of trees. Many lichens grow on soil and rocks; now under the snowpack. Others remain above the snow, on the tree bark; right out in winter weather. They may appear to be no more than gray, green, blue-green or yellow patches on the trees; almost looking like dried paint. But living here, lichens are able to cope with winter. A closer look at lichens reveals that they consist of a combination of algae and fungi. These two organisms live in a mutualistic relationship that allows them to thrive. Algae are green; with chlorophyll, and are able to make food in the presence of sunlight. The filamentous fungi cells will hold needed moisture. Though winter days may have plenty of sunlight, they are very dry and lichens go into a dormant phase; unless there is a change from the normal weather.

And precipitation did come during a couple late December days. The fungi component of the lichen growth did its part and absorbed the available moisture. I could see as I passed by that the wet lichens looked larger and more colorful. Several species grow here, but most obvious were common greenshield lichen (Flavoparmelia), gray shield lichen (Parmelia) and yellow sunburst lichen (Xanthoria). All were coated with available rain drops allowing their bodies to enlarge and show good color. It was also interesting to note that when the cold and dry weather returned, the lichens went back to their dormant winter phase; waiting for the next damp opportunity. But for a short time in late December, the local lichens thrived in the moisture.

January 19, 2020

Maybe It Is the Winter of Blue Jays

Like many in the Northland, I maintain bird feeders in winter. Sitting back and looking out on chilly mornings at activities of the feathered neighbors as they breakfast on sunflower seeds and suet is an AM delight. Typically, birds are the same kinds each day. Abundant black-capped chickadees mix with white-breasted and red-breasted nuthatches as they dine on seeds. The three (sometimes four) species of woodpeckers; downy, hairy and red-bellied, with an occasional pileated, select the suet. Together they reveal small, medium and large sizes. Nearly every day, a group of about a dozen turkeys comes walking from the woods to the feeders. They seem to prefer a diet of both sunflower seeds and corn. These large birds are often joined by a flock of rather big songbirds feeding with them; blue jays. It is the turkeys and jays that have been most numerous so far this winter. A surprise is what I have not seen at the feeders; finches.

Recently, I participated in the local Christmas Bird Count to find out what else has been seen in the region. Teaming with several others, we searched woods, waterways, fields, yards and feeders for a day. Compiling the results later, we noted that about thirty kinds of birds had been observed by the counters. This number is near average for this site. It included bald eagle, barred owl, wild turkey, ruffed grouse, a duck (common goldeneye in open water on the St. Louis River) and many kinds of songbirds. Some were represented by only one or two individuals: junco, shrike, mourning dove, brown creeper and cardinal. Most were in numbers beyond this; but not so numerous. What about the finches? We did see three kinds of finches; goldfinch, purple finch and pine siskin; none in large flocks. But I was glad that they did appear. A few birds did show up in good amounts; most notable, blue jays. They outnumbered their larger cousins, crows and ravens. They were behind only the abundant black-capped chickadees in how many were present. Apparently, my seeing a dozen blue jays at the feeder each day was being noted by others as well. We have a long way to go, but with fewer finches, this could be the "winter of blue jays".

Blue jays are well known in the region. They are a type of corvid; related to crows and ravens (and further north and west; gray jays and magpies). Being nearly a foot long, they are larger than most all the feeder or yard birds. Back and tail appear blue with black bars and white patches; they are quite easy to discern. Above the head is a stately crest, while a black necklace blends with a white underside. Like other corvids, blue jays are adaptable; diverse diets and homes. They have done well in the region and have learned to live and breed among people. Their loud "jay, jay…" calls are well known. And later in the year, we'll hear their more musical "weedle-eedle" sounds.

Blue jays may be migratory or permanent in winter. Flocks of migrants are seen passing through spring and fall. But others decide to stay. These wintering birds may be from further north or ones that live here. They may be adults or young of the year. But each winter, some blue jays remain during the cold. This year, jays' numbers may be up. With fewer finches at feeders now (this could change), I'm glad to watch these crested birds in what may be the "winter of blue jays".

January 26, 2020

A Winter Look at Evening Primrose

By the time we get to late January, the amount of daylight is noticeably getting longer. We have about nine and a half hours of light; quite expanded from the eight and a half at the solstice of a little over a month ago. Rapidly as we end this month and enter February, the light will continue to lengthen. This does not necessarily translate into warmer temperatures yet; that will be later. Late January can have some of our coldest days of the whole winter. Thanks to the substantial snowfall of early December, we also have a deep snowpack at this time.

Besides watching birds that usually come to the bird feeders, I take walks regularly in this season. Feeder watching is done mostly without going outside; but though I won't see as many birds at feeders while walking along trails and roads, these sites provide for other seasonal happenings. This winter has been a marvel for seeing tracks in the snow. They began with the movements of wildlife active in the snows of November. Snow not so deep and not so cold, critters were very active; leaving a plethora of tracks. After the heavier snowfalls, their movements changed, but with some looking, I was able to see them. This was followed by warming that made for wet snow; subsequent freezing provided a crusted surface. In this setting, animals that were struggling in the deep snow now could go over it. Many walkers and hoppers were able to stay above the crust. But there is plenty more to see in the winter landscape besides active birds and abundant tracks.

Sticking up through the snowpack of mid-winter are stalks of wild flowers that bloomed last summer. It is not unusual to find goldenrods, asters, thistles, tansies, fireweeds and milkweeds above the snow. Though plants have mostly died above ground, two parts remain alive in winter; one below, one above. Below, the roots are still alive of these mostly perennial flowers. And out above the snow many plants hold living seeds that could grow in the coming warmer days. Looking more closely, I see goldenrods and asters with fluffy seeds; to disperse in winter winds. Those of fireweeds, milkweeds and thistles are mostly gone by now. In swamps, cattails are also open for wind travel. The ubiquitous and not always appreciated tansies do well by just dropping their seeds. Another flower here in the snow is evening primrose.

They were part of the roadside bouquet of last July with milkweeds and fireweeds. Unlike these that had purple flowers, evening primroses opened four large yellow petals that bloomed at night; hence the name. (Instead of trying to attract diurnal insects, primroses entice nocturnal moths.) Differing from many flowers of the summer days, seeds of evening primroses are not fluffy to be spread by the breeze. Seeds are borne in pods that develop from the large flowers and mature to be tiny ball-like structures.

Last summer was long ago, but primroses with seeds are still here. After the pods developed and formed seeds within, they opened in the arid air of fall and winter. Now in the cold season, they stand with open pods and though not having seeds blowing in the wind, they are still being helped by breezes that shake the plants, dislodging seeds; falling onto the surface of the snow. Yes, last summer was long ago and next July is far away, but the evening primroses stand out here in January preparing for the coming warmth; whenever it may come.

February 2, 2020

Rabbits and Hares in Mid-Winter

Midway between the winter solstice of December and the vernal equinox of March is early February. Does this mean that we are half way through winter? February usually acts like winter with several cold (some even frigid) days, but can also warm to forties or above. Even though February is our driest months, significant snows can happen (February of 2019; record-setting 36 inches). We deal with weather fluctuations, but consistently we get longer days; earlier sunrises and later sunsets.

These longer days bring changes with local wildlife. One that does not change; the groundhog. Despite the "groundhog day" label, this rodent (woodchuck or marmot) does not wake from its hibernation. A couple others that sleep through the coldest weather are not true hibernators and will wake during mild weather and often take short walks outside of their dens. Best known of these are skunks and raccoons; often, we see, hear or smell of their presence at these times. Chipmunks will wake from sleep as well, but with a cache of food close at hand, they usually do not step outside. Occasionally, we might see a drowsy chipmunk on a winter day; but it quickly returns to its slumber. And mid-winter is when bear cubs are born.

Among those that stay active, tree squirrels were seen all winter during daylight hours. Now their activities increase. Gray squirrels in February exhibit pre-mating behavior. For the first time in weeks, those at bird feeders seem be interested in something besides eating the bird food; they begin to notice each other. True breeding season is still a few weeks away.

I have noticed while walking regularly through the last several weeks that wild canines; foxes, coyotes and wolves are now showing behaviors of their mating season. Tracks tell of movement within their territories; often leaving scent markers at the borders. With pups being born in a little over two months, they have an active breeding season now. Also, of note are the rabbits and hares.

Both are small mammals remaining active all winter. Often mistaken for rodents, their teeth are a bit different and they belong to another group; the lagomorphs. I have been watching both. I find that cottontail rabbits which remain brown for the winter are more common in fields and yards; frequently living in towns and cities as well as rural homes. Snowshoe hare turn white for the cold times; changing from the brown coat of summer. (Another name is varying hare.) They remain in the forest. Though most common in coniferous woods, I have often found them in mixed forests as well.

Both rabbits and hares are nocturnal and though they live among us, we may go weeks without seeing them. Both are hoppers and their tracks tell of activities during the night. Since they do not cache food for winter, they need to venture from shelters in the darkness to find meals. Gnawing and biting on branches and twigs will usually suffice. And cottontails will come to bird feeders to gather fallen seeds. Winter can be a hard time for these small mammals and with the current snowpack, they need to adapt. I found it interesting that while the hare have been able to go over the deep snow; making trails of much use, the rabbits followed routes others have made; often along roads. Now in the longer days, they begin mating behaviors. In early mornings of this month, we can see many more tracks; telling of their nocturnal activities as we move towards spring and the first litters.

February 9, 2020

Pileated Woodpecker Drumming

As we move through this winter month of February, we note signs of the season moving on. Though days can and usually are chilly, others may reach into the forties. And of course, the ample snowpack is still with us. But days are getting longer. By this date, we have reached a threshold in the annual cycle. With the sun rising at 7:23 AM and setting at 5:23 PM, we now have ten hours of daylight; up from the eight and one-half at the winter solstice. This lengthening continues throughout this month. By the end; we have eleven hours as we move towards the vernal equinox on March 19. It is hard to not notice these longer days even if they be cloudy and cold. Our commutes are brighter now. We who wintered here are not the only ones to notice such changes and any observing of local wildlife reveals their responses to the longer days.

Gray squirrels in my yard that have joined birds in dining on seeds during all the cold times are now looking more at each other. Their feeding is interrupted by some chasing each other in what appears to be pre-mating behavior. Also, a plethora of tracks from wild canines; foxes, coyotes and wolves, along with rabbits and hares tell us their nocturnal activities have increased. (Longer days equals shorter nights.) While true hibernators continue their sleep, those not so deep in slumber; skunks, raccoons and chipmunks, may make an appearance in our neighborhoods on mild February days.

Among the birds, it is too early for spring migrants, but with those that persisted all winter, there are changes. Ravens fly in family units, perhaps pairs. Crows are more gregarious and vocal. Blue Jays start to give their “weedle-eedle” calls. Chickadees begin singing “feebee” songs and nuthatches add “yank-yank” sounds to the scene. Out in the woods, I hear more owls at night and turkeys gobbling in early morning. But I find that it is the woodpeckers that are now most notable.

While many birds proclaim their breeding territories with a series of songs, most woodpeckers proclaim their ownership by using their powerful beaks to rap against the sides of tree trunks and branches; producing loud sounds, called drumming. Both downy and hairy woodpeckers that wintered here have been drumming for some time. I heard several during January (including January 1). What began sporadically has become more regular. Now during walks in February, I hear that the pileated woodpecker has joined them.

Among our four woodpeckers that winter in the northland, pileateds are by far the largest. Downy; about seven inches; hairy and red-bellied nearly nine inches; pileated are almost twice that. Though their bodies are mostly black, white marking are on wings and neck. Above the head, they carry a pointed red crest; in addition, males have red near the bill; "a red mustache".

Birds are very powerful and use the bill to dig through bark of trees to extricate insect larvae within. Often while digging, they discard rather large chips of wood on the nearby ground. This strong bill is also great for producing a sound that will loudly resonate through the forests now in mid to late winter.

Recently, as I walked on a silent cloudy mid winter morning, the silence was broken by a loud drumming from deep within the woods. I paused and waited for a repeat, which it did several times. We will hear from these giant woodpeckers many more times as we move through late winter into their spring nesting season.

February 16, 2020

The Owls of February

For some winter weary northlanders, the month of February, the shortest of the year, may seem like the longest. Chilly temperatures keep from melting the snowpack that has been more than a foot and a half for nearly eighty days. Mild days followed by cold gives us ice and crunchy snow. But with lengthening daylight, things are happening.

Birds that frequented the feeder are calling as they feed. Back in the woods, woodpeckers drum for proclamations of their territories and I heard turkeys gobbling. Ravens and crows continue their vocal flights. We may be looking for more changes. Some years redpolls have not appeared at feeders until February, but with finches very limited this winter, I do not expect to see them. But there is more happening.

February may be the best time to see a variety of owls. With some searching in the region, seven kinds can be seen or heard. These include permanent residents and migrants that came here from further north. These various owls range from small to medium to large. While many do the expected hunting at night, other prefer days.

While walking in the pre-dawn darkness, I have often heard calls of two resident owls; the great horned and the barred. Tufts of feathers above the head that are neither horns nor ears give the large great horned its name. They call a series of hoots, while the slightly smaller barred owl; named after dark lines on its underside, produce sounds that have often been paraphrased as "who cooks for you". A range of other sounds; screeches, grunts and laughs are theirs too. The tiny saw-whet owl, only eight inches, lives in coniferous forests. Here they may pierce the darkness with beeping notes; compared a backing truck. During the lumbering days, it was said to sound like a saw being sharpened.

Among the quartet that arrives from the far north, perhaps the best known is the white snowy owl. At nearly two feet long, this bird of the tundra is a regular winter visitor to the region where it searches for prey near the lake or in open sites further inland. Hunting is done day or night. Even larger, the great gray owl of nearly thirty inches, is a bird of the northern boreal forests and bogs. Here they feed on small mammals. Most winters, some come here to seek similar meals; many times diving into the snowpack to grab mice beneath. Being large and hunting in the daytime, they are often seen from roads. Some winters they can be abundant; if food up north is not.

The sixteen-inch hawk owl is a mid-size. Its long tail, unusual with owls, gives this name. They also breed in the bog country north of here. Nearly every winter a few hawk owls will arrive in the northland, but being solitary, they are never abundant. The smallest northern owl visitor and least likely to be seen, is the ten-inch boreal owl. This brown owl is also a resident of the northern conifers. With a deep snowpack or reduced small mammal prey, they may come to our region. Those arriving here at this time are often quite hungry and there have been late winters where many appeared.

These wintering owls are more common in the second half of winter; from February on. I find that with their diurnal hunting, this may be the best time to see them. And the Sax-Zim Bog west of Cotton, MN may be the best place around to locate all of the owls of February.

February 23, 2020

Late Winter Porcupine News

As we move through this last week of February, we notice the longer amount of daylight; eleven hours as we exit this month. Sunrises are now before 7 AM and the setting sun is at nearly 6 PM. We will have mild days with temperatures getting above freezing that send many us looking for signs of spring, but such days can be followed by chilly ones that remind us that we are still in winter; late winter. The vernal equinox that marks the passing of the cold season is March 19. Late winter can be a hard time for all living in the region. While humans may suffer from two timely maladies; cabin fever and spring fever, the local wildlife are dealing with more.

Two quite different happenings are in their lives now; mating season and hunger. Longer daylight and warmer temperatures have triggered mating time for many. With a gestation of weeks or more, they will be able to have their young born in weather conditions allowing for a successful birth. I have been seeing tracks and scent markings of the wild canine; foxes, coyotes and wolves for more than a month. More recently, the tracks and behavior of squirrels, rabbits and hare have joined in. In addition to starting families, these mammals are also hungry. With a sustained snowpack of two feet or more, food can be hard to find. Perhaps the most obvious of the hungry critters are the deer. They now mix with squirrels, rabbits and mice in feeding on seeds that were left for birds.

Tracks of bobcat, fisher, pine marten, otter and weasels (ermine), all seen recently, also tell stories of hunger as they travel over the packed snow seeking meals of smaller mammals or birds. With the exceptions of tree squirrels, I have seen very few rodents in the last couple of months. They are still here and maybe coping with the season better than many by staying below the snow cover. Here in the protection of the sub-nivean space, they can do quite well. Two aquatic rodents; beavers and muskrats, are mostly beneath the persistent ice. And then there are the porcupines.

These spiny rodents, feeding on inner bark of twigs find plenty of food throughout the winter. Their coats protect them from cold and predators. Typically, they find a good feeding site and a nearby shelter and go through the days in a feeding-sleeping pattern. Without much movement, we may not see them often in winter.

Such was the situation for me until recently. I was passing a nearby forest when I noticed a tree with many branches sheared of bark; the sign of a porcupine. Gnawing the branches for several weeks, the tree stood out as looking more bare than others. Indeed, the feeding activities of porcupines can kill a tree. At about the same time, I received an email from a local resident with photos of strange tracks in new light snow. Looking closely, I could see the waddling footprints indicative of a porcupine, but this one also had a tail dragging that swayed back and forth in a “snake-like” pattern. A few days later, I was on a trail that I frequently use. Passing under a white pine, I noticed that the snow was scattered with inch-long pellets; porcupine droppings. Searching the branches overhead, I located the dark spiny rodent on a horizontal branch; curled up in the cold wind. After much of the winter staying put, perhaps the porcupines are feeling the changes of late winter as well.

March 1, 2020

The Glow of Red-Osier Dogwoods

We arrive in March after a February that gave us interesting temperatures. We had more subzero readings this month than recorded in January; including the coldest for the whole winter. These chilly times were offset by days nearly reaching forty degrees. These temperature fluctuations were easy to note, but two other weather factors may have been less obvious. We were far below normal in both snowfall and precipitation. But the lengthening days has continued. Now as we enter March with about eleven hours of daylight, we quickly expand it towards the vernal equinox, March 19; and get into the days of more light than darkness.

Many critters are already responding to the longer days and as we move further into March, we may see the arrival of some very early migrants from the south. A flock of snow buntings may be seen along the road. Later we could note juncos at the feeder and a few robins and grackles in the yard. Towards the end of the month, the local red-winged blackbirds will be proclaiming territorial ownership at nearby swamps. A few raptors; red-tailed hawks, northern harriers and bald eagles are quick to return as are geese and mergansers in any available open water. Besides birds, we will soon also notice the waking of a few sleepers; chipmunks, skunks and raccoons. But the thirty-one days of March can also give substantial snowfalls and cold that can slow the progression towards spring.

Probably the most obvious of all the living community that wintered with us are the trees. They remained standing right out in the weather for the entire cold season. They dealt with temperature and moisture changes and now they also respond to the longer and warmer days as well. Each year, as we enter the month of March, I observe a phenomenon in the deciduous forests. At the base of trees; usually larger trees, where the snow has formed against the bark, it begins to melt in a circular pattern. I refer to these as "tree circles". What is happening is that the sunlight during longer days is getting absorbed on the darker bark; heating it a bit. This warmth is being reradiated back out to the surrounded snow and melting it; creating this circular affect. Thanks to the many clear days of this February, I observed tree circles a bit earlier than normal.

The sight of these changes at the base of trees is the beginning. Going up from the base, we may see more. Out on the branches of small willows, we can find the opening of buds revealing a furry type of growth. A little higher up, similar bud openings are happening on quaking aspens. Both the willows and aspens are starting to form catkin flowers that will slowly reach maturity later in spring. And soon, the sap will be flowing in regional maple trees.

But I also like to look at another small tree as we leave February; red-osier dogwood. One of several kinds of dogwoods in the northland, this shrub, usually less than ten feet tall, is common on roadsides, ditch banks and edges of wetlands. Though present all year, it is at this time, they are most obvious. Bark that was red during winter is brighter now. Demanding attention, these small dogwoods light up the roadsides. Some willows also have red branches in late winter, but the entire plant is red on red-osier dogwoods. These reddish glows along with buds of willows and aspens usher us into the changing spring month of March.

March 8, 2020

Following the Deer Paths

We are now in March and look forward to the coming season changes. Days have more than eleven hours of daylight, quickly lengthening as we approach the vernal equinox; beyond which light exceeds darkness. Temperatures vary greatly in this month, but there is a warming trend that comes along with the longer days. However, looking around, we are easily reminded of the winter when we see the deep and long-lasting snowpack. Typically, March is when the snowpack is at its greatest depth for the whole year, but this year it's a little different.

Going out now, we see a substantial snowpack as expected at this time but this year it has been here for a long time. It was back in early December that the northland received a heavy snow. The excess of twenty inches has persisted and with some subsequent snowfalls, the snowpack of at least twenty inches (much more in some places) has remained for the last one hundred days. This recent winter was not particularly cold; about 16 degrees compared to the normal of 13. The total snowfall for the whole season is about eighty inches; about a foot above normal, but nothing record-setting. But it was this lingering snowpack that has impacted us throughout the cold season.

During the one hundred days that the snow was on the ground, it underwent many changes. What began as powder, became wet during a warming time (even some rain in late December). Following this, chilly temperatures caused a crust to form over all. Some new snow on the crust brought on more changes. And when mild temperatures arrived again in February, the entire snowpack became sticky; only to freeze into a deep crust again.

The snow depth and various textures made it tough for much of the local wildlife. At first in December, it appeared as though many of the critters were caught by surprise; they had hard going. I marveled at the way the squirrels, rabbits, foxes, coyotes, fishers and deer dealt with the snow. Many were jumping into the deep snow and trudging through. As the season progressed, they settled into following hard-fought routes formed earlier. Later, the crusty covering allowed for smaller mammals to walk over the surface; but deer with their hoof feet were not granted this luxury. They kept to the existing trails.

It wasn't far into the cold season that these hungry deer spread out to numerous sites in search of meals; including my yard. Nearly every day some would arrive trying to dine on bird seeds. I noticed that they always came and went on the same routes. Their regular visits had formed well-packed paths in the woods.

Taking a break from the snowshoeing and skiing, I decided to see if the deer paths were substantial for me. And yes, I was able to walk on their wood routes with ease. As long as I stayed on the deer-packed path, I could wander far into the forests; stepping off brought me into a snowpack at least up to my knees. During recent walks on these paths, I noted that I was not the only one taking advantage of the deer routes. Tracks on or near the trails included squirrel, hare, porcupine, fox, fisher and turkey. And I was able to get great views of this arboreal landscape. The snowy March woods is marvelous to behold with the long shadows and melted circles at the base of most trees. Thanks to the hungry deer, we were able to move about better in this snowpack.

March 15, 2020

Spring Chipmunks in the Yard

We are in mid-March. Cold and snow may still be happening, but the springing things continue. Cold may be here, but subzero readings are far less likely. As we have seen from a few recent springs, snows may persist into the next several weeks. With all these changes, the longer days are consistent. Now with sun rising shortly after 7 AM and setting a little after 7 PM, we approach the vernal equinox. Following this astronomical event, daylight exceeds darkness each day. And nature responds to these lighted times.

These are the days in which we look out at the feeders of winter and try to locate some early migrants mixing with chickadees, nuthatches, blue jays and woodpeckers that wintered here. I have often seen purple finches and juncos near the house by mid-month while horned larks and snow buntings, birds of the fields, congregate along roads. It may be a bit too early for the anticipated robins, grackles and red-winged blackbirds to have returned, but other migrants are arriving. In open waters, it is not unusual to see some mallards, mergansers, geese and perhaps a few swans. Along the highways, red-tailed hawks, harriers and kestrels can be seen doing their hunting.

Looking elsewhere, I have been seeing the furry open buds of willows at a local swamp and quaking aspens with similar buds nearby. These buds remain in this phase until later in spring, but now they tell us of what is to come. And maple trees resume their sap movements.

March is the month of micro habitats and often in this longer-lasting sunshine, things happen in small well-lit sites. Bare ground can be seen along south-facing roadsides. Here too, the snow has gone from large ant hills. Close to buildings, in sunlit sites, along south or west walls, we can see the movements of early waking ants and flies; bringing out opportunistic predators of wolf and jumping spiders. Wolf spiders patrol the ground, jumping spiders search the walls. Here too is where we'll find the first dandelions and crocuses starting to bloom. And there is more in the springing yard.

Recently as I looked out, I saw a new arrival among the tree squirrels that had been so active all winter. Abundant gray squirrels mixed with a few smaller reds. But as I watched, I saw an even smaller one with stripes on its sides scamper across the yard; a chipmunk.

Chipmunks are a very well-known and usually well-liked type of ground squirrel that has learned to live near our houses. We watched last fall as they gathered seeds and nuts for their winter cache and then in late October, they were gone. While tree squirrels remain active all winter, ground squirrels for the most part hibernate. These include the deep-sleeping groundhogs (woodchucks), Franklin ground squirrels and thirteen-lined ground squirrels. Most are still in a deep sleep, but not so with the chipmunks. Theirs is a waking sleep. They went into a dormant phase last fall a couple of weeks before our lasting snow cover began and here, they remained for the coldest winter.

Unlike the deep hibernators, they wake some times. Usually not leaving their dens, they relieve themselves, have a snack and go back to sleep. However; on mild days, they may wander from the sleeping site. I have several times seen chipmunks in January and February. These drowsy winter sights do not last long. But now in mid-March seeing a chipmunk is a spring arrival and likely to continue activity in and near our yards.

March 22, 2020

Trumpeter Swans Returning

The first half of March has given us plenty to get in the mood for the changing seasons. The temperature has been several degrees above normal. March 8 gave us our first day of fifty degrees in months and returned us to Daylight Savings Time. (This happens each year on the second Sunday of March; the 8th is the earliest that it can be.) And the ample snowpack that has been with us for more than one hundred days has been shrinking. Moving into the latter half of March, we were greeted by the vernal equinox late on the day of March 19. This is the earliest start of spring in more than one hundred years. All of this looks like we are quickly exiting winter and moving into spring.

Such conditions get us out to look for spring happenings. And they are here. I have heard reports of sightings of waking winter sleepers and hibernators; chipmunks, raccoons, skunks and even a few bears. Not quite as obvious, there have been a few butterflies and moths seen. (One group of butterflies; the anglewings, hibernate as adults and on mild March days, they may take flight. Usually this means basking in sunlight or feeding on dripping sap of maple trees.)

With all this going on, I have been searching for some very early bird migrants as well. Temperatures have been mild, but the length of daylight and the persistent snowpack still slows their movements. But soon, I expect to see robins and grackles in our yard with juncos and purple finches at the feeders. By the end of the month, I expect to hear from a couple of early migrants in the wetlands; the "conk-a-lee" songs of red-winged blackbirds and the "peent" call of woodcocks.

Other early migrants have already been northing. Various raptors such as bald eagles, red-tailed and rough-legged hawks along with harriers are arriving and hunting; often along roadways. Besides looking for these roadside raptors, I decided to visit some open water locations on the St. Louis River recently. Closer to Lake Superior, even in mid-winter, water sites can often host hardy ducks like common goldeneyes, mallards and maybe some mergansers. But when I checked the openings on this March day, I found a few newly-arrived Canada geese. This caused me to look at other open waters. And here, I found white waterfowl even larger than the geese; trumpeter swans.

Many of these huge birds; length of about sixty inches and a wingspan of more than eighty inches, will winter at selected places in Minnesota; often at sites along the Mississippi River. They have become regular early spring migrants. It wasn't always so. Trumpeter swans (so named because of the loud honking sounds they make) were extirpated from the state about a century ago. A very successful reintroduction program has allowed them to not only be regularly seen in the last twenty years, but many also nest in the region.

They arrive here early, maybe breed nearby, but they do not travel in large flocks as tundra swans do; later in spring. Tundra swans are smaller (and more silent) than the trumpeters. They also just pass through here; wintering on the east coast, near Chesapeake Bay, and nesting, as their name indicates, on the far north tundra. Many will rest in the St. Louis River area while heading further north. It begins with the viewing of trumpeter swans, but here in the northland, we are fortunate to see both kinds each spring; adding more to this fascinating month of March.

March 29, 2020

First Dandelion Bloom; Good Sight

When we are concerned with our health and our safety, it is easy to become so enamored by thee difficult issues that we may miss what else is happening around us. Despite the present possible sickness, now in late March, spring is unfolding in the northland. The pace may be a little slower than what some of us desire, but the new season is happening. Since the vernal equinox of last week, the amount of daylight each day is longer than darkness; and continues so. A bit slowly, temperatures are rising and the snowpack that has exceeded fifteen inches for more than one hundred ten days is shrinking. We can see bare ground at many sites now. Some local wildlife responses to this have been slow, but they are here.

I now have daily sights of chipmunks in the yard. What began as occasional glimpses has become regular. During the morning walks, I have been seeing flocks of pine siskins and snow buntings along the roadside. A neighbor reported purple finches at the feeder and there has been a scattering of robin and red-winged blackbirds in the region. Crows are calling in flocks each morning and woodpeckers continue to drum on tree trunks. One day while walking, I heard the honking Canada geese flying over; and not to be outdone, the following day, I watched and listened as two large and loud trumpeter swans came by. Finding no open water here, they moved on. Raptors have also flown over and I've observed bald eagles often. Some of these large birds may have wintered, but others are northing. Also going north are a few hawks; red-tailed, rough-legged and harriers. Raccoons and skunks have been active for a while after waking from a long sleep. And I have heard a few reports of drowsy wandering bears in the vicinity. Northland wildlife are waking and migrating; spring is happening.

Passing by on streets and roads, I've also noted changes in the trees. Willows in wetlands hold branches of yellow or red while the small red-osier dogwoods are entirely red. The swamps also host pussy willows with scores of furry buds while the larger quaking aspen has theirs looking similar. Branches of the abundant shrubby speckled alder (sometimes called tag alder) take on a purplish glow at this time as their catkins expand; forming pollen that will be seen soon. Looking at the buds of silver maples, we can see they will soon be opening in female or male flowers; very common in early April.

Many northlanders have crocuses near their houses. These minute plants put up green leaves quickly and in the sunlight of late March will open blossoms of white, yellow or purple. While going by a building recently, I noted that the snow was all gone from its southside. March is a month of microhabitats and in these south or west-facing sunny sites, spring comes earlier than elsewhere. Taking a closer look, I saw greening of grasses and in its midst was a dandelion in bloom. Though often called a weed and usually not appreciated, I find the sighting of these yellow blossoms after the long winter is one that we are glad to see; nearly always the number one plant to bloom. A long taproot extending far into the ground allows this hardy plant to survive winter. There will be more dandelions, they may lose their appeal, but this first one seen in bloom at a time when other things can take our attention, was a good sight to behold.

Second Quarter

April 5, 2020

Alder Catkins Open in Wetlands

As we move into April, we are in a fickle month. During these thirty days, we may receive cold and snow (as in 2013), rains (including thunder showers) or dry and quite warm (70 or 80). Lengthening daylight mixed with warming temperatures revive plants that have been largely dormant for the winter and five months beneath the snow. At sunny snow-free sites, we might see dandelions in bloom. And it here that crocuses that began to open in March become more widespread and colorful. Grasses begin to green; new shoots pushing up from the soil. (At the edge of receding snow cover in our yards, we may also find patches snow mold.) But there is plenty to see in the trees around us as well.

When thinking of flowers in trees, we are likely to look for blossoms of apple, cherry, plum, juneberry or lilac; all of which we will be seeing during warmer days of May. These blooms are more of what we call a typical flower; one that has petals (the colorful part) around the female and male parts. In the center is the pistil (female) with stamen (male) surrounding. There is huge variety to this arrangement, but with tree blossoms of May, this is normal. Not so with the tree flowers of April.

Early blooming silver maple and, a bit later, red maples, have florets somewhat like this. They have some colors, but differ from the blossoms. Male and female flowers are separate and usually on different plants. The tiny female flowers (pistilate) are red-purple while the equally small male flowers (staminate) basically just produce pollen. With no leaves of trees, pollen readily drifts in the spring breezes from male flowers to female; assuring pollination.

Among many other kinds of trees, a different type of flower is produced at this time; catkins. These structures that are shaped long like "hot dogs" can now be found on the branches of willows, aspens, alders, hazels and birches. Those of willows and aspen opened as the furry buds a couple of weeks ago. These opening buds gave us a look at what was to come in the warming season. Though we may have used these as a remedy for "spring fever", they have been growing and now, in April, they mature as male or female flowers. Male catkins produce pollen and may appear more yellow; females are greenish.

With the alder, hazel and birch, male catkins were on the tree twigs all winter. Now in spring, they enlarge and swell with pollen. No leaves on the trees, the pollen blows in the wind. April is the month of catkins. By the end of the month, we'll see more, but now in early April, it is the alder branches that are filled with these developing catkins.

Alders (speckled alder, sometimes called tag alder) are small trees with numerous branches. They abound in the wetlands; along the edges of ponds, swamps and lakes, often with willows. We hardly take notice of them all winter. But during the longer days of March, the catkins take on a reddish-purple glow and when we take a closer look, we may see the tiny yellow grains of pollen. Female catkins are smaller and grow nearby; on the same plant. When they get pollinated, seeds form in the female catkins that later grow to be cone shaped. They also persist on the plant. (We can still see last year's cones on these trees.) The smaller alders of the swamps introduce us to the numerous catkins of April.

April 12, 2020

Mosses Begin the Woods Greening

April is a fascinating month of changes in the northland. Ponds, swamps and lakes that held an ice cover for more than five months are starting to take on their new look. Where we've seen ice for more than one hundred fifty days, we can now see some open water. This new aquatic world is quickly used by returning water birds; ducks, geese, swans and mergansers. Muskrats and beavers that had a confining winter now move about in this present scene. In the smaller ponds, frogs are waking from their long sleep to go on to their next phase of life; they will sing territorial and courtship songs though the water and air are still chilly. April can be warm or cold with either rain or snow.

Besides ice-out time, we also see the loss of an ample snowpack that has been with us since late November. (A simple observation of the northland weather is that in most years, snow cover will persist from Thanksgiving until Easter.) Though this winter was not particularly cold or snowy, we did have a snowpack of at least fifteen inches for nearly four months. The amount of snow on the ground may have hampered our activity during this time. This snow went from wet to dry to crusty. Now, in the last few weeks, it has shrunk much; revealing the ground beneath. In our yards, we can now see some new shoots of green grass poking up from the soil in sunny and damp sites. In this same location, we may also see a few dandelions showing circular yellow flowers and maybe a few crocuses. Perennials, such as rhubarb and day lilies, are emerging for another season as well.

The April spring is happening in the woods too. With trees giving more shade, melting of the snowpack is a bit slower; but it is happening. With some searching near the ground, we can see that the forest is beginning to green. May is the greening month in the region. It is during this time that bare trees at the beginning open their leaf buds and by the end, foliage overhead is nearly complete. The greening of the woods in May, starts near the ground with many small plants in April. First of these are the mosses.

With longer days of sunlight in March, trees absorb warmth from this solar source and reradiated it out to melt snow at the base. Trees form circles near the ground devoid of snow. In these small circular hot spots, tiny green mosses that weathered the winter and remained green throughout the ordeal are quick to take advantage of this available sunlight.

Mosses are abundant in the northland; especially in the forests. Due to their small size, they are often overlooked even though they grow near us on soil, rocks, logs and trees. Probably the two best times to observe these miniature growths are in fall before the snow covers them and now, as the snow goes. Recently, while wandering on a woodland path, I paused to look at the base of a large tree. Here was a green leaf of hepatica; a spring flower, but here too was a large growth of mosses. Not only were they green, they were thriving and many of these tiny plants were putting up new growths of leaves and spore capsules. Small and often not noticed, mosses begin the greening of the woods; now in April. Soon wild leek and other vernal plants will be greening too, but it starts with mosses.

April 19, 2020

Vernal Ponds Formed by the Melting

We are now in the second half of April. This is a time of longer days (daylight; fourteen hours) and warmer temperatures. Melting happens not only with snow (The snowpack lasting from late November to late March, is gone), and we see plenty of melting of ice. April varies greatly, we expect ice-out during the latter half of the month. (Early in 2017, it was April 7; late 2018, May 1. Ice-out in 2019 on April 21 was more "normal".) We who wintered here look forward to this event, but so do others. Muskrats and beavers that were mostly within lodges for the duration of the cold now swim about again. Migrant geese, swans, mergansers and ducks are quick to find and settle into any open sites. Just as freeze-up last fall began with ponds and swamps before lakes, so does the melting.

Each year in early April, I take a walk to check the conditions of several small vernal ponds. Such vernal (spring) ponds abound in the northland. Being shallow, they are quick to melt the ice and snow cover in their low sites. The result is a space of open water early in spring. These ponds appear with the melt every spring and when this warming season passes and morphs into summer, many will lose their water, mostly through evaporation. Filled with water in April; empty in August. In this short period of time, these vernal ponds hold special adapted forms of life. For many this is only a temporary home.

As I walked by the ponds, I noted their variety. Thanks to rains of last fall and the winter snowpack, all have plenty of water. Some still were covered with snow and ice. Others were partially free of the winter coat and one was nearly one-hundred per cent open. Standing here at this ice-free pond, I heard the creaking call of a chorus frog. There are many residents of vernal ponds, but perhaps best known are the vocal frogs. It is a trio that sing spring songs of courtship from these wet sites each April. Joining the beginning one-inch chorus frogs are larger wood frogs and tiny spring peepers. While chorus frogs make creaking calls, wood frogs produce a quacking type of sound and spring peepers punctuate the area with peeping songs. The frogs are quite loud and easy to notice, but there is much more here than these songsters.

Another amphibian is silent when it comes to ponds to breed; the blue-spotted salamander. Quiet and cryptic in its movements, we do not usually see them. But gazing into this clear water of a recently-formed vernal pond, I see plenty more. Several insects have their immature stages in water. These include some flies, mosquitoes and beetles. All are easy to see as they swim here. Like frogs that will go from eggs to tadpole to adult in a few short months; so, do these insects need to grow up before their homes dry up. Other critters here are a bit different. Orangish fairy shrimps swim about. On the bottom among the fallen leaves, are some snails and even a minute kind of clam.

At the edge of the ponds aquatic plants are growing. Marsh marigolds and water calla unfold leaves leading to spring flowers. Wood ducks are frequent visitors as are grackles and red-winged blackbirds. The ever-present raccoons come by to dine and drink. Taking advantage of warming April days, a plethora of wildlife; large and small, make use of newly-formed vernal ponds in the northland.

April 26, 2020

New Migrant Arrivals in Woods

Late April is a delightful time to walk in the woods. With the snow cover nearly all gone (only patches on the sheltered north-facing hillsides), the wandering can be easily done on or off trails. The less-appreciated insects are not yet here; thanks to recent cold temperatures. In fall there is a period of time after the leaves drop from the trees and before the snow cover that I refer to as AutWin. So now, the time after the snow has melted and before the greening of the forests, I like to call WinSprin. At the base of trees, on logs and rocks are greening mosses. With some searching as I walk, I find green wild leek emerging from the ground. Also, I see leaves of hepatica, pyrola and wintergreen; all these stayed green under the snow. But mostly, the green woods is yet to be.

As I wander, I hear singing frogs from the vernal ponds. The early spring trio of chorus frogs, wood frogs and spring peepers blend well together. Also, I hear the drumming of local ruffed grouse, gobbling of turkeys and the resonating sounds from pileated woodpeckers. All have wintered here. I'm searching for the next group of migrant birds. Migration has already been going on for several weeks. In open waters, a variety of aquatic birds have settled either to rest or nest. These include geese, swans, mergansers, ducks, grebes and pelicans. Great blue herons and the first shorebirds are appearing along the edges of wetlands. Many are quite large or colorful and fairly easy to see. Raptors also have been flying over for weeks: eagles, hawks, harriers and vultures; along with the loud sandhill cranes.

Among the songbirds, red-winged blackbirds and robins seem to have set the pace. Both are into their territories and singing. Their arrival was quickly followed by groups of sparrows. Often in flocks, the gray-black juncos fill the roadsides and often our yards. Song, fox and tree sparrows frequently scatter with junco flocks. We have seen plenty of these early arrivals. Now, in late April, comes the next migrants.

As I walk, I listen and look for two diminutive songsters. Ruby-crowned kinglets and winter wrens, both about four inches long, are tiny bundles of energy and both sing long and loud songs upon arriving here. Also, there is a pair of migratory woodpeckers that have recently returned from wintering in the south; flickers and yellow-bellied sapsuckers. The latter, coming into our yards and giving its drumming on trees in the early morning, may annoy us. But I'm looking for two other migrants of late April in the woods. The first warbler of the season is always the yellow-rumped warbler; I have never seen an exception. And I seek to locate another thrush; the hermit thrush. Unlike their cousins, robins and bluebirds, hermit thrushes live up to their name and remain deep in the forests. Mostly brown with a reddish-brown tail (which they often pump up and down), these six-inch birds, smallest of northland thrushes, mostly stay under cover. Occasionally, they will appear in our yards where they hop in a manor like that of a robin. Despite their small size and secretive ways, hermit thrushes sing a very pleasant flute-like song; often letting us know of their presence. (Maybe why it is the state bird of Vermont.) As I step from the woods, I hear a calling loon; telling me of ice-out conditions on the nearby lake. Yes, migrants; songbirds and others, are here and more to come during May.

May 3, 2020

Elderberry is First of Greening Trees

The month of May shows many natural happenings in the northland. It's during these weeks that we'll see an expanded influx of migrating songbirds. The sparrows, woodpeckers and the earliest of the warblers that are present before April ends are just the start. Now, in this new month, we'll see swallows, wrens, orioles, grosbeaks, vireos, hummingbirds and a huge variety of warblers. With lakes open, the resident loons have moved in. Many earlier arrivals have gone on to the next phase and bird nests are being constructed. Among mammals, the early litters of squirrels, rabbits and mice are present in yards and parks. The frogs that called much during the latter days of April will be joined by other species in May and the toads seen last year in our yards and gardens take their annual trip to water to court and lay eggs. We've seen a few butterflies so far this season, but now in May they will diversifying and becoming easier to see. Other insects such as bees, flies and dragonflies are also now active. And by later in the month, we note the presence of mosquitoes and black flies.

Along with all this happening with the local animal wildlife, May is also the month of flowers. The forest floor becomes crowded and colorful as we move through these coming weeks. Spring wild flowers that survived the winter underground now emerge as green leaves and soon will flower in the sunlight that penetrates through the forest canopy above. Hepatica, bloodroot, spring beauty, trout-lily, violet and bellwort, just to name a few, will soon be showing a vernal bouquet that is sure to catch our eyes. But these wild flowers are often called ephemerals (short-lived) and are quick to fade in the shade of the leafy woods. May is also the greening month.

In our yards, we've been seeing the grass and garden plants greening. In the woods, this color change starts low with the mosses that were present under the snow all winter. Soon among them are the new leaves of wild leek (ramps), trout-lilies and spring beauty; preparing to flower. Going higher, the woody plants forming new green leaves are small. Bushes of gooseberry, raspberry and honeysuckle open new leaf buds to grab the needed sunlight. The first trees to green are also small. Setting the pace for the greening woods is the shrubby tree; elderberry.

Also known as red-berry elder, these small trees are common at the edge of the woods; reaching only about fifteen feet tall. (A close cousin, the American elderberry; more common to the south, has dark berries.) Being a shrubby tree among the taller ones can mean that it will often not be noticed. Now, the huge leaf buds open before the other trees and we see their large compound leaves unfold. Once these leaves with five to seven leaflets open, they are quickly followed by a cluster of white flowers that bloom later in the month. It is common to see the leaf and flower buds opening together on these trees in early May.

Once the elderberry has shown its leaves to the new warming season, it is as though others were waiting for one to start the greening, and they are quick to follow. Cherry, hazel, willow, alder and lilac are soon to follow. Quaking aspen are the first taller tree to form new green canopy. By the end of this greening month, the forests will be full of green trees; but it begins early with the small elderberry.

May 10, 2020

Return of the "Teacher Bird"

With a sunrise now at 5:40 AM and setting at about 8:30 PM, we are approaching fifteen hours of daylight. This means that the daily morning walks begin earlier. May days are long and though can be chilly with snow (as seen in 2019); but also warm with much happening.

As I step from the house on this cool clear calm May morning, I note that I'm not alone in greeting dawn. Chipping and white-throated sparrows are in the yard. Both the local phoebe and robin are proclaiming territorial songs. Using another method of sending its ownership, yellow-bellied sapsuckers are pounding away on yard trees. As I pass a swamp, the recently hatched Canada geese family goes into hiding. Red-winged blackbirds, male and female, are nesting here. He continues his singing that began weeks ago. A spotted sandpiper, just back from the south, bounces along the shore. And overhead, the winnowing of a snipe adds this sound to the landscape. This persistent bird has been doing its flight for a couple of weeks; dawn and dusk. The frogs are silent at this hour and temperature. Recently, leopard frogs with their snoring call, have joined the earlier ones; while the quacking songs of wood frogs are waning.

Passing a field, I hear the songs of song sparrows again. They are joined by the arrival of Savannah sparrows. Flying over the field are a couple of kinds of swallows; tree and rough-winged, breakfasting on any insects available. Coming to a woods, I hear the ruffed grouse still drumming on its favorite log. I've heard it daily since beginning on March 28. And then I hear the sound that I have been hoping to hear during morning walks lately; the loud song of the ovenbird.

Ovenbirds are a kind of warbler. These small birds abound in the northland and each spring, twenty-six species will arrive; most coming back from a winter spent in Central America. Before this month is over, we may see all of these nearly two dozen kinds; some in large numbers. Though in spring (breeding) plumage and though all will sing, not many are as vocal and as easy to recognize as the ovenbird song that I hear now. We often turn bird songs into phrases of words that they may sound like. This one sounds like it is saying "teacher-teacher-teacher…" and for this reason, it is often called the "teacher bird".

As it is this morning, the song is loud; often repeated and easy to hear, but since the singer is small (about six inches), brown on its back and spotted beneath, it may be hard to see. (The only other color is an orange cap; visible only if we see it closely.) And seeing it closely (or at all) can be hard. Not only is the bird small and brown, it stays near the forest floor where it will be nesting; easy to hear, hard to see.

The ovenbird name comes from its nest being a hollow beneath leaves on the ground; reminding early naturalists of a Dutch oven (not like our ovens of today). They are not the first warbler to return to this woods; a few that winter in southern states have been here already, but their announcement of arrival is loudest. Others will be present too in the next couple of weeks along with many May happenings. When walking in the woods to see spring wild flowers and tree blossoms, we may hear orioles, grosbeaks and thrush songs; listen to also hear the teacher call.

May 17, 2020

Blossoming Begins with Small Trees

Most of the tall trees have not yet grown new leaves for the season. And so, as I walk through the woods on this May day, I note that the sunlight is penetrating through the trees and reaching the forest floor. The plants that call this their home are taking advantage of the sunlight when they can. Within two weeks, leaves will be full in the overhead canopy and this site will be shady. These short-lived spring wild flowers, often called ephemerals, are fast to sprout from the soil, develop leaves and produce new flowers for the season. Once pollinated by early-flying insects, they will fade. Some keep their leaves through the coming months, but others fall back to the soil and in summer, we cannot tell that they were even here.

But they thrive now and during my walk I find about a dozen kinds; hepatica, bloodroot, spring beauty, wood anemone, white and yellow trout-lilies, bellworts, wild ginger, marsh marigold, toothwort, trillium, Dutchman's breeches and violets. This list is normal for a deciduous forest in May. Growing with them are some fern fiddleheads. Looking up, I see that many trees are forming new leaves. Near the woods edge, I find some of the trees are forming flowers of their own. We often call tree flowers blossoms.

Tree flowers have been with us since late March and many trees; alder, hazel, aspen and willows have held catkins; flowers of a different sort, through most of April. Silver maple was followed by red maple to show their pistilate and staminate flowers; some with red colors. But it is during the second half of May that we see the blossoms from other trees; many of which we are very familiar with. Now this arboreal show begins with three small trees. Common at the woods edge or roadsides where they get enough sunlight, these little trees, all with white petals, put on quite a show of their own. This early tree trio is composed of wild plum, juneberry and pin cherry. Each tree is small and each has flowers with five petals. They frequently grow near each other.

I find the first to bloom is wild plum. The small, nearly circular, petals will open on the branches before leaves develop. Within a couple of days, juneberry (also called shadbush and serviceberry) will open its blossoms with long thin petals at the same time that leaves are forming. Pin cherry with its clusters of small flowers is next; also, with leaves. All three are common on roadsides and we see plenty as we pass by. We usually do not realize how abundant they are until seen in bloom at this time. After being pollinated, each forms fruits and berries ripe in summer. Though small, the colorful berries are eaten by many of the local wildlife. Bears (and some of us) find juneberry to be quite tasty on hot July days. (It is interesting to note that although we call them Juneberry, they have blossoms in May and ripe berries in July.)

Soon others will add their blossom colors to the late May landscape. Elderberry, hawthorn, apple, choke-cherry and lilac will be giving plenty more petal colors late in the month. The blossoming of trees that we so associate with late May begins with the early tree trio of wild plum, juneberry and pin cherry as seen now along the roadsides.

May 24, 2020

The Morning Roadside Songster

Walking on a morning in May is a terrific way to see and hear what is going on in the surrounding spring. The calm conditions are cooler than what will happen in the afternoon, but in this wind-less time, bird songs and sounds permeate the air. And there is plenty happening at this hour. Without leaving the yard, I note the presence of robins, phoebes and three kinds of sparrows; chipping, song and white-throated. The local woodpeckers drum from trees in the adjacent woods. Each tries to make its call resonate through the morning. As I pass a swamp, I hear calls of Canada geese that are loudly protecting their family. In the nearby waters are ducks; ring-necked, wood and bufflehead and a hooded merganser paddles about. A camouflaged bittern sends out its weird squelching sounds; while a loud calling sandhill crane flies over. Here too, I listen to the red-winged blackbirds that are nesting in the cattails and swamp sparrows along the edge. A far-off mourning dove calls and the local loons of the nearby lake add sounds of their own. Over the wetlands, a few tree swallows do their acrobatic flights and feeding while a snipe winnows in an aerial performance.

Going by a forest, I stop to watch a hermit thrush; silent this morning. Movement in the nearby trees causes me to pause and look more closely. A few active, but silent, warblers are finding insects among the opening tree buds. I note three early arrivals; yellow-rumped, palm and orange-crowned and they are joined by black and white and Nashville warblers. None are singing, but one that I do not see is singing loudly; the local ovenbird. Others are a bit easier to locate. The patient ruffed grouse sitting on its favorite log, continues the wing-beating sound that he began weeks ago. Recent additions to the avian AM crowd are the rose-breasted grosbeak and Baltimore orioles. Both of the colorful males sing musical vocals with enough emphasis to be heard well. But it is a different avian songster along this morning route that demands attention; a brown thrasher.

Thrashers are a regular part of our local bird life, though not really common. Related to the smaller cousins and more common thrushes, brown thrashers are about a foot long. They are more closely related to the gray catbird (also here this morning) and the well-known mockingbird (state bird of several states in the south. The brown thrasher is also a state bird of a southern state; Georgia.) Birds are reddish-brown on the back, streaked below with an extended tail and a slightly curved bill. But it is not the size or color that catches my attention each time I pass by. It is the long loud song. Birds find an exposed branch and sit here to sing a series of varied melodious phases. Each phrase is usually given two to three times; not normally imitating other birds as the catbird or mockingbird does.

Returning from a winter in the southern part of the country, the brown thrashers seek thickets for their homes. Here they nest on or near the ground. And here they walk about using their long-curved beaks to find meals of insects and seeds. But when it comes to singing, they select a high open branch to perform. With binoculars and patience, I look forward to more spring morning walks and many more songs from this brown thrasher along with other birds living here.

May 31, 2020

Turtle Time; Basking on Logs

The bay is mostly in a north-south direction. On spring days, if the wind is from the east, this bay offers protection from the cool air. Coming here on this windy May day is a pleasant and warm site to stop and observe seasonal happenings. A few wood ducks, ring-neck ducks, Canada geese and a couple of hooded mergansers take shelter in these calm waters. Sometimes, the local loons move in from the main part of the nearby lake. Many times, I've watched the fishing activities of herons and kingfishers in this bay as spotted sandpipers patrol the shore. Newly arrived warblers of various species feed on the plethora of insects in opening leaves of adjacent trees. They are joined by phoebes, flycatchers, catbirds, song sparrows, veeries and a few vireos. Avoiding cool east winds, they find solace and meals in lakeside woods.

The bay has a long log of about forty feet protruding out from the shore. Years ago, a tall dead white pine came down into the lake; changing the scenery. This dead log resting on the water's surface has proved to be a great addition to the local wildlife. I have seen beaver, muskrat, raccoon, bobcat and otters (as recent as this morning) on the log. Many birds; aquatic and others, have come here too. And I've enjoyed seeing the abundance of spider webs in the morning mist. But now, on this afternoon in late May, the log belongs to the turtles.

Western painted turtles are our most common turtle in the northland and it may be hard to find a lake without them. They hold a shell; dark above (carapace) and reddish below (plastron). It is this red that give the name. Winter was spent mostly on the bottom of the lake in a highly slowed down phase near dormancy; carrying on little respiration. Following ice-out, they can return to the surface. A clear day seen above the chilly water in May is inviting for these aquatic reptiles to climb up and bask in the sun. Air temperatures may be warm; water is still cool. These days of late May or early June, might be the best time of the year for us to see turtles "sunning" themselves.

The apparent inactivity and resting in the sun is very important for turtles. While here, they make needed vitamins and the dry heat helps to rid their bodies of parasites; and of course, raise their body temperature. Logs, like this one, are very important for the local turtles. It is quite common on days similar to this to see about a dozen here; but there have been times in late May that I have noted more than fifty at once. Nearly always, they are painted turtles, but occasionally, a larger and darker snapping turtle climbs aboard too.

Basking turtles is just one of three happenings to observe in the lives of turtles at this time. Spring is when the young that hatched in buried nests last year will emerge and crawl towards a wetland. We may find these one to two-inch critters as they cross our roads and paths. As we get into June, adults come ashore to dig holes for a new batch of eggs. They may choose shorelines, but also driveways, roadsides, yards and parks to dig into the soil and deposit eggs. But on these clear days of late May, they appear inactive as they passively bask in spring sunlight.

June 7, 2020

More Green: It's Luna Moth Time

The growing month of June is upon us. Long days, including the summer solstice, with moisture (statistically, June is our wettest month) and warm temperatures cause quite a response of growth with plants. We witnessed the greening of the woods during May. What began as a time of bare branches and twigs on trees ended with an intense green foliage. Spring ephemerals on the forest floor succeeded in grabbing available sunlight at about mid-month; giving quite a floral display. These were followed by ones that tolerate the shade of the leafing trees. Despite the present shady woods, the forest floor remains green. Many other plants now flower at the woods edge. Soon flowering will be in open spaces. We observed the avian migration during May. May was migration; June is nesting. The region now has many diverse daily choruses as the feathered residents sing their territorial proclamations.

This amazing month has much more happening. June is also the month of insects. Anyone spending time in the northland is well aware of the "bugs of June". But besides black flies and mosquitoes, June is also when we see dragonflies emerging from their aquatic youth. The diversity of these fast-flying insect predators continues in these weeks. In addition to the diurnal dragonfly dazzling display of flight, we can see more after dark; when fireflies make their appearance. Often these living lights will begin in May and continue into July.

Colorful "flying flowers"; butterflies, show their diversity of size and color at this time too. Two of our largest kinds flutter about now: tiger swallowtails and monarchs. While the latter migrates, the former wintered in its chrysalis here. Both take nectar from the many flowers of June. But other large insects are here as well.

June is the time of the biggest moths. Four types of silk-worm months; family Saturniidae, can be seen in the region now. They are mostly nocturnal; resting in the daytime. Each has wingspan of at least four inches; far beyond other moths. Three of these; *Promethea, Polyphemus and Cecropia* are brown to reddish-brown with "eye spots" on wings. And the other large moth; the *Luna,* is green.

During a woods walk in June, I wandered on a trail that had a thick growth of leafy shrubs along the edge. As I looked, I noticed that not all the green was leaves. I was seeing a Luna moth with pale-green wings and long hindwing "tails". Eye-spots are on both forewings and hindwings. On the underside, the stout white body can be seen. Like many other moths, antennae are feathery. It may be hard to see the connection between this moth and the moon; Luna, except for night flying. Supposedly, they are called Luna because someone noted that the arc made by the long hindwing "tails" were in the same shape as the waxing and waning crescent phases of the moon.

The adult state is short. They mate and lay eggs at this time; not even eating meals. The plump green caterpillars with light lines and red dots, feed on leaves of birch. When ready to form a cocoon, they drop to the ground and make a brown papery cocoon where the pupa winters. Though we may not see the caterpillar or the cocoon, now in June, we may be fortunate enough to find the green adult as it rests on leaves in the daytime; as I did during a June woods walk.

June 14, 2020

Pines Show New Growth on Branches

During the last two months, the northland deciduous trees that stood out in the cold all winter without any foliage have put on quite a show. It began with the formation of catkins in early April. These long-shaped unique flowers on branches of willows, aspen, alders and hazels developed pollen. And taking advantage of the breezes at this time, the pollen scattered about. Silver maples and then red maples took this to the next step as they developed small reddish (pistilate) flowers on female trees and staminate flowers with plenty of pollen on male trees. April remained without tree foliage.

As we entered May, the leaf buds began to open on local woody plants. Beginning with smaller ones, like elderberry and gooseberry, the greening rose on taller trees with quaking aspens. Throughout the thirty-one days of this month, the greening continued. As we exited the month, even the trees that were slow to open their leaves, were greening as well. By the first week of June, the woods is fully green.

In the midst of all of this greening, many deciduous trees put on another show of their own; this one was floral. Shortly after mid-month, a trio of small trees; plum, juneberry and pin cherry opened up flower buds of another type. Often called blossoms when on trees, these attractive clusters of petaled flowers also started appearing in other trees and by the time we reach June, blossoms have shown up on elderberry, chokecherry, crab apple, domestic apple and lilac. For the last couple of weeks, we have been able to see plenty of forest flora without looking at the forest floor. (In the shade of the greening woods, the early spring wild flowers have faded.) Willows and aspens that were early to form catkins, now give an encore. The seeds that developed from the April pollination have matured. With coats of fluff, they drift in the breeze at this time; a "warm-weather snowfall".

Meanwhile the coniferous trees waited until all of this change from the deciduous trees had passed and now it is the conifer time. Walking by pine trees in mid-June, we see new growth of this season as extensions of branches stick up in a vertical pose. Being a lighter color, it is easy to discern this new growth. Such growths, often called candles, are most obvious on pines though new growth happens on other conifers too.

What is happening is that the trees; regardless of their age, are growing new branches (twigs). Trees never stop growing their whole life and do so in three ways. They grow down in the soil from the roots; wider on the trunks, and longer on the tips (twigs) of branches. Taking advantage of the conditions of June; warm, wet and plenty of sunlight; they put fort a new growth that last a couple of weeks. And we now see it clearly at this time. (Deciduous trees also grow longer branches, but are not as obvious as the coniferous ones.)

With conifers, this is quickly followed by the formation; growth and maturation of pollen cones with pollen drifting in the air. We often see this yellow dust on lakes. But now, we see this new growth on pines telling us that the trees continue to grow. The pines are one of many trees and flowers that grow much in June.

June 21, 2020

Flowers Tell of the End of Spring

Many of Northlanders who spend winters here have learned to look forward to the vernal equinox; the first day of spring, usually about March 21. After the cold of forty or more days of subzero and a snowpack that remains on the ground for about one hundred fifty days, this new season of spring is a relief. Getting out and watching the snow subside along with rising temperatures and the longer days, we get plenty to see during the months of April and May. Late lingering snows and below normal temperatures may slow things a bit, but overall, this season grows by very rapidly. Along with ice out and bird migration, we may take note of the changes on the forest floor. After being covered with snow for months, the site gets spring sunlight and rapidly, myriads of wild flowers take advantage to put forth leaves and flowers in this early-season sunlight; and just as quickly, they fade. These ephemerals with a short flowering time, took advantage of the sunlight that penetrated the forest trees.

But overhead, leaves came out on the trees during May and cast shade over these sunny sites where the early spring flowers were. Their place was taken by a batch of flowers that did well in the shade. Clintonia, starflower, wild lily-of-the valley, bunchberry, Solomon's-seal and yellow lady-slipper orchid tolerate the shade of the darkening woods and last for a couple of weeks; May into June. But their time is also passing and the nearby ferns, growing a few feet tall, will thrive for the summer. But the floral season is not over. It has moved.

Anyone driving some of the area roads at this time is quick to notice that there are many wild flowers in bloom. No longer in the woods, they are now out in the sunlight of the open spaces. Whether it is roadsides, unmowed lawns, fields or even parts of wetlands; a plethora of wild flowers are now adding color to the scene, and they do not need to compete with trees.

There are more than a dozen kinds here now; clovers, sweet-clovers, vetches, cinquefoils, buttercups, fleabanes, yarrow and goatsbeard. They blend in colors to make the roadside bouquets a rainbow variety. But it is four kinds that seem to be most noted.

Daisy with a yellow center (disc flowers) and surrounding white (ray flowers) are abundant now. About as numerous are the hawkweeds of both yellow and orange. (Orange hawkweed is sometimes called Indian paintbrush. The true Indian paintbrush grows more in prairie country further west and is quite uncommon in our region.) And there are the tall spikes of lupine; varying in color, but mostly blue-purple. White, yellow, orange, red, blue and purple invite us for a closer look. These abundant field flora tell us that spring has ended; the flowers in the open outnumber those in the woods at the time of summer solstice.

It is interesting to note that when the huge majority of woodland spring wild flowers are native, many of these field wild flowers are non-native. Despite their colors, some are not appreciated; even seen as noxious weeds. These summer wild flowers now in fields are often composites, spring wild flowers rarely are. Whether native or not and whether they are seen as pretty flowers or nasty weeds, they now add a lot of color to roadsides and fields, as we enter this new season of summer.

June 29, 2020

Yellow-Throated Vireos Sing and Nest

Early morning walks in late June are a delight. Temperatures tend to be pleasant; often with calm winds and sometimes a dew. Though uninvited companions; mosquitoes and black flies, will frequently accompany me, the discoveries at this time are worth it. It seems like each day there is more flora in bloom. The small trees; three kinds of viburnum; nannyberry, highbush cranberry and arrowwood flower now and they are joined by a few kinds of dogwoods. Smaller bushes of rose, raspberry, thimbleberry and blackberry add to the scene. And there are the summer wild flowers on the roadsides; mostly daisies and hawkweeds. Closing for the night, they open with the sunrise.

Also greeting the new day are the plethora of songbirds. By the house, I hear a robin. In the nearby forest, two other thrushes, hermit thrush and veery, provide other songs. As I move along the road, I hear from grosbeaks, orioles, flycatchers and about a half dozen kinds of warblers. Coming to a field, I hear songs of Savannah sparrows. And as I reach a wetland, I note swamp sparrows, song sparrows and singing red-winged blackbirds, still proclaiming their territorial ownership; something that they began in late March. A mother wood duck is here with her growing family while a couple of tree swallows feed over the water and kingbirds call from the shore. But there is more to hear than birds; the summer frogs, mink and green frogs, are calling. Out in the water, the yellow pond-lilies that have been open since May are now joined by the larger white water-lilies; while irises glow along the edges.

During such a walk at daybreak, I expect to see and hear these avian songsters. In their breeding season, these sounds are a consistent part of my walks. But when it comes to consistent singing, none can outdo the vireos. Vireos are small birds, maybe a little larger than warblers. They are not particularly colorful and all kinds seem to have dark feathers on much of their bodies. In the northland, we can see five kinds of vireos each year; red-eyed, yellow-throated, blue-headed, Philadelphia and warbling. Of this group, two kinds; red-eyed and yellow-throated, are residents of the forest that I wonder through. In the persistent pattern as found with these birds, both sing repetitive songs among the deciduous trees where they live.

The red-eyed is better known and very common in the region. Within their home territory, they construct a small nest in the fork of branches. Nests may be quite low and are not hard to find since they frequently live in our yards. The two-phrase song; often heard now sounds like "see-me; hear-me" and is sung hundreds (or more) times a day.

Lesser known is the yellow-throated vireo. With bright yellow under the head, they are much brighter than the drab red-eyed vireo. Nests are similar to the red-eyed, but high in the trees, where most of their singing takes place. Songs of the yellow-troated are also of two phrases, but their voice is more slurred. Yellow-throated vireos are more common to the south of here; it appears as though we are on the northern fringe of their range.

As the day warms, most songbirds sing less, but not the vireos. Both vireos are regular songsters now and in the weeks to come. When most birds will slow or cease their singing in July, vireos, especially, the red-eyed, will persist through the summer.

Third Quarter

July 5, 2020

Ringlets; Brown Butterflies on Flowers

Along with the heat and sunlight of this summer month of July, we see plenty of roadside flowers in bloom. The daisy and hawkweed abundance of June may still be lingering during this month, but many are being replaced by summer flora that will continue throughout the coming warm weeks. The yellows of hawkweeds are giving way to black-eyed susans and oxeye sunflowers. Cow parsnip with white umbels, maybe eight feet tall, stands above others on the roadsides. Blends of purple are seen in Canada thistles, fireweeds and milkweeds. Whether it is the plants of June still present or those of July, roadsides and fields reveal plenty of color each day.

I find that walking the same route regularly is far from boring and I see a new story each time I come by. These wild flowers have my attention and as I look closer, I see that I'm not the only one to be attracted to these colorful summer bouquets. Myriads of insects gather here too for various reasons. Plants buzz with activity of bees, wasps, flies, moths and butterflies. From sunrise to sunset, these open flowers host plenty of visitors. Most come to take nectar; often with pollen as well. Others, predators, take advantage of the insect gathering for some hunting. The patches of flowers also abound with the flight antics of dragonflies.

Recently, when I took a field flora walk in the sunlight and heat, I stopped often to look over the scene. Insects gathering nectar were oblivious of me and I closely observed them. Their potential predators surveyed the region too. Dragonflies seen were pennants, corporals, whitefaces, emeralds, gomphids and darners. These winged hunters were joined by crab spiders that stayed on the rays of daisies and black-eyed susans. (These spiders that were white on the daisies of June are now mostly yellow on the black-eyed susans of July.)

The flowers were not the only colors out here today. Fluttering over them are colorful insects; about a dozen kinds of butterflies. The two largest, yellow tiger swallowtails and orange monarchs were easy to see. But there is plenty more. Mid-sized but also colorful are the checkered black-orange fritillaries. I see two kinds; atlantis and silver-bordered. Nearby, is the white and black; white admiral. Smaller orange butterflies; crescents, checkerspots and skippers were frequent flyers and feeders as well. Easy to overlook were the brown ones.

We expect colorful insects when seeking butterflies; and they are (even sometimes called flying flowers), but some not as colorful are also flying now. During my walk, I found three kinds of brown butterflies. Two of them; little wood satyr and northern pearly-eye were along the wooded trail that I took to get to the field. But out here among the blooming field flowers, I also see the orange-brown common ringlets. Mid-sized butterflies, these less-colorfuls are closely related to the brighter ones. When the other two brown butterflies in the woods were feeding on rotted material and sap, ringlets chose nectar. Many butterflies open wings while basking in sunlight; not so for the ringlets. They are lateral baskers; wings remain closed as they feed and sit in the sun. We'll see many more kinds of butterflies among the flowers this summer month. They will be various colors; many quite bright, but let's not overlook the ringlets and other brown butterflies also flying now.

July 12, 2020

Swamp Candles Glow from the Shores

My daily walks take me past forests, fields and wetlands. During my wandering now, the roadsides abound with plenty of summer wild flowers. By the time we get to July, grasses are tall, but the varied wild flowers are able to bloom with them quite well. Some flowers from earlier in the season can still be found; daisies, fleabanes, yarrows, clovers, vetches and buttercups. But as we get into the days of mid-July, a whole new batch of summer wild flowers takes over these sites.

During my walks in June, I watched many of these plants growing. Now, triggered by the amount of daylight, warm temperatures and even though it has been dry, enough moisture, these wild flowers have grown and opened for a mid-summer bouquet of note. Here we see the yellows of black-eyed susans, yellow sweetclovers, mulleins and evening primrose (flowering at night, but the four-petaled flowers are still open in the early morning). Purples of Canada thistles, milkweeds and fireweeds add more to the scene that I pass regularly and looking at these plants, I note their changes each day as well. Robust cow parsnips and white sweetclovers mix theirs with the other colors. The roadsides and fields are not the only open spaces now available and I field plenty of colors among the waters in the wetlands of lakes, ponds and swamps. Out in the open waters, the colors of yellow pond-lilies and white water-lilies abound. The yellow pond-lilies with elliptical floating leaves that began to flower in May are still with us. The large white water-lilies with the circular leaves did not begin to blossom until late June. I watch them open each morning. These yellows and whites add to the wetlands, but there is more. Often, it may be hard to notice, but a smaller floating-leaf flower is here too. Water shield with its little oval leaves and tiny flowers can get missed. In the shallows are other small flowers sticking up from submerged leaves. The yellow flowers of bladderwort attract insects while the hollow leaves catch insects at the water's surface to feed on them.

Looking along the shore where the irises and water calla were growing earlier are a couple of summer flowers; small blue marsh skullcap and the tall white water hemlock. Soon Joe pye weed and arrowheads will be growing and blooming here too. And then as I take a closer look at this space near the water, I see the delightful yellow loosestrife.

With a single spike of five-petaled yellow flowers sticking up above the leafy stem of one to two feet tall, it is easy to see why they are also called swamp candles. They appear to glow a yellow color from this lush water's edge. This yellow plant is just one of several kinds of loosestrifes that we have in the northland during summer. In the shaded woods, whorled and fringed loosestrifes open large five-petaled flowers on tall plants. Also, in the wetlands is the small clustered flowers of tufted loosestrife. (The purple loosestrife, an un appreciated and unwanted flower of the swamps, is not in this family of native loosestrifes.) These yellow loosestrifes whether in the woods or the wetlands are desired and add much to the days of mid-summers. And the candles continue to grow and glow in the swamps.

July 19, 2020

Ebony Jewelwings Flutter by Streams.

July, especially one that is above normal in temperature, is a good time to see insects. Though we may not always appreciate the heat, these six-legged critters that share the region with us, do quite well. Perhaps it is a couple of the lesser-loved ones that we are most aware of. Mosquitoes continue to be with us, mostly at dawn or dusk, while the larger deer flies circle us during our moving about in the daylight hours. But there are myriads of other insects here too.

In the sunlight on these summer days, we can see many butterflies as they visit flowers. The large and well-known monarchs take nectar from a variety of flowers, but they select milkweeds, now in bloom, for egg laying. Those flying at this time will die by the end of the summer; their young will make the long south flight. Another large butterfly of the northland, tiger swallowtail, is unlikely to be seen now; more common in June. Others out among the flowers of yards, gardens, parks, roadsides and fields include fritillaries, crescents, checkerspots, white admirals, yellow sulphurs, cabbage whites and brown ringlets and wood nymphs. Tiny, but abundant, are the orange skippers. A few moths fly in the daytime, but they are much more diverse after dark. Bees, wasps and flies abound now and of course, taking advantage of this scene are the predacious spiders; more and larger webs each day.

Also feeding on insects, but not as the sedentary spiders hunt are species of dragonflies that use aerial patrolling and excellent eyesight to locate and catch prey. Spending nights in plants, they bask with open wings in the early morning hours. During my walks, I have seen darners, whiteface species, gomphids, emeralds, pennants, and the dazzling whitetail and twelve-spot skimmers. I expect to soon see meadowhawks as the season progresses. But their cousins are here too.

Not as big or as well-known are the damselflies. Dragonflies and damselflies make up the insect order of Odonata. A simple rule (with exceptions) is that when the dragonflies rest with wings sticking out perpendicular to the body, damselflies hold wings parallel to their thin bodies. Probably the damselflies that we are most likely to see are the small bluets as they fly along the shoreline. They may land on a dock, boat or even us in these flights. These pond damselflies may be the first ones that we see in summer. The exception to the rule are the spreadwings that hold wings out from their body at about a forty-five-degree angle. They are usually later in the season.

Recently, during my morning walks, I have located a site of broad-winged damselflies. Along a small stream, they sit in the morning light. Known as ebony jewelwings, they have black wings and a head, thorax and abdomen of bright metallic green; reaching about two inches long. They are a delight to behold. Instead of quick flights as seen with dragonflies, ebony jewelwings flutter about almost in the manor of butterflies. But unlike butterflies, these beautiful and delicate-looking damselflies are predators and seek meals of other insects. While the wings of the males are all black, females have white marking on the tips of wings. Though a regular part of the summer insect population, they are more confined to these stream habitats and not seen as often as their cousins. I was fortunate to observe these delightful insects.

July 26, 2020

Late July: Tiny Toad Time

As I walk to the lake this morning, I see some mushrooms near the trail; a testimony to the recent rains and the season moving on. At the edge of the woods, I note that raspberries and blueberries have become ripe. They both contribute to my breakfast on this clear July day. In the dew, spider webs are easy to see. In recent weeks, these snares have become more numerous and larger as the spiders grow in summer. I have seen that spiders tend to be larger during hot weather. Apparently, they find more food in these conditions. Arriving at the lake, I watch the local loon pair with their young chick. While the adults dive, the little fluff stays on the surface. Again, there is more happening at the lake. From along the shore comes two sounds of the season; "knock-knock" calls of mink frogs and plucking sounds made by green frogs. Both of these frogs are summer breeders and mark the end of anuran (frogs and toads) reproductive time. Laying eggs late in the season here, their tadpoles are able to winter in this large body of water; reaching maturity next year.

It's been a tough time for some of the frogs that were breeding early in the spring. Wood frogs: mid to late April; chorus frogs: mid April to mid May and spring peepers: mid April to late May. Many vernal ponds that appeared so full of water and ample for frog breeding in spring could not handle the arid conditions of the next couple of months; drying up. No water in the vernal ponds; no sites for tadpoles to grow. Fortunately, not all ponds had this harmful happening.

Leaving the lake and taking the path through the woods to the yard, I see that there were many successful products of the season. This region has an abundance of tiny toads. Minute versions of adults, these very young toads are barely one-half inch long. Seeing them in this setting is a regular occurrence of late July. This year, it is also a very welcome sight; it tells me that some toads found safe places to breed and despite the dryness of May and June, they were able to develop.

American toads have a short breeding period; usually less than a week. This year, I noted this time to be between May 20 and May 30. During this lively week, male high-pitch trills punctuated landscapes surrounding the wetlands and seemed to be heard any hour day or night. As I see now in mid summer, they apparently have chosen well to lay their eggs; mostly avoiding drying ponds. Unlike frogs that place eggs in masses of jelly, toads string theirs in the water. Quickly the larvae develop within and the dark tadpoles scatter in the shallows. Here, they feed on algae and grow so rapidly that they are able to leave the water in less than two months. During their development, they grow legs; hind ones first, front ones later. They grow lungs for breathing in their new terrestrial lives; no longer needing gills. And one day, they go from wetland homes as metamorphosed tiny toads. With rough skin, they keep from desiccating as they move through the woods and yards. They find food in the myriads of insects that live here, but they also can become meals for other predators. It is a good sight on a hot July day to see numerous tiny toads after a dry May and June.

August 2, 2020

Lichen Spider Comes to Stay

The month of August is an amazing time in northland nature. We are still in summer, and often have hot days, but the later sunrises and earlier sunsets each day show that the season is moving on. With birds, it is a time of early migrants and late nesters. Gardens give us produce while new wild berries ripen each week. Mushrooms of various sizes and colors abound in the woods and the wild flowers of late summer, most notably sunflowers, goldenrods and asters prevail on the roadsides. Tall and robust, these flowers often persist to fall. In these warm days, insects continue to reveal their diversity. Butterflies, moths, bees, wasps, flies, grasshoppers and late-season dragonflies continue their movements among the grown flora. And when there are many insects, so there are predator spiders. These eight-legged critters abound now and for us, August is prime web-watching time.

Many of the local spiders do not make webs, but others that do are easy to see on these dew-covered mornings. Each day, I see their snares. I often see all four types; orbs, sheets, funnels and cobwebs during a single walk shortly after dawn. Perhaps the best known of these webs (and most photogenic) are the orb webs. Constructed in circular shapes, these insect catchers are known as orb webs. Though there are exceptions, typically orb-weaving spiders build their snares at dusk; intent on catching night-flying insects. After being out in the night, the webs are frequently knocked down by winds the following day, but in the calm of early morning, these dew-covered marvels stand out. Using tall grasses, wild flowers or tree branches as substrates, spiders form their webs. Each day when I walk, I expect to see them; often wearing a necklace of dew. Frequently, I go looking for these webs, and sometimes they come to me.

Recently as I was putting the car into the garage, I glanced into a nearby tree and saw a Wow of a Web. The circular sticky part of this web (only the spiral threads in the center are sticky) was about two feet in diameter and nearly four feet above the ground; where it was anchored. Threads also held the web from above in branches to the right and left, both about three to four feet long. What a huge web. The web-maker was not in its web, but with some searching, I located the large body curled on an adjacent branch; next to a growth of lichens. The blue-green color of the spider's abdomen blended with the color of the lichens. This is fitting since this kind of spider often makes webs in trees with lichens and hides there. It is known as the Lichen Orbweaver. Using its sedentary hunting style at night, it sits in the center, the hub, of the web in the darkness. When not in use, the spider may take down the web by consuming the threads; recycling the material to make a new web the next day.

With this delightful addition to the yard, web watching, always interesting, has added much to the summer. Though most catching happens at night; primarily moths did see it snag a dragonfly one day. I'm thankful to this lichen spider for deciding to build such a huge web in my yard and I hope that it will stay; revealing more interesting web watching during this amazing month of August.

August. 9, 2020

Arrowhead time now along Shores

Calls of mink and green frogs greet me as I arrive at the lake on this clear and calm summer morning. I scare up a mink frog and get a good look at it. These aquatic frogs are not often seen out of water. Out in the lake, a pair of loons swim in unison as they escort their young one. Plants along the shore hold many circular spider webs. These orbs, constructed last night, show good catching of night-flying insects. Here too are a couple of dozing meadowhawk dragonflies; they are waiting for warmth of sunlight. Over the water's surface, I watch a group of whirligig beetles scatter and do their gyrating movements. Paddling away from shore, I see that I'm not alone. A beaver comes by; going under when I get too close. A kingfisher rattles its call and flies ahead of me. Bobbing motion on a log followed by a low flight above the water tell me of a spotted sandpiper. At one site, I come up to a group of phoebes (probably this year's family) breakfasting on insects.

As I paddle near shore, I see plenty of summer wild flowers that take advantage of this sunlit location; near water. White flattop asters thrive as well as a patch of yellow goldenrods and sunflowers. All will continue through the coming weeks of late summer. Nearby, I see more whites; boneset and pearly everlasting Three kinds of flowers, more associated with earlier in summer are still lingering here; yellow loosestrife (swamp candles), purple joe pye weed and orange jewelweed. A bit further up on shore are pink and white spirea; some flowering, but mostly forming seeds.

As I move through the floating round leaves of white water-lilies; many with flowers now emerging from under water in the morning sunlight, I see that they are not the only emergents. Most of the flowers on shore are out of the water, but there are those that begin under water and grow above to flower. Not only the white water-lilies, but near them are small yellow flowers of bladderworts creeping from below. And there the hard-to-overlook arrowheads.

When many plants are named after their flowers, arrowheads owe their label to the large leaves. The stalks of both the flowers and leaves stickup from the water. Floral spikes which hold many blossoms rise above the water with no leaves attached. The large flowers of two inches are white and of only three petals. (Among the aquatic plants, three-petaled blossoms are not very common.) Also rising up from the subsurface are the rather robust leaves. Highly variable, these leaves may be only six inches long or maybe a couple of feet; and they can be narrow or wide. All are roughly shaped like arrowheads; a point on the apex of the highest leaf part while two other parts are turned down; making the shape of an arrowhead.

I consider arrowhead flowering time in the wetlands to be in mid-summer; early August. Leaves have been present for some time, but only recently have the flowers joined. Most of us refer to this plant as arrowhead, but it may also be called "duck potato". The tubers beneath the water are edible and may be gathered by those who go through the bother to dig them. As I paddle by the shores, I'm satisfied with just looking at these white flowers with the tell-tale leaves along with all the other aquatic plants on this mid-summer morning.

August 16, 2020

The Swans of July

Since March, much staying at home has meant taking a closer look at nearby nature. What evolved out of this was regular, almost daily, walks along a nearby road. The route takes me by woods, fields, swamps, ponds and a river. Walking in the morning, I have been able to see plenty of local wildlife. And I have been able to watch the seasons change. It might be wild flowers, tree leafing, insects or songbirds, but each day; each week, the seasons unfold during these walks.

A site that I pause at for a closer look is a roadside pond. This wetland of maybe five acres is near the road and grants me ample opportunity to observe changes occurring here. One group of birds that has clearly shown the seasonal happenings are the water birds. In the early spring, shortly after ice out, migratory waterfowl began to appear. Mallards, shovelers, buffleheads, ring-necked and wood ducks all settled in for some resting before moving on. Other waterfowl were seen on this site as well; pied-billed grebe, hooded merganser and Canada geese. Despite the nearness of the road, they learned that passing cars were harmless, but a walker coming by was harder for them to accept. Most birds rested and then resumed their northing flights, but a few; geese, wood ducks, hooded mergansers and mallards found nearby sites for nesting and proceeded to bring their young onto the pond. Many an early summer walk was made more interesting as I stopped to watch these families swim through growths of water-lilies. A protective mother kept the fluffy young ones with her.

During June, the immatures grew and dispersed (or maybe they hid well) and I saw fewer. Only a solitary wood duck, mallard or hooded merganser (and once a black duck) came by after the summer solstice.

But on July 1, that changed as a couple of trumpeter swans arrived. I had seen these large white birds here before, but usually in passing. This pair was different. They found the shallow pond with an abundance of aquatic plants; water-lilies, water shields, cattails, arrowheads and more to be a fine place. They settled in for the next phase of their life. This was not to be nesting; too late for that, but these unmated birds were molting. Molting happens each summer and often during July. The birds shed their old feathers and grow new ones. This includes the flight feathers on the wings; the primaries. And for a couple of weeks in summer, the are flightless. This usually corresponds with the nesting time for trumpeter swans and parents remain with the young; no need for flying. But with these non-breeding birds, they chose a pond that was protective enough with secluded sites to stay. This pond also provided plant material; giving adequate food for these large birds. They spent all of July silently resting, feeding and pruning.

Many passersby commented on the swans that came to stay. I also observed them during my daily walks. I noted how they settled in and I wondered if they would last into the fall. But then came August. When I wandered by on August 1, they were gone; an observation easy to see. Apparently, using their new flight feathers, they flew to another location. One month to the day; but what a wonderful addition to the summer these swans of July made.

Aug.23, 2020

Northern Toothed; An August Fungus

The rains of July followed the dry months of April, May and June (third driest June or record) and by the end of the month, the total precipitation was above normal. Though the rains were a great help for the berry season and the beginning of mushroom time, July ended in a dry spell. During the last third of the month, we received almost no rain. August started the same way; for the first week. This changed radically during the night of August 7 – 8 when a downpour came by. My rain gauge held four and one-half inches of rain! Others in the region recorded even more. Once again, we (at least some of us) were back in a wetter-than-normal month.

Awesome August with its garden produce, berries, bird migration, insects and spider webs has much to offer. But I find one of the greatest happenings at this time is the plethora of mushrooms. The August rains were well accepted by these quick growths in the woods. A walk in the woods following these rains became one of forest fungi finds. I easily located more than a dozen kinds of mushrooms and other fungi without leaving the trail.

Mushrooms are often known only by their Latin or scientific names; that does not take away any of their discovery delights. My mushroom finds began in the yard with brown *Marasmius* and gray *Coprinus* (inky-caps). Soon after entering the woods, I found several kinds and colors of *Russula*; especially white, red and yellow. White *Lactarius* (milk mushroom), red and yellow *Hygrocybe* (waxy-caps) and gray *Mycena* were here too. Not far away, I found a patch of golden *Cantharellus* (chanterelles). Large *Amanitas* of yellow and white were conspicuous off the trail. All these mushrooms hold gills or folds under their caps where reproductive spores are formed. But there were others here too.

Boletes; mushrooms that do not have gills under the caps, but instead have tiny holes for their reproductive spores; and so are called porous mushrooms, are also very common in the woods. I found several boletes; including *Leccinum* (scaber stalks) and *Strobilomyces* (old man of the woods). On logs, were tan and gold *Ramaria* (coral fungi); near a growth of yellow-brown *Pholiota* (scaly-caps). On another downed log, I found a thick growth of white *Pleurotus* (oyster fungi) and a fresh batch of *Laetiporus* (sulphur-shelf; chicken-of-the-woods). This orange-yellow growth seemed to light up the dark log. I had gotten used to looking down to see all these fungal finds, but higher up on a stump, I found the biggest growth of all; *Climacodon* (northern tooth fungus).

The white shelf fungus was layered in several "shelves" as it extended for a foot tall and nearly as wide. This long fungal growth is a type of shelf fungus. Many kinds of shelves are on trunks and stumps throughout the northland. These have either gills or pores on the undersides; beneath the robust shelves, where the spores are produced. Northern tooth (also called "shelving tooth") differs by having spine-like structures, known as teeth, that give the northern tooth its name. Many of the porous shelf fungi will last for months; some are perennial and survive winters. This thick and rough-looking northern tooth does not. It will turn from its present white color to become yellow-brown when aged and fading. But for now, the northern tooth adds height and delight to mushroom woods walks.

August 30, 2020

This is Great Web-Watching Time

Late August continues to be a remarkable time. With fewer than fourteen hours of daylight, we are seeing migration of warblers, geese, nighthawks, raptors at Hawk Ridge as well as monarch butterflies. The woods still has a plethora of mushrooms. Roadsides and fields abound with tall yellow native goldenrods. Not only do they add much floral colors to the scene, they are also the site of myriads of insects and spiders. And, these days are the best for spider web-watching.

Several conditions come together in late summer making this prime time for web watching. Spiders have been growing all summer and are now full grown. Abundant insects provide plenty of food. Days are warm enough for their activity. But it is the nights and early mornings that allow for us to view these webs. A clear night sends out spiders to construct their insect-catching snares. As night progresses into cool mornings, dew settles onto plants of fields, roadsides and swamps; and the webs. The rising sun provides for illumination for us to observe and photograph these droplet-covered marvelous works. Web watching in early morning is best done as we move towards the dawn; giving a back-lit scene.

We tend to think of webs for spiders (the word spider is a derivative of "spinder"), but many of these eight-legged hunters do not make webs; using other methods to catch prey. Among those making webs, four types exist. Common indoors and out are cobwebs; looking like a mass of threads; they are more complicated than appear. Looking like cloths on grass are funnel webs. A central hole where the spider stays gives funnel its name. Frequently in evergreens are sheet webs; often looking bowl-shaped. But the one that I look for at this time are the circular orb webs. And conditions are just right now for these webs.

Though there are exceptions, most orb webs are formed at dusk; intending on catching night-flying insects. They remain during the calm night and into the dew-covered cool mornings before being knocked down by winds. Most are constructed in a vertical position; easier to catch flying insects. Moths appear to be the intended victims, but other nocturnal insects are accepted too. The orb webs are truly remarkable formations. Several kinds of silk go into the making of a single web. The protein silk comes from glands within the spider's abdomen. Each gland has a tube to carry silk to the spinnerets on the "tail" end of the body. When exposed to the air, liquid silk become threads. These threads are pulled from the spinnerets by the spider's hind legs.

Orb webs have threads going towards the center (hub). These radii (spokes) provide the structure of the snare, but are not sticky. Spiral threads attached to the radii are sticky. Insects hitting spirals get stuck. The web-maker sits patiently either in the hub or to the side. Prey are usually wrapped in threads.

Webs vary in size, number of radii and spirals for different species. With some practice, we can determine the kind of spider by just seeing the web. Spiders construct webs on most evenings of late summer and do so in a pattern; taking about one-half hour to complete. Nearly all the webs that we see are made by females and she is nearly blind; relying on feeling to locate the prey. From now until frosts of mid-September is prime time for us to get out in dew-covered mornings and observe orb webs in these grasses and goldenrods.

September 6, 2020

Migrating Autumn Warblers

Early September follows the last weeks of August by being a time filled with nature happenings. The woods still abounds with mushroom species. Roadsides and fields have an abundance of blooming late summer flowers; especially sunflowers, goldenrods and asters. These plants host myriads of insects; often buzzing with activity. Opportunistic spiders build webs here to feed on the available prey. Days can still be quite warm, but these days are also getting shorter. With sunrise at about 6:30 AM; setting near 7:30 PM, the thirteen hours are moving towards the autumnal equinox. Though the summer was hotter than normal, decreasing daylight tells of other changes; as seen with migrants in early September.

It started slowly in mid-summer with sporadic movements of tree swallows and shorebirds, but as we went through August so did more bird migration. Now, in early September, migrants are a daily occurrence. Being where we are, near Lake Superior, we frequently see this autumn avian phenomenon as birds, heading to the south, choose to fly by us rather than cross the big lake. Each day now, during my morning walk, I hear and see flocks of Canada geese. Starting with just a couple about a month ago, these flocks have enlarged to more than twenty. Ducks of different kinds are appearing and resting in wetlands as they fly by. Along the roadsides are groups of robins, blackbirds and waxwings. Mostly these are families that feed before going south, but the numbers regularly grow. Groups of flickers, a kind of woodpecker, are here too; but often they pause to feed on ground ants. At Hawk Ridge, raptors; especially sharp-shinned and broad-winged hawks along with bald eagles are on the move. But I like to sit in the yard and watch the warblers as they pass through.

Late last May, warbler waves; composed of several species, provided much interest as they traveled north. Of the nearly two dozen kinds coming by, about one-half remained to breed. And as I observe these small five-inch birds flitting through the branches at this time, I see that the ones who nested here are most common; ovenbirds, yellowthroats, redstarts along with chestnut-sided warblers, golden-winged warblers, black and white warblers and Nashville warblers; all seen regularly. The families feed as they move through the trees often in the company of nuthatches, chickadees or vireos. Unlike their visits in spring, they no longer sing, they have molted from their breeding plumage and adult birds have their young accompanying them. Such conditions make warbler watching in fall a little harder than spring. Fortunately, most of the resident ones have not changed their plumage much; still looking similar to the way they appeared earlier. Others from further north; Cape May warblers, bay-breasted warblers, blackpoll warblers and pine warblers may be more of a challenge to recognize. In fall feathers, they may look quite different.

Birds flit through the branches as they move and feed. Usually, the families of warblers are mixed with other families; making groups of several species, known as waves. With binoculars and patience, the different kinds of warblers can be discerned and they are a joy to watch. Such warbler waves will continue through at least the first half of the month. Later, two species; palm warblers and yellow-rumped warblers, will show that the warbler flight is waning. But now, in early September, we see plenty of kinds of these moving warblers.

September 13, 2020

Growth of a Hornet Nest

We have been able to watch plenty of insect happenings throughout the warm months. Shortly after the arrival of black flies and mosquitoes in May, we saw the night glow with fireflies. Dragonflies prevailed during June and their diversity and population was seen again this year. (Species vary from April to October and we are never without them. Now, small red meadowhawk dragonflies abound.)

Later in the summer, butterflies got our attention. These “flying flowers” showed us how abundant they are in mid-summer. Varying in size and color, they fluttered through these hot days. (Like dragonflies, we still have some with us late in the season; notably white cabbage and yellow sulphurs.) And there was the annual flight of mayflies; abundance depends on our location, but we all see some. Now with the lesser amount of daylight, there are other insect activities.

Bird migration is easy to see now, but so do a couple of insects. Best known is the monarch flight; going to south of the border. Not as long of a flight or as well-known is the migration of green darner dragonflies. (Some days at Hawk Ridge, more darners are pass by than raptors.) Another strange phenomenon at this time may be in our yards; the flight of ants. As a way of dispersal from the populated colonies underground, they take to the air; the only time in the ant's lives when they have wings. To our surprise, we may notice "a bunch of bugs" flying up from a hole in the ground.

I was fortunate to have a nest of hornets on the side of a nearby building this summer. As the season progressed, this structure grew. Beginning about the size of a golf ball in June, it reached maturity; nearly the size of a football in August. Throughout these days, there was constant movements of hornets; in and out of the nest opening. Hornet nests are often referred to as "bee hives", but they are quite different. Whereas honey bees make their structures to raise young and to store food for winter (honey), hornets make theirs only for raising young. They are also called wasps which they are related to, but differ by forming large colonies. Hornets that I observed are cousins of yellowjackets. The black and white bodies are about one inch long with strong white jaws; called Bald-Faced Hornets.

Following the warming temperatures of spring, the queen, the only survivor of last year's colony, wakes from hibernation; usually under a log. Impregnated last fall, she proceeds to chew wood fibers and start a new nest. This small nest holds her first batch of a few eggs. They grow into workers that proceed to enlarge the dwelling as the queen continues to produce dozens of eggs.

Inside the nest, are three or four layers of maybe one hundred hexagonal chambers. Each holds one egg that hatches to be a larva. Workers catch insects to feed the larvae; forming pupae that mature to become hundreds of workers. This summer pattern continues until we approach fall.

Triggered by shorter days, the queen lays no more eggs. The worker females are no longer needed and so they disperse until succumbed by the cold. Males and new queens are produced and leave the nest to prepare of the next year. Usually placed on tree branches, these abandoned nests become easy to see when leaves drop in autumn. I've been able to watch this change of the hornet nest and growing colony throughout the season; until abandoned.

Sept. 20, 2020

Two Seasons of Stay-at-Home Nature

The vernal equinox, the first day of spring, was chilly with more than a foot of snow on the ground. It was also the beginning of "stay-at-home" due to the corona virus. I would be walking and watching nature here; not driving anywhere. After a return to zero degrees a few days later, the temperature continued to rise; reaching fifty by month's end. Also, as we exited March a couple of migrant birds arrived to stay. While red-winged blackbirds and woodcocks performed in wetlands, robins came back to the yard and ruffed grouse drummed in the woods.

As I walked and watched the season unfold in April, I noted the snowpack demise, the formation of vernal ponds, followed by ice out on a nearby lake. Vernal ponds at this time appeared to have plenty of water and waking wood frogs and chorus frogs called from them. (Unfortunately, limited precipitation in April, May and June dried some of these aquatic homes.) During April, the return of hawks, ducks and various sparrows along with loons and the first warblers added to the season. Beavers and muskrats swam in swamps while willows and alders on the shore revealed catkins.

Walking in the woods of May, I was surrounded by thick growths of spring wildflowers; beginning with hepaticas and bloodroots and ending with starflowers and bunchberries. In the midst of tree leafing and blossoming, large warbler waves passed through; a dozen kinds at one site. Grosbeaks, orioles and tanagers added color to their melodies. The swamp that held ice recently now hosted water-lilies and nests of geese and blackbirds. More frogs called and we saw the last frost.

June wanderings showed wildflowers of daisy and hawkweed blooming in open fields. (This tells of spring's departure; sixteen hours of daylight at the summer solstice.) Turtles crawled up on shore to lay eggs and I found nests of veery and warblers in the woods. Dragonflies climbed out of their water-world youth to perform aerial hunting in daylight; fireflies glowed at night. Bear and bobcat were observed crossing the road while twin fawns and a star-nosed mole came to the yard. June had above normal temperatures, but far below normal precipitation. In the arid heat, birch leaves curled and berries struggled.

As expected, July was hot, a few days above ninety degrees and the rains returned; just in time to help some of the berry crop. In cool morning walks, I watched fireweeds and milkweeds produce new flowers each day. Two trumpeter swans spent their molting time in a nearby pond. With bird songs waning, summer frogs began; tiny toads emerged from surviving vernal ponds. Butterflies stole the daytime show; Comet NEOWISE gave us a nighttime treat.

Continuing the rains of July, more came in August (for some of us). (On August 8, we recorded more than four inches in one storm.) Mushrooms responded and were abundant in the woods; easily two dozen forest fungi on a single walk. And I found two kinds of salamanders under one log. Roadsides filled with flowers of goldenrods, asters and sunflowers while those of July formed seeds. Spiders that matured in previous weeks now built large orb webs. Nighthawks showed impressive evening flights.

Thirteen hours of daylight; shortens to twelve by the autumnal equinox; the start of fall. September gives more changes. Red and yellow leaves of maples, dogwoods, birches, basswoods and ashes are filling the woods. Apples are ripe as are hawthorns, highbush cranberries, acorns and maple seeds. Flocks of geese, blue jays, flickers and warblers fly over as well as groups of raptors. Insects such as monarchs and green darners migrate while others continue to buzz with activity in goldenrod patches until the return of frosts. Barred owls and coyotes provide sounds in the cooling nights.

These two seasons of spring and summer with no travel were different from the normal and not what was planned. But, as I saw with regular wandering and watching of wildlife, stay-at-home nature had much to offer. I was never bored. Nature is here and now. There is a new story here every day. Will we also stay-at-home in autumn? If we do, I'm sure nearby nature will provide much more to observe.

Sept. 26; A Couple of Late-Season Yellow Flowers

Late September is a very colorful time in the northland. Roadsides and woods glow with plenty of shades to mix with the persistent green. Red seems to stand out as the brightest and the most sought after. The trees do not disappoint us as we gaze at bright large scarlet red maples. Smaller trees of dogwoods, sumac, cherry and young red oaks combine with the vine Virginia creeper; often draped on trees, to give quite a scene. It is interesting to note that of our two hazels; American hazel is red, beaked hazel is yellow. Though reds are most dramatic, these dazzling colors are far outnumbered by yellows. While reds are usually seen in open areas or woods edge, yellows are anywhere.

In the woods now are yellows of a few large trees; birch, basswood and sugar maple; and in the wetlands, ash and willow also glow. The leaf color for our neighboring trees began early in the month. Yellow pigments of xanthophyll were present all summer and now can be seen when the dominating green chlorophyll is breaking down in the shorter days. Red anthocyanin is produced in leaves of many trees late in the season. Colors will continue and though trees change, we can expect September and October to be colorful. But there is more than trees.

I have noticed lately that the road and trail sides have also glowed with colors of late summer wildflowers. They are basically of three groups; asters, goldenrods and sunflowers. Asters persist with rays of white and purple and remain despite some frosts. Though about a dozen kinds can be found here, a large purple aster, New England aster, recently seen, appears to be the last of these flowers to open its rays.

With the goldenrods, also about a dozen kinds can be found in the region, some quite difficult to discern. They began about mid-July, and with various species continue to bloom until now. Some grow in bogs and woods, but more likely goldenrods are flowers of roadsides and fields. I find three kinds that recently started to bloom; zig-zag (mostly in woods), stiff-leaved and showy. The latter two are most common to the west of here; more in the prairies, but getting established in the region. During recent biking, I have seen many. Showy goldenrod lives up to its name with flowering clusters of numerous small yellow florets. They grow on branching stems and fill the three-foot tall plant with an abundance of yellows; hard to not notice along the roadsides.

Sunflowers have also been with us since mid-summer. These yellow flowering plants can grow to be quite robust and persist well into the autumn. During my wanderings, I have found two that bloom later than the rest. Now adding golden glows to the scene are Maximilian's sunflower and sneezeweed. The former may grow to be eight feet tall with many flowers on an ascending stalk. The latter is usually three to four feet tall holding many smaller flowers. Sneezeweeds have a rounded disk surrounded by lobed yellow rays. Both plants are more common in prairie country, but I see them regularly here late in the season. The unusual name of sneezeweed may have come from its use (flower and leaves) to induce sneezing. Whether tree colors or flower colors; whites, purples, yellows and reds will be with us for weeks and though we've seen this annual show before, it is worth seeing again.

September 26, 2020

A Couple of Late-Season Yellow Flowers

Late September is a very colorful time in the northland. Roadsides and woods glow with plenty of shades to mix with the persistent green. Red seems to stand out as the brightest and the most sought after. The trees do not disappoint us as we gaze at bright large scarlet red maples. Smaller trees of dogwoods, sumac, cherry and young red oaks combine with the vine Virginia creeper; often draped on trees, to give quite a scene. It is interesting to note that of our two hazels; American hazel is red, beaked hazel is yellow. Though reds are most dramatic, these dazzling colors are far outnumbered by yellows. While reds are usually seen in open areas or woods edge, yellows are anywhere.

In the woods now are yellows of a few large trees; birch, basswood and sugar maple; and in the wetlands, ash and willow also glow. The leaf color for our neighboring trees began early in the month. Yellow pigments of xanthophyll were present all summer and now can be seen when the dominating green chlorophyll is breaking down in the shorter days. Red anthocyanin is produced in leaves of many trees late in the season. Colors will continue and though trees change, we can expect September and October to be colorful. But there is more than trees.

I have noticed lately that the road and trail sides have also glowed with colors of late summer wildflowers. They are basically of three groups; asters, goldenrods and sunflowers. Asters persist with rays of white and purple and remain despite some frosts. Though about a dozen kinds can be found here, a large purple aster, New England aster, recently seen, appears to be the last of these flowers to open its rays.

With the goldenrods, also about a dozen kinds can be found in the region, some quite difficult to discern. They began about mid-July, and with various species continue to bloom until now. Some grow in bogs and woods, but more likely goldenrods are flowers of roadsides and fields. I find three kinds that recently started to bloom; zig-zag (mostly in woods), stiff-leaved and showy. The latter two are most common to the west of here; more in the prairies, but getting established in the region. During recent biking, I have seen many. Showy goldenrod lives up to its name with flowering clusters of numerous small yellow florets. They grow on branching stems and fill the three-foot tall plant with an abundance of yellows; hard to not notice along the roadsides.

Sunflowers have also been with us since mid-summer. These yellow flowering plants can grow to be quite robust and persist well into the autumn. During my wanderings, I have found two that bloom later than the rest. Now adding golden glows to the scene are Maximilian's sunflower and sneezeweed. The former may grow to be eight feet tall with many flowers on an ascending stalk. The latter is usually three to four feet tall holding many smaller flowers. Sneezeweeds have a rounded disk surrounded by lobed yellow rays. Both plants are more common in prairie country, but I see them regularly here late in the season. The unusual name of sneezeweed may have come from its use (flower and leaves) to induce sneezing. Whether tree colors or flower colors; whites, purples, yellows and reds will be with us for weeks and though we've seen this annual show before, it is worth seeing again.

Fourth Quarter

October 3, 2020

Flight of the Giant Water Bugs

By the time we get to early October, we have been in autumn for about ten days and it continues to unfold. With less daylight than darkness, we have sunrise after 7 AM and setting before 7 PM. Though days are shorter and cooler, dazzling colors continue. Reds, present for a couple of weeks, are waning a bit, but yellows are in no hurry to pause. This leaf glow prevails until later in the month when the foliage will be dropped. But more is happening.

Walks at dawn reveal changes each day. Besides new leaf color or more fallen, lingering wildflowers often hold crystals of frost. And there are the migrants. In addition to daily flights of passing Canada geese and ducks, there are southing songbirds. Varieties of sparrows abound now as do yellow-rumped warblers. Since many songbirds migrate at night, we can see them in the morning.

Besides walking at dawn, I like to go to a nearby swamp at dusk during these days. It is about a quarter of a mile walk along the road to get there. As I wander, I often have passing acquaintances with bears and deer. Barred owls and coyotes call to welcome in the evening while a distant flock of Canada geese tell of their travels. Despite the cooling temperatures, when I settle in to observe the "night fall", I am greeted by some insects. Moths fluttery by, a few crickets scratch out tunes and the latest mosquitoes are glad to find me. Looking over the water of the swamp, I frequently see the local beaver patrolling his estate. And I'm surprised to hear calls from a couple of lingering frogs.

After Sol disappears in the west, ducks of various species; probably migrants, fly over from west to east. They come from an undisclosed daytime site to another undisclosed location for night. Nearly every evening, I also see the flight of a woodcock. But it is the flight of two others that brings me here; one mammal and one insect.

About twenty minutes after sunset, big brown bats will circle over this wetland in search of insects that are active here since water may be warmer than air. Most of the insects are too small for me to see, but one I can; the giant water bug. It is on autumn evenings; these huge aquatic insects rise from swamps and ponds for a dispersal flight to a larger body of water.

The giant water bugs belong to a group of insects that are correctly called bugs. They are about two to three inches long and one-inch thick; truly robust. Huge hind legs are well adapted for swimming and front legs are like pinchers; for catching prey. In addition to this, their mouth is piercing; like a nail. They are voracious predators to other aquatic insects and tadpoles. Living under water all summer, we usually do not see them; until now.

As cool weather moves in, their homes get chilly and they move to larger bodies of water for winter. This emigration flight happens at night. And yes, I'm able to see them take wing at dusk. The destination is deeper water of a lake. However, flying at night, they can get distracted by lights on porches or parking lots. Confused, they fly until exhausted. We may find them the next morning. But what I see during these autumn evenings is the flight of large powerful insects.

October 10, 2020

Honey: An October Mushroom

September gave us much to see in the world of nature. We had plenty of arboreal color; reds came out bright, but eventually gave way to yellows. This color dominates the scene in early October. Besides looking at leaves of woodland forests, we could also note the colors of roadside wildflowers. Goldenrods, asters and sunflowers all contributed plenty of glow before succumbing to the cooling and shorter days; after the autumnal equinox. Morning walks early in the month dripped with dew and a plethora of spider webs showed up at dawn; giving great photo opts. As the dew became frost, some of these webs held sparkling crystals. Bird migration of many kinds headed south. Whether it was geese and ducks in the wetlands, raptors over Hawk Ridge or the roadside gatherings of warblers and sparrows, we never stopped seeing this avian movement. But September was also very dry.

With everything that this month was able to give us, it gave us very little moisture. Less than one inch of rain was recorded for the whole thirty days; one of the driest Septembers. Responding to arid conditions, the woods that showed much color had very little to see with mushrooms. Our time of abundance of these fungal growths is late summer and thanks to rains of August, my woods walks were full of pauses to take a closer look at the various mushrooms. They ranged in sizes from those barely above the ground to nearly a foot tall, and diverse colors; nearly all the spectrum shades appearing here. This rainy time, was followed by a return to dry days.

During much of September, forest fungal finds were limited. Though I found *Marasmius, Amanita and Agaricus* in lawns, the only ones that I could discover as I continued to woods wander were a couple that grew at the bases of trees. Scaly-cap *Pholiota* formed attractive clusters on stumps along with new growths of puffballs. I found almost no other mushrooms, But the month exited with some days of scattered showers; not a lot, but the nearby woods responded to an inch of rain,

October is not too late for forest mushrooms. They may be hidden by fallen leaves, but they are present. Such was what I discovered during an early October woods walk. The rains brought them out and at the base of several trees, I found clusters of the autumn mushrooms that I was searching for; honey mushrooms.

Honey mushrooms (*Armillaria)* are a diverse group and may be seen as several different species, but what I located here were the "typical" ones. The group was composed of several growths, mostly about four inches tall with brown stems and caps. The caps were darker in the center, lighter around the edged and scattered with scaly growths. (It is the color of the caps that gives the name of "honey" to these mushrooms.) Stems have an obvious ring around; near the cap. Under the caps are gills where the reproductive spores are formed. Seeing the dropped spores, especially the color, can help identify a mushroom. Due to the tight growing clusters, the light-colored spores from some fall on the caps of lower ones.

Honey mushrooms are a regular in the autumn woods; often in October. Some years, they are abundant with clusters in the dozens, other years they are sparse; but they are here every fall. I'm thankful for the light rains of late September that allowed this October mushroom to show up in the woods; adding more to autumn walks.

October 17, 2020

October Sparrow Watching

During the days of mid-October, it is hard to not notice seasonal changes. We now have about eleven hours of daylight. The trees that were so colorful a couple of weeks ago are now dropping this same foliage. This annual arboreal event opens up the landscape. We can see further into the woods. Not all deciduous trees become defoliated at this time. Those still with leaves will be shedding by month's end. In addition to leaves leaving, there continues to be the avian migration; myriads of birds are heading south.

Canada geese that began their fall flight nearly two months ago are still on wing. It's an unusual morning walk without hearing these loud honkers. Ducks of several species, along with grebes and coots are also on the move. I have watched many as they pause on route, but they don't stay here long. At Hawk Ridge, the raptor flight has changed but continues. While the large numbers of broad-winged hawks flew over a month ago, they were replaced by hundreds of sharp-shinned hawks. These accipiters do not fly in big flocks as seen with broad-winged, but they do come by regularly and low enough to be seen well. October is a great time to see bald eagles and turkey vultures. And at night, the diminutive saw-whet owls are also migrating.

Not as large as the waterfowl or raptors, songbirds are southing too. Flocks of blue jays have been obvious, but groups of robins are passing as well. Warblers that migrated in much of September left us with quite a show as the month exited. The final species to move through, the yellow-rumped warbler, was also the most abundant. And often with them were the sparrows.

Early October may be the best time of year to see a variety of sparrows. We have a blending of these small birds; ones that nested here still lingering with others that were breeding further north. The local residents still present include song, swamp and Savannah sparrows. They may be joined by northern arrivals; pausing on their migration flight. Among these visitors are white-throated, white-crowned, fox, Harris, tree sparrows and juncos. Their stay is temporary and after feeding and resting (maybe for much of the month), they will be going further south; not wintering with us. While here, they can be seen in a variety of places; often along roadsides, but woods, parks and yards will provide needed shelter and food for the travelers; maybe our feeders.

To many, sparrows look like little brown birds; all similar. No doubt, they can be difficult to discern, but with binoculars and references, they can be identified. Except for the gray/black juncos, nearly all have much brown on the body and are from five to seven inches long. But noting the colors on the head and spots (or lack of) on the undersides, they can be discerned. One of the most common is the white-throated sparrow. Often seen in yards, including feeders, they are a good one to get to know. They do have the diagnostic white on the throat, but also white markings on the head (sometimes with yellow) and can be confused with another present visitor; the white-crowned sparrow. While both have white above the head, the former has a white throat. These two, as well as other sparrows now here add much to the fall. By this time next month, they will nearly all be gone; now is October Sparrow watching.

October 24, 2020

Asparagus Glows on Roadsides

September, like several of the preceding months, gave us less precipitation than usual. Nearly a foot below normal for the whole year, we began October. The first ten days continued this pattern. And then there was October 12. (Until this date, October had virtually no precipitation.) Starting at about midnight, thunder showers accompanied by wind and steady rain passed over. After consistent rain for the rest of the night, at dawn I noted almost two inches in our rain gauge. The weather service in Duluth recorded a bit less; a little over one inch; however, this one rain was more than any of the months of May, June or September.

Besides this needed moisture to the soil, the rains that were followed by winds of the next several days had a huge impact on the local foliage. A week earlier, trees still held most of their leaves and even though red leaf colors had been waning and seen only sporadically, there still was plenty of yellows. But not after these days of rain and wind. Now, looking out into the landscape, we see the bare defoliated trees. Yes, the annual arboreal event that I call the leaf drop, had occurred. And with this happening, we began AutWin. (The time after leaf drop and before lasting snow cover.)

With the open woods around us, the daily walks take on a new perspective. Some red oaks, sugar maples and lingering quaking aspens still hold a scattering of leaves. In the swamps, the coniferous tamaracks give a glow of their own. Unlike other conifers, they drop all their needles at once in fall, but not before turning a brilliant yellow-gold. Besides these limited yellows, the only leaf colors that I see while walking are the roadside reds of some small bushes. Raspberry, blackberry, blueberry and wild rose continue to hold their colorful leaves after most trees have shed theirs. Movements of migrant flocks of sparrows mix with the blowing leaves; adding a sense of motion to the scene. But there is more color.

While driving some routes nearby recently, I noticed yellow-gold from a shrubby-looking plant along the roadsides. Unlike most of the color at this time, the glow did not come from a woody plant of a tree or a bush. Taking a closer look, I realized that this showy plant of about three to four feet tall was an asparagus.

Best known by most of us as a garden vegetable, this plant is and has been grown in the region for a long time. Usually, we eat the tasty new stems as they develop in spring. Before they get too tough, they make for excellent additions to our meals. And then, we let it grow. Plants have extensive branches with minute, almost scale-like, leaves; all of which are green. Later in the season, after growing taller, they form tiny green-yellow flowers that eventually lead to small red berries. The flowers and berries could get overlooked, but not the yellow-gold of the entire plant, not just the leaves, as seen now in late October. No longer only in the garden, many asparagus have escaped and find the openness of the roadsides as a fine place to grow. Even though plants may reach more than four feet tall, were it not for this late fall (AutWin) color, we would not notice the plant or realize how common asparagus (wild asparagus) is in the region.

October 31, 2020

Arrival of a Rusty Blackbird Flock

The calendar says that today is in October, but when I step outside this morning for a walk, it looks and feels more like a day in November. A cloudy day with snow on the ground; temperatures in the 20's seems to be ahead of the date. The bird feeder has been active lately with blue jays, chickadees, nuthatches and a couple of woodpeckers. A few juncos and active fox sparrows keep searching for seeds on the ground.

As I walk along the road, I'm met by a large flock (about 80) of juncos and tree sparrows. The snow cover has sent them to seek seeds along the roadside. As I pause to take a closer look at the flock, I note a couple of other sparrows here too: white-throated and white-crowned. Crows and ravens fly over as they do each day, but I also see two bald eagles; both are immatures, not yet with the white head and tail of adults. Ice is forming at the edges of swamps and ponds as expected, but here are a few chilly, but active yellow-rumped warblers. Earlier this season, they were frequently out on the lily pads where they could catch insects. They appear to be trying the same hunting today.

I leave the road to walk a trail in the woods. This route takes me near a swamp. In the shoreline alders, I see movement of tiny birds. Looking more carefully, I can see that they are kinglets and with patience, the colors on the heads tell of both the ruby-crowned and golden-crowned kinglets. Despite there small size of four inches, their activity and constant wing flapping, makes them fairly easy to discern. But here, near this wetland, I see other birds. Flitting about, they head for the edge of the swamp. Most are staying low. About the size of robins (which I have also seen flocks of recently), I note that their bodies are mostly dark. Clearly seeing the light brown heads, I realize that I am watching a flock of rusty blackbirds.

Rusty blackbirds are one of several kinds of blackbirds that can be seen in the northland. Perhaps the red-winged blackbird, with its loud singing in spring is best known. But grackles, Brewer's blackbirds and cowbirds might be observed as well. Some stay to nest, others move further north. Of all the members of this group, perhaps it is the rusty blackbird that is the northern-most nesting species; breeding in the boreal forests of Canada. Their appearance here every spring and fall is to be expected, but like other breeders in the taiga, they do not remain long. The name of rusty blackbird refers to the rust-colored feathers on much of the body at this time. They are more uniformly black in breeding season.

The flock that watched moved and fed along the edge of a wetland in silence. A few days earlier, I discovered a flock of their cousins, the grackles, that were anything but silent. Loud creaking calls emanated from this group as they fed. Often such flocks of grackles are mixed with other blackbirds. But what I see here today is this small flock is only rusty blackbirds. They'll rest and feed here for several days or more before resuming their trip to wintering sites in southern states. They may be gone the next time that I walk here, but for the time being, I'm glad to be watching these northern birds as they pause on their southing flight.

November 7, 2020

Watching Cold-Weather Moths

Usually early November is a time of AutWin; after the leaf drop of October and before lasting snow cover. But this year, AutWin was shortened a great deal. We had barely a week between the leaf drop (October 12) and what appeared to be a lasting snow cover (October 20). (This could change with recent mild weather.) I expect when I walk in the woods at this time, to see plenty of mosses, clubmosses and ferns that are still green among the brown fallen leaves. Though a few trees; ironwood and some sugar maples and red oaks have not shed their brown leaves, nearly all the rest have. A few willows in swamps and lingering tamaracks have retained their yellows, but mostly what I see during my walk today is bare trees and a snow-covered scene.

The day is cloudy and calm with chilly temperatures in the twenties. Instead of looking at the forest floor and seeing some greens, I'm looking at the tracks of local critters that tell of their activity; mostly at night. Deer tracks and trails reveal stories of their wandering and at many locations, they have been digging among the fallen leaves in search of acorns that were so abundant this year. They are joined by local turkeys also scratching in the leaves. Fox and coyote tracks go about the woods too; seeking prey. Squirrels, hare and mice that could become their prey, have been moving actively. Raccoons and bears that will be sleeping in the deeper cold are still moving; trying to satisfy omnivorous diets. Their tracks show travels into a variety of places. One of which is near a beaver pond where the owner of the lodge comes ashore for more twigs before the freeze-up. We don't usually see beaver tracks in snow. This is a bit of a surprising find, but not like the one that I see next.

As I wander one of the woods walks, I see some flitting in the air. I pause to watch and I realize that I am observing the flight of a moth. After some of the cold that we've had, snow cover and ice on a nearby pond, it seems almost surreal to see this critter. Looking more closely, I recognize this insect as a "winter moth". This flight is not of a confused or displaced individual. This is their regular flying time.

The name of winter moth may be applied to a couple of late-season moths. Two in particular that I see often in late October or early November are the spanworm and the basswood (linden) looper. Both are small with wingspans of less than one and a half inches. Spanworm is mostly gray;

looper is brown. Each can be very cryptic among the present trees. They are common in the late-season woods, but also frequently seen on windows of our house; attracted by the indoor lights, or maybe noted in the headlights of our cars as we commute home. It is the spanworm that I see today.

Flying at a late date is a bit strange for these moths, but they have adapted. With little food available, they do not eat. After seeking shelter under bark, they shiver to warm the body temperature in order to fly. With fewer bird predators in early November, the flying males can locate females. This flight time is a bit unusual, but the spanworm that I watched on this chilly day, is also part of the woods community.

Nov. 14, 2020

Clubmosses Abound on Forests Floors

October of 2020 was a month that gave unpredictable weather. Looking back at the month is very interesting. The first half was warmer than normal with a record-setting 80 degrees on the ninth. Except for a hard rain on the twelfth, it was mostly dry. This rain and subsequent wind brought down leaves in huge amounts. After the leaf drop and before snow cover (AutWin) began at this time. Normally, I expect this interlude to last a couple of weeks. But the second half of the month was quite different. By the twentieth, we had a snow cover with cold temperatures that made the snow appear to be lasting. After only one week, it looked like AutWin was over. This snow and cold continued and by the end, we noted October to be the second snowiest October and the fifth coldest. And then things changed. November began with temperatures far above normal with clear skies. In mild sunlight (seventies a few times), the snow cover (and ice) melted and we returned to AutWin.

The present open woods reveals much of the forest that will not be seen later. A few northern birds; redpolls, grosbeaks and crossbills may be seen. But I watch other small critters during these days. Crane flies do their undulating flight in the afternoon sunlight. A few late-season moths flutter about. And it seems like many branches hold threads; telling of traveling spiders; dispersal flights called ballooning (kiting).

In addition to these AutWin animals, I like to see the plants that will soon be wearing a covering of snow. The big leaf color on trees is long past, but I see red leaves still on bushes; raspberry, blackberry, blueberry and bunchberry. Others remain green; hepatica, pyrola, strawberry and wintergreen on the forest floor. Besides green leaves on these flowering plants, there are many greens of non-flowering plants.

There may not be a better time of the year to see just how abundant mosses are in the woods than now. In many locations, it looks like every log, rock or base of trees are covered by these small green plants; diverse species as well as numerous. But mosses are not the only ones still green. Clubmosses of several kinds abound on the forest floor. Called clubmosses, they are more closely related to ferns. And I find a wood fern, that continues to be green in AutWin while others have turned brown and faded. Lichens coat tree trunks while many trees also hold various fungi.

Taking a closer look at clubmosses, I note that they are mostly about six inches tall. Like ferns, they grow from underground branches called rhizomes. Unlike ferns, the part that we see above ground will stary green all winter; even when buried beneath snow. Most clubmosses have green spiny or scale-like leaves on branches. Above this leafy part, many hold candle-like spikes (clubs); why they are called clubmosses. It is in these structures that spores (seeds) grow. They are also called lycopodium, princess pine, ground pine, ground cedar and firmoss. One of the most common looks like small branching trees and known as prickly tree clubmoss. The Latin name of *Dendrolycopodium*; essentially means tree-like. I find that they grow in groups of maybe hundreds and seem to do best on cool north-facing slopes. Thanks to the recent warming weather and the return of AutWin, we can now see large numbers of these clubmosses and realize just how common they are in the northland woods.

November 21, 2020

Deer Mice Seek Winter Shelter

November is known as a changing month in the northland and this November has given plenty of weather variations. We expect to begin with a scene devoid of snow and often fairly mild temperatures. We began without a snow cover; snows of late October quickly melted in climbing temperatures. Highs in the forties or even fifties are not that unusual in the first half of the month, but reaching into the seventies for a couple of days made us feel like a return to summer. (Interesting to note that seventy-five degrees recorded on November 6 was not only a record temperature for that date, it was the warmest November temperature ever recorded at the Weather Service. Exactly a year ago we had freeze-up in many lakes.)

The changes continue and once the warm days passed, rains came. After virtually no precipitation in the previous two weeks, the Weather Service recorded 1.18 inches rain on November 9 (a record rain for that date). With cooling temperatures of the next day, snow moved in. Ending around midnight, this snowfall recorded 7.3 inches (and yes, a record snowfall for this date). In the wake of the snowfall, we may have finally settled into a "normal November".

Though not as dramatic as seen earlier, November is when we see some big changes. During the second half, I expect three very important weather happenings to take place in anticipating winter. This is often when lake freeze-up takes place (ponds and swamps freeze earlier). With subsequent frozen ground and ice cover, falling snow will remain; often setting the pace for the next several months.

Critters that live here respond to winter in four different ways. Some lay eggs and die; especially seen with insects. Many migrate to warmer locations; mostly noted with birds. Others hibernate, waking next spring; bears, chipmunks, snakes, frogs are some examples. And there are those that stay active throughout the cold. This group is of mammals and birds are the ones that we see in winter. Keeping active in the cold means adjusting in both physical and behavioral ways. Fur and feathers can provide the physical protection. Behaviorally, they may need to vary their diet and find sufficient shelter.

One small mammal, the deer mouse, copes well. (Deer mice are very similar to white-footed mice; also, local residents.) When walking in the morning after a recent snowfall, I noted the tracks of mammals that are active in the woods. Among the deer, squirrel and weasel tracks, I found the hopping gait of deer mice. While some small mammals stay under the snow, this one travels over; leaving its hopping tracks with a tail marking. The tracks told of this rodent going among logs and stumps; seeking shelter. But when I located similar tracks near outbuildings and the house, I was reminded that the shelter that they may be seeking could be ours.

I have found that deer mice with light brown backs, white undersides and big eyes are common. Among other native mice; voles have short tails, jumping mice extremely long tails and deer mice have a tail about the same length as their body. By this time in November, they spread out to find shelters and our homes could be their homes. Indeed, the indoor movement of these mice is also a regular November happening. Eventually, with our disapproval of their influx, we take back our homes and they seek other shelters in the snow. But in late November, we see how abundant deer mice are.

November 28, 2020

White Clematis; Vines With Fluffy Seeds

The roadsides appear bare as I walk on this late autumn day. Temperatures are cool and along with the lessened amount of daylight, the season is advancing towards winter. In front of me, off to the edge of the road, I see an active flock of redpolls. These small birds from the far north have just recently arrived in the region and they will come to feeders later. Now they go to other sources for food; often seeds of alders and birches. But this flock is feeding on the seeds of a patch of tansies; growing on the roadsides.

Tansy is very common at these sites and though not always appreciated, it does provide numerous seeds that can be chosen for bird food; as seen with the redpolls on this day, A few other plants here may also provide food for birds, but some are avoided. Many roadside wildflowers hold seeds, formed a couple of months ago, attached to fluffy growths. Such growths make the plants very easy to see now and very easy for breezes to pick up and transplant Using wind-dispersal, they do not need to rely on providing a meal for birds to transfer their seeds. Instead, the breezes of autumn and winter will carry off their hope of the next generation.

The fluffy growths that make this travel possible grow from the flowers of last summer and fall and now these seed-holdings abound in open sites. Most common are goldenrods and asters that filled these locations last summer with flowers of yellow, white and purple. Earlier ones; fireweed and milkweed that added their flowers to the roadside botany in mid-summer, have mostly emptied their pods of wind-blown seeds by this time. And there is the clematis.

During the days of late July and August, this vining plant showed its numerous white flowers to this scene. Like many vines, it grew in the open sunlight along the edge of woods, and hung onto branches of nearby trees as it reached far above the other roadside plants. White clematis (also called virgin's bower and old-man's beard) is a regular, though usually not common, plant along these edge sites. The woody vine is perennial and I have learned that where I find them one season, I'll see them again in the next. Flowers are in clusters; each one is about one-inch across. They appear to have four white petals that are actually sepals; no petals. (This happens with some other members of the buttercup family as well.) Plants are dioecious and either male or female. Both flower in summer among their green leaves that are in groups of three. In autumn, it is the female plants that stand out as they hang onto the substrate. Once pollinated, the female flowers produce seeds that grow long plumes on them. Each flower has many of these fluffy plumes that appear as huge furry growths on the vines in fall (why called old man's beard). And like the one that I found; they may be more than ten feet above the ground; hard to not see.

White clematis (*Clematis virginiana)* is one of two wild clematis in the northland. The other, a purple spring flower (*Clematis verticllaris),* is a vine but not as large. The beautiful growth of flowers on a long vine in summer, white clematis continues to be noticed in autumn with fluffy seeds that are also very showy.

December 5, 2020

Turtles Under the Ice

Late November has three important seasonal events happening in the region as we move towards winter. I expect the ground to freeze during these chilly days. Also responding to the colder temperatures, we get the freeze up of bodies of water. This usually starts in October with ice coating shallow ponds and swamps. As we progress through November, the shorter days and sub-freezing temperatures causes ice to form on lakes. Beginning at the edge, extending into bays and finally encompassing the entire lake. Several of the smaller lakes freeze in November, larger ones, maybe not until December. (With moving waters, rivers freeze later in winter; usually December.) It is interesting to note that with temperatures fluctuating between early morning and afternoons, many form ice only to have it melt later; refreezing the next night. With ample ice on ponds and swamps; along with frozen ground, the stage is set for the next of the seasonal happenings; lasting snow.

As we have seen this year, snow often comes before the ground and water are frozen; and these early snows are not usually going to remain. But eventually, frozen substrates hold this cold precipitation and we get a lasting snow cover. New snows on ponds and swamps are delightful settings for seeing animal tracks. Every day there is plenty of news out here. And though I usually do not see the critters themselves, tracks tell of their presence. Such wetlands are wandered by minks, weasels, deer, foxes, coyotes, mice, raccoons, shrews; sometimes muskrats and otters. But more is happening here as well.

There is a period of time each year between the new ice forming and before it gets snow covered. This is the time of clear (and often slippery) ice; lasting a few days to maybe a week. No snow on the ice at this time; but it is worth looking at anyway.

Pausing during my walks and looking through this clear ice can give a view of what is going on under this cold cover. In the shallows, we can see to the bottom; and what is happening here. Recently as I looked, I noted movements that morphed into a couple of wintering turtles. I was a bit surprised to see them initially, but once I got used to it, I found that it was not that unusual to find turtles under this newly-formed ice. I have several times watched the wanderings of both the snapping and painted turtles.

We have only two common species of turtles in the northland. Both are readily seen in the warmer months. Though each will bask in sunlight, painted turtles are most likely seen. With the coming of autumn, they seem to disappear. Winter is spent in a dormant phase on the bottom of the lake; often in groups. Their metabolism slows down and they are able to survive on dermal and rectal respiration. (Turtles do not have gills.) However, as I watch these turtles on this late November day, I realize that this dormancy does not happen immediately after freeze-up. Sunlight coming in through the clear ice may invite the turtles to search in these shallows for food. And maybe they find air here too.

The freeze-up has occurred as a regular part of our annual cycle. And as often occurs, it means much to see. Turtles swimming under ice may be a bit unusual, but is just one of these happenings; as cold moves in.

December 12, 2020

The Visitor on the Porch

As we go through the snowy season, we enjoy having some companionship in these dark and cold times. I find it pleasant to note the presence of some local wildlife each day. These are most obvious with birds that arrive and make use of our bird feeders. From the confines of a warm living room, we can look out to watch these fluffed-up avian neighbors as they feed in the cold. Usually, we have the regulars that come by each day; jays, chickadees, nuthatches and woodpeckers and they may be joined by turkeys and finches later in the season. Especially delightful is observing the energetic antics of flying squirrels after dark. Using their big eyes and gliding skills, they move in shortly after sunset. But there is also the presence of nearby wildlife that we usually do not see.

With regular coatings of snow, we can find tracks of the others that are active here too. On a daily basis, I expect to see tracks of squirrels, deer, mice, foxes, coyotes, shrews and hare or rabbits during my winter walks. To these can be added occasional weasels, minks, martens, fishers, porcupines and raccoons. Except for squirrels and maybe deer, I normally do not see these critters, though they appear to be common. Most are active at night, but thanks to the cold coating of snow, they let me know that they are in the region.

One set of tracks that I expect to see probably every week of the winter is that of weasels. Their activity and agility leaves footprints and trails that are unique. With a coordination that most of us can only imagine, they leap through the snow in such a manner as to place their hind feet in the same track where the front feet were. The result is a pattern that appears as though the weasels move about on only two feet. Not only are their tracks common, they also reveal the movements of an energetic predator. Weasels hop in the snow, but they also climb branches and burrow under the cold blanket. Tracks abound, but again, I rarely see the weasels themselves.

We have three kinds of weasels in the northland; small, medium and large: least weasel, short-tailed weasel and long-tailed weasel. All are smaller than other members of their family; mink, marten, fisher or otter. During cold times, they put on a white coat; the only predator to do so. Though all turn white, it is usually only the short-tailed weasel that takes on a new name. When in its winter attire, it is known as the ermine. The entire body now holds white fur except for a black tip on the end of its tail.

One of the joys of watching wildlife is that they often surprise us. Such was the case a few days ago when an ermine (short-tailed weasel) came out of the woods, hopping over a driveway and without a hesitation, scampered onto our porch; in the daylight of late morning. This behavior revealed just the opposite scenario as expected; the critter was visible and easily seen while in the crusty snow, the tracks of this five-ounce mammal did not show up. It avoided the bird feeder but chose a porch where mice may be found. Most likely it was the mouse odor that caused this hungry ermine to go hunting in the daytime. It did not stay long in this predacious pursuit, but its sighting added much to a northland winter day

Dec. 19, 2020

Slipping, Sliding Deer on the Ice

The first part of December has fit into the weather patterns as seen in October and November. Each of these months started off with temperatures that were above; sometimes far above, normal. Indeed, both October and November posted record-setting temperatures early in the month. Besides having these readings above usual, each of these autumn months were dry; limited precipitation. If these conditions sound familiar, it is because December has been following a similar temperature and precipitation patterns. December has begun warmer than normal with less precipitation (almost none). Even as we now approach the winter solstice, snowfall in this month has been limited. A recent weather service map of snow cover for the state revealed much of Minnesota is without snow on the ground. Thanks to snows of mid-November (a month ago), the northeast does have some snow cover.

Temperatures in the second half of November did drop enough to produce a freeze-up. Some lakes froze over by the 20th; only to have a melt and a return to freezing late in the month. I noticed ice anglers taking up their activity in early December.

With mild temperatures fluctuating between above freezing in the afternoons and below freezing at night, the ice conditions on area lakes have been a bit hard to determine. However, I noticed that the local wildlife that share these conditions with us were venturing on lake surfaces in recent weeks. The lack of snow on the ice and previous freeze-thaw cycle made for some strange tracks (and ice conditions).

Ice without a snow cover on regional lakes happens about every year for a short period of time, but usually this ice is also covered; by snow. This year the bare ice has remained for a couple of weeks; cold enough for ice to form, too dry for snow. And with now snow cover, ice skaters went for their winter activity; ironically, something not common here.

It wasn't much, but we did get a light snow coating on the ice a few days ago. I went out to see if tracks were recorded. (Snow on ice is perhaps the best place to observe animal tracks at this time of year.) And yes, as I stepped along the edge of the swamp and lake, I noticed how mink, squirrels, voles (field mice; quite common in swamps), foxes, coyotes, raccoons, hare and even a crow did some wandering here. Like me, all left tracks revealing slipping and sliding, but none like the deer.

Deer tracks were plentiful in the nearby woods, but they seemed to avoid the lake ice. I did; however, find where a couple of adventurous ones stepped onto the hard slippery surface. The light snow cover told of their sliding, loss of balance and quick movements to regain their stature. At the two sites that I found, these deer showed that hoofs, so good in the woods, are not as agile on the ice. In each case, the slipping deer appeared to do a bit of a dance before regaining composure and quickly moving back to terra firma. I wonder if these icing deer learned a lesson to stay off the ice for a while longer. I expect the weather pattern that we are in will give us more snow and I plan to do much more tracking on the swamp and lake.

Dec. 26, 2020

Carlton County Christmas Bird Count

It's a chilly six degrees under a partly clear sky when I step outside at dawn for my walk. I go along the road, passing woods, fields and swamps. As expected, I hear ravens, crows and a calling pileated woodpecker. I return and in the comfort of the house, look out at the feeders to see that plenty is happening. The usual birds are present; black-capped chickadees, white-breasted and red-breasted nuthatches, downy, hairy and red-bellied woodpeckers along with blue jays and a few turkeys wandering in from the woods. All of these birds, plus more that I see later, are part of the today's Christmas Bird Count.

These bird counts began early in the twentieth century and have spread throughout the country. Each year during a three-week time between mid-December until early January, a day is chosen to conduct a bird survey. Though called Christmas Bird Counts, they have become a look at what kinds of birds are present here in winter. In Carlton County, we have conducted such a count for more than thirty years. In recent years, it was done about January 1, but this year; mid-December.

Many people maintain bird feeders in winter and with weather conditions of the season and with less mobility, birds observed may be those at the feeders. However, with the help of some volunteers and some movement within the designated area (count circle) more birds can be seen. About fifteen of us wandered the region for the day and later reported our findings. We usually locate about thirty species. This year was the same; thirty-four species (nearly 1800 individuals). Birds are identified and the number present are counted.

Each of the four bird groups were represented. Raptors: bald eagle, rough-legged hawk, barred owl and great horned owl. Gallinaceous birds (chicken-like); ruffed grouse and turkeys and one aquatic bird; a duck, common goldeneye, was in the open water of the St. Louis river.

By far the most numerous birds were the songbirds. At feeders were the same seven kinds that I saw. Not surprising, black-capped chickadees were the most abundant. Other birds seen at feeders included cardinals, pine siskins, goldfinches and some redpolls (a bit early for these birds to be at feeders). And a few feeders had unusuals; mourning doves, rock pigeons, a grackle, evening grosbeaks and a rose-breasted grosbeak (first time ever).

Crows, ravens and pileated woodpeckers were also seen, but not at feeders as was the raptor-like shrikes. A good number of crab apple trees with plentiful fruits attracted the attention of others; pine grosbeaks (nearly seventy were seen this year after none last year), starlings, robins, Bohemian waxwings (these berry-eating birds often form large flocks and numbered in the hundreds) and one cedar waxwing. A couple of boreal birds were also present; a lone gray jay and flocks of white-winged crossbills in spruce trees.

Because of limitations that might exist on the day of the count, some other birds seen three days before or after (count week) may also be part of the list. A brown creeper and a surprising Wilson's snipe, a shore bird (also a first-time sighting) were added.

During the thirty years, there have been some changes of note. Both red-bellied woodpeckers and turkeys were not seen when we started, but are common now. House sparrows have not been seen in last couple of years. Evening grosbeaks that were absent for years may be returning. Yes, the annual Christmas Bird Count did succeed it letting us know what kinds of birds are present locally in winter.

Average Temperature: 43.9° F

Highest Temperature (June 5): 94° F

Lowest Temperature (Feb 13): -35° F

Total Precipitation: 25.71 Inches

Total Snowfall: 60.1 Inches

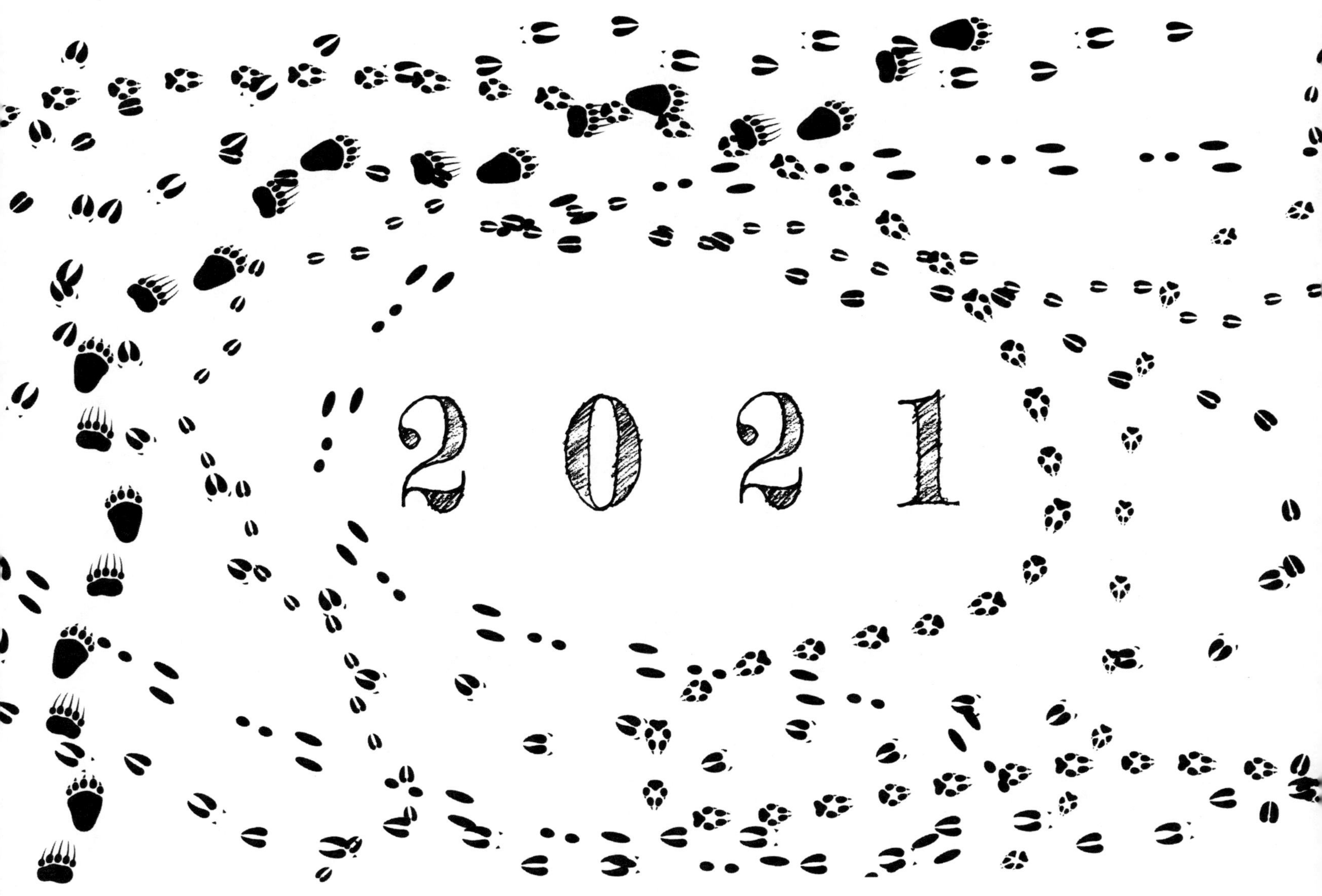
2021

First Quarter

January 2, 2021

Evenings with the Flyers

Entering the new month of January, we continue the cold and snow, but the new year gives us other happenings. After months of sunrises regularly getting later, nearly 8 AM; during the first week of January, they begin to get earlier; a pattern that goes on for the next six months. We are also at the time of perihelion; when we are closest to the sun in our annual trip around Sol. We will notice longer days soon, but mostly January is a month of cold and snow. We deal with these winter conditions in many ways. For some, it is keeping bird feeders. Like many northlanders, I regularly maintain these feeders that I usually start in October and keep filled until spring. Sunflower seeds and suet make up most of the feeding. If winter finches move in, I add thistle seeds.

Local avians will breakfast here each day. Chickadees, nuthatches, woodpeckers along with blue jays are regular attendees with sporadic visits from turkeys and pileated woodpeckers. (Later in the winter, perhaps some finches.) Their antics and energy in coping with the cold are a delight to watch each day. Subzero mornings bring in many birds while milder times have only a few. This lets me know that they really don't need the feeders to survive. We need them. With late sunrises, early sunsets and cold nights, they will spend much of the daylight hours feeding. They are gone to roost by dusk. Sunsets in winter are early; often by 5 PM. We may have nine hours of daylight followed by fifteen hours of darkness. Snow cover is an excellent place to record the tracks and movements of those critters active during the night even though we do not see them. But some are seen.

I go out at dusk to fill a platform on a nearby tree each in anticipation of the night feeders. Illuminated by an outdoor light, I can look onto this feeding site and watch the arrival and activities of the local nocturnal flying squirrels. Usually, at about 6 PM, I'm able to see them move about as they feed.

They are a type of tree squirrel; a little smaller than red squirrels and much less than grays. Like many other nocturnal mammals, they have large eyes; helping in this scene. As tree squirrels, they spend the night among branches. Using a large fold of skin going from front legs to hind legs allows them to glide through the growths of trees. A flat tail acts as a rudder and they steer and maneuver around the forest at night. The typical behavior for flying squirrels is to glide in from a neighboring tree to the one that holds the food. Landing on the trunk above the platform, they descend to it. Soon they are joined by others. Being gregarious, they seem to tolerate each other and the site may hold nearly a dozen. Time is spent gobbling seeds or running off to cache them; quickly returning for more. (When a boot was left outdoors recently, it was found the next day with many cached seeds inside.) The northland is at a location where the ranges of southern flying squirrels and northern flying squirrels coincide. Southerns are common in deciduous trees and the larger northern ones mostly live in conifers. We have both kinds at the feeder.

While birds bring delightful watching to winter days, so do the flying squirrels add to the long cold winter nights.

January 9, 2021

The Crab Spider on the Wall

During January in the northland, we obviously take note of the snow conditions; always on the lookout for the next storm. And the temperatures that frequently drop to zero degrees and below forces us to deal with nature around us. We may need to alter our plans or behavior while commuting in winter weather. Our neighboring wildlife copes with the cold as well, many of which remain active. We expect to see birds at the feeder and find the tracks of active wintering mammals. These warm-blooded wildlife remain well insulated with feathers and fur. But we do have some of the smaller critters that are also active in winter; insects and spiders.

During a few of the mild days a month ago in December, I paused in my walking in snow to observe a small fluttering insect. At first, it looked a lot like a mosquito; an insect that we are quite familiar with. But at this time, with temperatures in the 30's, it was not a mosquito, but a cousin; a type of crane fly. About the size and shape of a mosquito, these winter crane flies reach maturity in this season and flutter about as expected. Also, while crossing the ice of a swamp on another day, I stopped when I saw movement of a small critter on the frozen surface. Looking more closely revealed a wolf spider. Slowed by the cold, it was persisting in its crawling to nearby snow. (Wolf spiders remain active all winter in the subnivean zone beneath the snow. Insulated by the snowpack, they are able to move about here throughout the cold; occasionally, they come to the surface; walking on the snow.)

But there are times when we'll see insects and spiders indoors. It is not unusual to see the activities of house flies and ladybugs in our house. We may not appreciate them, but with an interrupted sleep or dormancy, they don't want to be here either. Ants showing up are a little different. They remain active in winter in sheltered sites (normally underground) and may wander into our homes; searching for food.

Besides these insects, their predators; spiders, may be present too. Every winter, I expect to see two web-making spiders in the house. In corners of the basement frequently are the triangle-shaped webs of funnel-web spiders (Agelenids). They may remain for weeks waiting for meals to come by, and their webs may last for months. Cellar spiders (Pholcids) are so well adapted to human habitats that they almost never live elsewhere. They make webs usually near the ceiling. Here they catch prey and they also continue to make egg sacs all winter.

Spiders that do not make webs may be a little less common indoors, but recently when I saw movement on a wall, I examined it more closely. Since it had outstretched legs, I could tell that it was a climbing crab spider (Philodromid). Crab spiders are well known to be in flowers where they use their camouflage to do sedentary hunting of visiting insects. The climbing crab spiders are more active in their pursuits. Outdoors, they are often found in trees. Coming indoors, they do the climbing again; this time on walls. I watched it carefully for a while as it moved along the wall. I wished it well and hoped that "Phil" would have a good winter in the shelter of this house.

January 16, 2021

Trail and Tale of an Otter

In the northland, we get used to having a snow cover for several months each year. When we get to mid-January, we have had a snow blanket for at least two months. This constant white coat varies much; especially due to ambient temperatures. I always see snow as a substrate that holds tracks; revealing the activities of local wildlife that winter here with us; even though we usually do not see them. This became apparent to me when I went for a walk about a month ago on a morning following a new snowfall. Such conditions are great for reading recent critter news. I was not disappointed. Right in the yard, I saw where squirrels and mice were hopping. Here too, I noted the nocturnal movements of deer and I found where a porcupine waddled by. In the driveway, I saw that a shrew pushed through the snow and a rabbit hopped. The local flock of turkeys also passed this way. Along the road, fox and coyote tracks told me they were here before me; as well as a snowshoe hare. I went over a swamp where voles were active and their predator; a short-tailed weasel (ermine). Continuing along a lake shore, I found that both a mink and a skunk were present.

Taking a path through a woods I noted signs of two more predators; long-tail weasel and fisher. The night was clear; early morning temperature was near zero and many critters were out. I did not see them, but they let me know of their movements.

Recently, I went for another walk after a new snow. The snowpack of January was different from that of December. Wildlife were still leaving their messages in the snow, but things varied. Instead of seeing tracks of nearly twenty kinds of wanderers as in last month's snow, I found only about half that in this January walk; with changes.

One local wild mammal that I had not seen the tracks of in my earlier walk was that of an otter. But during my January outing, I came across the tracks and trail of this aquatic member of the weasel family as it hopped and slid through the snow scene. It looked a little out of place here in the forest where I discovered the trail. I decided to follow the route of this mobile otter to see what was happening.

It came out of the south from an unknown site and was heading north towards a lake. But its trip was not direct. The critter took many turns and twists as it went through the woods. At a couple of places, it doubled back on itself. Nearing the lake, it went under the length of an inverted canoe. When finally reaching the lake, its trek was not done. It needed to find a location to go below the ice. Coming by two docks, the otter went under; but to no avail. At long last, it reached a swampy shoreline where the ice was not as strong and here it proceeded to make a hole; reaching its goal of going beneath the ice.

Otters are very at home in water and though the cold of an ice-bound lake may not seem attractive, I'm sure that it did well here. Not as many tracks on my January walk as that of December, but I was able to read the tale of this wandering otter's trail. There are new nature stories out here every day.

January 23, 2021

Walking on Calm Winter Mornings

Going for a walk at dawn on winter mornings has been a great experience that I have enjoyed for years. It is not unusual to step out of the house into a frigid northland temperature of subzero or to negotiate a route through newly fallen snow. Some mornings, snow is still falling and may be accompanied by strong winds. However, the walks are not canceled and each venture in the winter AM offers more into the insights of northland nature. During the first half of January 2021, the walks continued, but under different conditions.

Temperatures were far above normal and with this pattern, the month could be in contention for one of the warmest Januarys on record. Not once in the early weeks of the month did the mercury dip below zero. On the other side, forty degrees was also not exceeded; something that has happened during other years in this first month. What we have been having is repetition of cloudy (sometimes fog) and mostly calm days. Not what is expected at this time of year, but I find that such days are good for walks and offer plenty to see and hear.

Calm with clouds or fog are great conditions for hearing what is happening in early morning. Just as bird feeders settle in with the usual birds, so too it is along the road. Each day, I listen to sounds of the local crows and ravens as they fly over open country. In woods, chickadees, nuthatches or blue jays call as they begin the day. And there are the woodpeckers. Tapping and pounding on trees to dislodge a breakfast is a regular sound, but nearly every day, I also hear drumming from some woodpeckers; usually hairy woodpeckers. Such is the proclamation of ownership done by these birds; more common in late winter.

Roadside tracks reveal the activity that happened when I was not here. Tracks of deer, squirrels and mice are daily seen. Some routes often used; I call trails. Snowshoe hares and coyotes in addition to deer show these paths. And there is other news. Recently I noted fox tracks that included a scent marking. (Many canines begin breeding in January.) But for about a week earlier in the month, it was the trees that demanded attention.

For several days in succession, my morning walks were greeted by forests, swamps and roadside plants that were coated with crystals of frost. Apparently, temperatures in the daytime were warm enough to allow for vapors to rise from the snowpack (sublimation). They formed droplets in the air; we call fog. These droplets settled onto the branches of numerous trees and in the cooling temperatures of early mornings, they formed frost. This condition of "frozen fog" is often called hoar frost, but what I was experiencing on these days, was a bigger build-up of crystals, some nearly one-half inch long and often in a spiney arrangement; a formation that is known as rime.

Rime is not that unusual; we see some most every year, but as the day warms in sunlight and winds pick up, it usually dissipates. But for several of these January days, it did not warm enough for that to happen; and they remained cloudy or foggy and calm. Walking here was like going through a fantasy forest. Whether seen from a distance or close-up, the trees cover was a delight. This unique situation was not what we expect in early January, but still a welcome delight to behold.

Jan. 30, 2021

Cecropia Cocoon Prepares for Spring.

It's a long time from late January to late May. The days are getting longer and we might see some different behavior with birds and squirrels at the feeders. Canine breeding season is beginning to happen in the region and baby bears are born about this time. But we still have weeks of cold and snow ahead of us as we move in that direction.

However; there are several nature happenings now that are preparing for spring. Most obvious are buds on local deciduous trees. Within the small scaly coverings out on the twig are the new leaves; already green. Also, of note are seeds of many roadside plants; tansy, sweetclover and mullein; just to name a few. This cold time with less light is important for their growth. Opening buds and seeds too soon could make problems for the plants.

Another example of a preparation for the spring time was made apparent to me when I was shown a large cocoon that was recently discovered. It was attached to the stem of an alder growing near a swamp. Exposed to the cold without any apparent heat, the resident inside was alive and getting ready for its next phase of life.

Cocoons are made by moths; using silk and leaves to fold over their pupated body. (Butterflies form a chrysalis from their skin.) We all are familiar with the moth metamorphosis; a caterpillar (larva) goes into the cocoon and comes out as an adult, looking quite different. (It is interesting to note that we might know moths better as caterpillars; such as woollybears or armyworms, than we do as adults, but with butterflies, it is the opposite.) Though we see the beginning and the end, we mostly don't know what happens to make these changes within the cocoon. Often referred to as a resting stage, the first weeks inside the cocoon are not resting.

The caterpillar does dramatic altering to become a moth. The body of the caterpillar is essentially digested from the inside. Once secure in the shelter of the cocoon, hormones trigger enzymes to do the digestive changes. Organs used by the caterpillar are reduced and replaced by others. Cells known as imaginal discs form to produce completely new body parts that the caterpillar did not have. Antennae, eyes, wings, legs and related muscles need to develop. Adult moths will lay eggs and so reproductive organs are formed. And since many adults do not feed, their digestive system is altered as well. (Caterpillars seem to eat all the time.) What begins as a "worm" becomes a winged insect within the cocoon. The development is then followed by a period of dormancy in cold temperatures so adults do not emerge too early. They need to be in synchrony with the spring season.

Cocoons vary with different species. The cocoon that I was shown was of a large moth; the cecropia. If we are fortunate to see this magnificent moth of a reddish-brown color and a wingspan of about five inches, it would be in late May or early June. As adults they do not eat and so flight time is short. They seek a mate and lay eggs. Their caterpillars of summer change from dark color to green over a period of five molts; growing to about four inches long. Cocoons are formed in fall. If we see them in winter, it is best to leave them. They need to experience cold to complete the development from caterpillar to moth.

February 6, 2021

Canine Scent Marking Time

The number of days from the first day of winter; winter solstice on December 21, until the vernal equinox, March 20 this year, is ninety days. One half of that; forty-five days, brings us to the first week of February. In different words, according to the calendar, we are midway through winter. Calendar winter is not always what we experience in this region; and so, if we look at the snow season; starting in mid-November and ending in mid-April (both dates are a bit nebulous); early February is also the middle. Either way, we are beginning the second half.

Subzero temperatures in the mornings are common at this time; still cold and we'll see more snow. But despite the weather phenomena, other things are changing. We began February with about nine and a half hours of daylight; we'll have eleven by the end of the month. Days rapidly get longer. Sunrise moves towards 7 AM; setting well after 5 PM. And many critters respond.

I notice chickadees singing their "feebee" song while nuthatches get more vocal and hairy woodpeckers continue to drum. Crows and ravens do more calling now during their morning flights while the nocturnal owls are heard in the darkness. Among the small mammals, squirrels that appeared to be interested only in food at the bird feeders are now becoming interested in each other. Tracks of rabbits and hare tell of their nightly activities as well.

Recently, while out along the roads and trails in the woods, I noticed that larger mammals are also reacting to the lengthening daylight. Despite chilly days, I saw the trails of foxes and coyotes at these sites. One location is so pronounced with their tracks and trails, that I call this place the "coyote crossing". They appear to be traveling far in their mid-winter wanderings; crossing the roads to fields and woods and even going onto a nearby lake. The fox trails were more common in the woods and as I passed this way on my daily outings, I noticed plenty of their tracks. But both of these canines had something else to show along their route; besides footprints. They both had done some scent marking at selected sites.

The fox had zig-zagged on its wandering through the woods, but twice along the route, I saw that there was a yellow stain in the snow. The fox had chosen a place near small trail-side plants; likely to be found by others, and here it deposited a bit of urine. With ample odor, it sent a scent message to others of its kind; this territory was taken; an olfactory "no trespassing" sign. With weather changing, the sign will need to be renewed occasionally. I went further along and out onto the lake. I found where a coyote, crossing this body of water, came to shore to give a scent-marking sign of his own. It then went back on the lake. The scent at the lake's edge would be enough to tell other coyotes to stay away.

Both, the fox and the coyote, will make their rounds again. What is happening is that early February is breeding time for these canines. Scent marking is part of this annual event. Coyotes have a gestation of about sixty days and foxes, maybe a week less. Mating now can assure of springtime births and plenty of time to raise the new family in their territories. It's early February, but wild canines are preparing for spring.

Feb. 13, 2021

Mulleins Above and Below the Snow

Mid-February; the days continue to get longer. We are near ten and a half hours of daylight. While the sunsets move towards 6 PM, rising approaches 7 AM. Though often cold, February can also bring temperatures in the forty-degree range.

Birds (and squirrels) arrive earlier at the feeders now and during my dawn walk, I hear more sounds from crows, ravens and woodpecker drummings. It seems like there are more crows here each day lately. Also, besides these, tracks of deer, coyote and fox abound along the road and hare are more active in the woods.

As we ease into late winter, we are not only entering the time of changes, this is also the time of the greatest snowpack. Typically, late February and early March is when we have the deepest snow on the ground. And though February does not usually give us much snow; not much has melted either. This winter has not been a particularly snowy winter, but the Weather Service has recorded a seasonal total of about sixty inches (close to normal). We have had a continuous snow cover for nearly one hundred days.

I was looking at this snowpack recently as I walked along the road. The depth was about one foot and that was enough to cover the myriads of wild flowers that bloomed here in the open last summer. At that time, the roadsides flourished with a diversity of colors from daisies, black-eyed susans, trefoils and clovers; all presently buried under this snow. But as I passed by, I noted that several of the taller plants could still be seen; goldenrods, asters, sunflowers and the ubiquitous tansies. They were so common in late summer and can still be seen here now. These plants are holding seeds to be dispersed by winds or birds. Nearly all are perennial, with roots still alive underground, they will be in this location again next summer. But there is one biannual among them. The tall mullein that bloomed here last summer has a life of two years.

Reaching above the snowpack, mulleins may be five feet tall. Not only do they have an impressive height, they are also robust. With a stem thick and tough, the plant not only stands above the snow, it seems to be also as solid as wood. During its flowering time in summer; usually coming to bloom in early July, they are hard to not notice. Besides rising above the other flora, they also are full of large leaves. Wide and long, the leaves are coated with a furry growth; giving a soft coating. (One of the other names for this flower is velvet-leaf; and I have heard it called "calf's tongue".) Leaves are mostly low on the plant, but higher on the stem are numerous flowers. Ironically, such a tall and robust growth has tiny yellow flowers; easy to overlook even when we see this roadside plant.

This flowering phase is the end of its second year. Seeds are formed and the plant fades in fall. Mature seeds drop in these open sites along roads. Growing during its first year, the plant stays low and spreads its leaves forming what is called a rosette; spending winter in this stage. Doing some digging under the snow here, I was able to locate a rosette with leaves that were still largely green; preparing for the coming spring. In the snowpack of mid-February, we can see the mullein of last summer and the one preparing for next summer.

February 20, 2021

Thanks to the Same Seven

When both December and January registered temperatures that were considerably above normal, it looked like, with only one month to go, the meteorological winter (December, January and February) would continue to be warmer than the norm; a bit of a mild winter. It was hard for any of us weather watchers to predict a rapid change that we experienced. (The first few days of February showed this mild pattern; even some thirty-degree days). And then we got the "arctic week". Beginning on February 6, the winter statistics changed.

It seems like the pattern of recent months is to have quite a difference in weather in the first half to the second half. We may be seeing that again now in this month. Thanks to the recent frigid air, the first half of these twenty-eight days, was almost minus two degrees; far under the usual of fourteen. We frequently have negative temperatures during this month, but usually not this long. Getting in the positive numbers after nearly ninety hours of less than zero degrees, we returned for more than one hundred hours of subzero. Such cold certainly impacted us. What did it do to the local wildlife?

I continued my walks at dawn; nearly every day at twenty to thirty below. Skies were consistently clear, bright sunlight and most days with a wind. Only a few ravens and crows were company as I wandered along the road. One day, I saw a bald eagle and another time, a barred owl called. Fewer tracks told of many critters remaining sheltered in the cold. Most tracks I saw belonged to deer, squirrels and white-footed mice. As the days passed, foxes, coyotes and weasels ventured out. While most of the local wildlife waited out the cold, I'm glad that the bird feeders gave plenty to see.

I kept the feeders well-fortified with sunflower seeds and suet. And the feathered neighbors responded. I have not seen the variety of birds at the feeders this winter as usual; none of the several kinds of finches that often find meals here. Turkeys that started the season with us, have gone back into the woods; apparently finding shelter and acorns. This has left us with visits from the "same seven".

Seven kinds of birds were here for the whole winter. On mild days, some would not be present at all. But once the recent cold moved in, so did the regulars. Each day, with the sunrises continuing to get earlier (now about 7 AM), they begin to arrive. Consistently, it is the black-capped chickadees that are first to come to breakfast. These little bundles of energy are followed by the two kinds of nuthatches; white-breasted and red-breasted. Later, three species of woodpeckers make their entry. Usually, it is the hairy woodpecker first, then its smaller look-alike; the downy woodpecker, and finally a pair of red-bellied woodpeckers. (The woodpeckers and nuthatches seem to be in pairs.) Last of the seven are several blue jays; some days a half dozen.

Though they gobble sunflower seeds that I replenish each day, it is the suet that is most in demand now. This animal fat hanging from nearby trees holds much energy to help the birds deal with the cold. Such foods and their behavior of fluffing-up feathers to provide for more insulation allows the birds to cope with subzero. These same seven have been consistent through the cold and though it may appear as we are helping them, their arrival each day helps us too.

February 27, 2021

Deer Mice Hop During the Cold

At the end of February, sunset is at 6 PM; we have eleven hours of daylight. Moving into longer days of March, we will reach vernal equinox on March 20. Many of us are looking forward to the coming season change. But February of 2021 is worth taking a look back at as well. It was not a record-setting month, but after the December and January that we had, it was a bit of a surprise. For nearly two weeks, we moved through an arctic winter pattern. It is not unusual to get subzero temperatures in February, but rarely lasting this long.

From February 6 until February 17, we saw below zero each day. February 6 to 15, it remained there nearly the whole time. Of the 240 hours during this time, the warmest was two above. I found that the early morning low temperatures on these days were quite impressive. During every one of these "good mornings", we recorded colder than minus fifteen. (Eight of the twelve days were more than minus twenty; two record setting!) Before this, the coldest for the whole winter, was minus fourteen. Yes, a cold snap to remember.

We coped with these conditions quite well and we survived. Perhaps it is the extension of the ice cover on Lake Superior that would be our lasting reminder of this time. But we share the region with much wildlife and they needed to deal with this cold as well.

Going for walks and other treks during these days, I noticed far fewer tracks. (The consistent sunlight and no new snowfall made tracks a little hard to discern.) Deer and squirrel remained active. Deer trails in the one-foot snowpack were easy to make and use. Squirrels still came to the feeders, but fewer than usual. When only about five came during the cold, their numbers quickly grew to more than twenty when the temperature rose. Foxes and coyotes that were so active before the cold, made limited movements in the frigid time. Hopping gaits of weasels appeared at a few sites in the woods, but it was another hopper, much smaller, deer mice, that remained active.

With an ample covering of snow on the ground, many wildlife sat out the chill. I did not see tracks of rabbits, hare or grouse at this time. All most likely found shelter in the snow. Voles and shrews moved beneath the white blanket. Here they could easily go through and under the dry February snow. Another small mammal, the deer mouse, chose to hop on the snow. Deer mice; often called white-footed mice, are very common in the region. They will take shelter under the snow as other mice do, but when it comes to moving about, they go above.

They quickly move over this cold substrate in their normal hopping gait. Hopping cannot be done under snow and so to really go somewhere, they hop over the surface. They remained very active in the snow and I found their tracks each day. Plenty of other mammals will hop in snow, but these mice are the only ones that leave a tail mark along with footprints as they hop. Deer mice have a tail about equal to body length; long enough to leave a mark as they hop in snow. Typically, the mice covered an open space to take shelter, usually under a log or the base of a tree. And they continued to hop throughout the cold. It was good to see their activity during this cold snap.

March 6, 2021

The Bug Walking on the Snow

The divergent pattern of recent months continued through February. We saw it well as the month waned. After ten days of frigid temperatures; two with record-setting cold, the situation drastically changed and we warmed. Though I did see a temperature of minus forty on the thirteenth, the same thermometer spoke of plus forty on the twenty-second. Again, we had a month where the weather of the first half was much different from that of the second half. February overall was colder than normal, but not a record.

I found it very interesting to see the responses in nature as the days changed. During my walks in the cold, I noted persistent tracks of deer, squirrels and deer mice. Fox and coyote moved about occasionally, but mostly not. Once the days warmed to freezing and above, the roadsides held tracks that showed activities of some absent during the cold; snowshoe hare and raccoons.

Feeding the birds, I also noted changes. The feeders that were active with the same seven kinds that came by each day in the cold, were mostly empty. Again, this showed that feeder birds were able to find food elsewhere and wanted a change of diet. During the morning walks, I heard the usual ravens and an increasing number of crows. They were joined by blue jays. Woodpecker drumming, including the pileated, became more consistent. And several times, a barred owl called; often in the daytime.

As I passed by a nearby stream, I was surprised at how quickly the ice cover gave way to some open sites. These enlarged each day, revealing the movement of this waterway. On south-facing hillsides, some patches of bare ground emerged as well. But despite these happenings; including the eleven hours of daylight, we are two weeks from the vernal equinox. Early March is still winter.

This was pointed out to me recently when "bugs" were seen in the snow. These days in March are when we have freezing and thawing making for wet snow. Sometimes in these settings, we might see what looks like pepper on the snow. A closer look reveals that these black dots are moving. What we are seeing are numerous springtails (Collembola) that live under the snow, but come onto the surface when days warm. Due to their hopping, they are also called "snowfleas".

What was reported to me was larger and walked alone over the snow; no hopping or flying. This is another insect of winter; a wingless winter crane fly (Chionea). Also living beneath the snow, in the subnivean zone, through the coldest times, they come to the surface when weather permits; usually temperatures near thirty degrees. (Forty seems to be too warm for them.) Unlike nearly all other insects, they reach maturity in winter. I find them mostly in late winter. Another winter crane fly (Trichocera) flies about in early winter. With no wings, Chionea walks over the snow. The dark body is easy to see on the snow. Here, they seek food and mates. Not being in groups, they are often overlooked; though they are common. Chionea has been confused with winter scorpionflies (Boreus); also active on late winter snows. As they walk, they may have a slight resemblance to spiders; but they have six legs, spiders have eight. So now, in late winter, if we see a bug walking in the snow, it is probably a wingless winter crane fly (Chionea).

March 13, 2021

Horned Larks Are Early Migrants.

As we approach the halfway point in March, we have seen, during the early weeks, quite a change from the previous. Daylight is eleven and a half hours long now; the vernal equinox is only one week away. Sunlit days have also been accompanied with warmer temperatures and after a long absence, 50 degrees appears on our thermometers.

The responses to these changes are amazing. Among the trees that have stood out in the open during the dark and cold season, there is plenty happening. Buds of willows and quaking aspens have opened to reveal a furry growth beneath. Later, these buds will develop into catkins, but now they are just interesting to look at and serve as a remedy for cabin and spring fever. Willows and maples also show yellow and reddish twigs. But the deepest reds are on the small shrub of red-osier dogwoods; the whole plant above ground is now bright red. With the deciduous trees, sunlight has been absorbed on the bark of trunks and reradiated out to the surrounding snow; forming open spaces around the trees. I like to call these "tree circles" and they seem to appear at about the same time as maple sap begins to flow. On a sunlit site, near a building, I found chutes of crocuses emerging; soon to bloom. Here too, in these hot spots, are the first dandelions.

Among animals, early spring also happens. In the yard, I've noted the return of waking raccoons, skunks and chipmunks. During my walks, I see and hear flocking crows; probably migrants. Early movement is also going on with raptors: eagles, red-tailed hawks, harriers and kestrels. Searching for some open waters are returning geese, swans and mergansers. And we may also see some migrants right in our yard.

After watching the wintering birds that regularly arrived at the feeders all winter, we might see some different ones in March. It is not unusual that passing redpolls, pine siskins, goldfinches and purple finches will be here. Early sparrows, such as song sparrows, fox sparrows, tree sparrows and juncos can be seen too. Though many robins winter with us, I usually find their first migrants during March. Soon, my morning walks will sound with songs of red-winged blackbirds at swamps and grackles calling from roadside trees. After dusk, the strange woodcock ritual of calls, dance and flight takes place in the wetlands.

One place that we are not as likely to look for early migrants is out in the fields and open spaces. Here, the snow tends to be drifted and may linger longer with cool March winds. But here and often along the roadsides, are a couple of hardy field birds. Flocking as we saw them in late fall are snow buntings; showing white in flight. Also, in small flocks or alone are the inconspicuous horned larks. These larks are more likely to stay while snow buntings move north.

Horned larks get their name from black feathers sticking up above the head. Birds are about seven inches long and though they have some yellow on the throat, they are mostly brown and likely to be overlooked. They tend to stay on the ground, often walking instead of flying. Feeding on seeds of field plants, they now are mating and preparing for the new season. Not as well known as many others, but horned larks are regular early March migrants.

March 20, 2021

Fall and Winter Nature at Home

The vernal equinox on March 20 marks the beginning of spring, but also, I see it as an anniversary. It was at last year's vernal equinox that we seriously took note of the pandemic. Tournaments, conferences and schools began to get canceled. And our lives changed. We started wearing masks and we learned that the safest thing to do was stay at home. I decided to do just that and watch nearby nature.

Many nature observers have wondered what it would be like to see the changes in nature while staying in one place for an entire year. Though we continue to watch nature, we often go elsewhere to see other natural news. Here was that opportunity, even though unintended, to remain at home for the whole year; observing nearby nature. I have done some traveling in recent years, but COVID changed that. From mid-March of 2020 until mid-March 2021, I stayed home.

At the time of the autumnal equinox of 2020, I reflected on what it was like to watch homebound nature throughout the seasons of spring and summer. There was constant happenings with local flora and fauna. I was never bored. Now, at the vernal equinox, I can reflect on two more home seasons; autumn and winter.

Weather made much news. After a very dry September, more moisture returned. October started off warm (80 degrees on the 9th), it morphed into a chilly ending (5th coldest) with the 2nd most snowfall for this month. Early November, also warm, had record-setting days (75 degrees on the 6th); melting the October snows. But snow returned; starting a snowpack that lasted more than 120 days; and the lakes froze. Early December, we saw subzero and freezing of rivers. Lake ice was devoid of a snow cover for weeks. Good for skating and seeing what is under water. Jupiter and Saturn gave quite a show in this dark month. January followed December's pattern; being warmer than normal and less snow. Early in the month, we enjoyed a wonderful winter crystal scene; "rime time". The mild winter took a change for ten days in February when the temperature never got above 2 degrees; including a record cold of minus 35. By the end of the month, the days had warmed and we ended the winter with melting mild March days (record setting; 55 degrees on the 9th). More snow and rain as we moved on to the vernal equinox.

In the midst of all these weather happenings, much was seen with local wildlife. During late September mornings, I searched for and photographed spider webs. Draped in dew, these constructions were very photogenic. When temperatures fell, I extended my web search, not just covered with dew, but frost. This marvel is seldom seen, but in the waning days of the month, I located a few such webs.

Bird migration of fall was again excellent. I did not need to go to Hawk Ridge, but saw flights right near home. Besides raptors, there were flocks of geese and various songbirds. Early October was filled with sparrows, blackbirds and the last of the warblers. I went to a swamp in October to watch the evening flights of bats. While seeing these mammals, I noted plenty of ducks (mostly wood ducks), flying from where they spent the day to their night sites. I kept coming back for this show; nearly every dusk for a month.

The leaf color and drop was dramatic at mid-October. Not only did leaves fall; many acorns dropped in the woods. This satisfied squirrels and turkeys. While wandering here, I also saw a couple of late season mushrooms; honey (Armillaria) and scaly-cap (Pholiota) and the waning fall wild flowers. In the light of a lower sun of October and November, I found myriads of tiny spiders ballooning (kiting) in their dispersal.

When colder weather came the flight of snow buntings and two kinds of finches not seen last year; redpolls and pine grosbeaks. A snow fall on frozen ground and ice in December provided for great tracking conditions. And I found tracks of about twenty kinds in one walk. Settling down with feeder watching in January and the cold of February, I noted chickadees, nuthatches, jays and woodpeckers actively here each day (no finches); flying squirrels at night. In March they were joined by raccoons and chipmunks. Willow and aspen buds opened and crocuses emerged in nearby soil as we returned to the vernal equinox.

My year of stay-at-home nature watching was a great experience. I continually observed happenings and whether it was hot or cold, dry or wet, day or night, the nearby nature show was continuous and never boring; always more to see. "There is a new story out here every day." Will there be more stay at home to come?

March 27, 2021

A Pair of Pileated Woodpeckers

The morning is cloudy, calm and cool with a temperature in the mid- twenties. Later in the day, the skies may break to be partially clear and the calm could become windy; as often happens in March. But as I walk at dawn, I think conditions are great. With calm and cloudy, I find it is very good for hearing the sounds of the local wildlife. During my walk, I pause often to listen. The snowpack, receding much is still present at many sites; especially on the north-facing slopes. Snow is crusty now in the chilly morning, but becomes wet with the warming afternoon.

Before leaving the yard, I see that a recently-awaken chipmunk has joined the squirrels here. Deer are easy to see as they go in the open sites scattered among the melting snowpack. Among the birds, it is the usuals that I hear first. Ravens, crows and blue jays have been companions in my recent morning walks. Now, their sounds are joined by white-breasted nuthatches calling in the woods. These small birds that have been here all winter, mostly silent. now give their nasal "yank, yank" calls. In the distance, I hear flocks of Canada geese and vocals from trumpeter swans. Occasionally, I see them fly over. Turkeys that have been so active in the woods and yard recently have started gobble in the calm early morning. A barred owl gives an encore call to the passing night. Late March is also when I hear another sound in the receding darkness; the call of a displaying woodcock. Welcoming the new light are songs of red-winged blackbirds and drumming of ruffed grouse. But it is the drumming of a different kind that is a regular part of these early spring morning walks; the drumming of woodpeckers.

Having a long and powerful beak, these woodland birds find a branch or trunk to hold on to and with repeated hits, they send out a sound that permeates the forest. Such sounds are usually noted as proclamations of territory. Woodpecker drumming has been happening for weeks. The mid-sized hairy woodpeckers began to drum already in January. I have heard them in very cold, but usually clear, winter days.

This drumming noise has become more common as we progressed into early spring. Hairy woodpeckers have been joined by three others that wintered with us: downy, red-bellied and especially the pileated woodpeckers. When these large birds find a location to pound on, they make sounds that resonate throughout the woods and beyond. As winter residents, they made sporadic appearances at the feeder, where they remained mostly silent. But now, in the longer days, they drum and often give their "wicker, wicker.." calls to get a territory to nest in, but also to attract a mate.

I've seen them often, but usually alone. That made a recent visit more interesting since it was a pair that arrived in the yard. Male and female are about the same size. Males have more red on the crest and a red "mustache" under the eye. Instead of going to a tree trunk, they landed and stayed on the ground. Here they appeared to feed on seeds under the feeder, but more likely fed on insects. They used their long tongues in the soil to catch a meal. This mated pair appeared to be feeding together on this spring day. It was a great sight to see and I expect that they will also nest nearby.

Second Quarter

April 3, 2021

The Waking of a Garter Snake

April in the northland is an amazingly varied time and it is hard to believe some weather happenings that we have had during this spring month. Subzero temperatures are quite unusual, but have occurred a few times. At the other end of the thermometer, temperatures in the eighties have been recorded. It is a month that has had both thunderstorms and snowstorms. Some Aprils have been very wet while others may be fire-hazard dry. Most years, we get some snow, but April of 2013 set a record of nearly fifty-one inches; April of 2010 had none. We'll see what this April will give us.

Looking back at March, we see a month with an above normal temperature; not record setting, but one of the warmest. Along with mild days, we saw the demise of our snowpack. The month that normally has the greatest snowpack, had virtually none when we exited. Instead of huge snowfalls, we received rains that gave moisture to snowless fields, forests and helped to replenish vernal ponds. Following the chill of February, March was a month of spring, not winter. It is not the earliest spring in the northland, but in response to above normal days, things began to unfold a bit ahead of time.

Along the south-facing side of buildings; early-season hot spots, crocuses opened and a few dandelions took advantage of this sunlit site. Nearby, a recently awaken chipmunk scampered across the yard an onto the deck. And the anticipated bird movement happens.

As I walked on the road, I noted the flight of returning raptors; especially bald eagles. At one swamp, the resident Canada geese settled onto the ice while in nearby open water, a pair of mallards swam about. More geese and trumpeter swans gave loud vocals as they flew over. Hiding among roadside shrubs was an early-arrived song sparrow. The first red-winged blackbird sang from a swamp. Ruffed grouse drummed and turkeys gobbled in the forest while loud guttural calls of a sandhill crane sounded beyond.

One day, as I passed by a sunny site in a woods, I spied a basking butterfly. This orange-black Compton tortoise-shell is a kind of anglewing; butterflies that hibernate in winter as adults. Members of this group are first to be seen in spring. Best known is the mourning cloak. With all these sights of late March, it was no surprise to see the presence of a garter snake on a sunny hillside a few days ago.

Another member of the northland fauna that hibernate through the cold season, garter snakes will frequently gather at a site; a hibernaculum, for winter. It seems like every spring this is the location where I see these striped reptiles. Upon waking and basking in the springtime sunlight, the smaller males will try to mate with the larger females. They become very active at this time and we may see several. Following this, they disperse into the region for the warmer months. Garter snakes and red-bellied snakes are the only kinds of snakes that are common in the northland. (I have also seen a few ring-necked snakes.) Though some garter snakes can reach two feet in length, our snakes are mostly small and harmless. They do not lay eggs, but have live birth at a later time in summer. Usually, I see the first wakening snake in April, but with the other recent happenings, this early-waking garter snake was almost expected. Following the lead of this snake, I hope to see more reptiles and amphibians in April.

April 10, 2021

The Woodcock Flight at Dusk

Early April moving into mid-April is a time of much change. Temperatures frequently get into the sixties, but mornings are often below freezing. The anticipated ice-out appears reluctant. It is a time of lawns beginning to respond; maybe with the help of a shower (rain or snow). We begin the month with thirteen hours of daylight; more than fourteen by the end. Crocus and daffodils join early dandelions in the yard while the garden reveals the new crop of rhubarb and the growth of day lilies reach up from the soil; even though they do not bloom until July. Spring wild flowers are a bit later in the woods, but here we may see greens of wild leek (ramps).

April is the month of catkins; long growths holding pollen on alder and hazel. Willows and aspens have their furry buds of March now developing into their catkins. Silver maples show flowers; male (staminate) or female (pistillate); usually on separate trees. Red maples will be flowering a bit later this month.

The warming weather melts winter's snowpack creating vernal ponds in any low sites. Quickly, they are the home of waking frogs as they sing of courtship and territory. In other wetlands, red-winged blackbird males continue singing begun a couple of weeks ago; females arrive in a few more weeks. In yards, we may see grackles along with robins, juncos and a variety of sparrows (maybe four kinds: white-throated, song, fox and tree). White-throated and song may breed here, fox and tree go far north; after resting. Junco flocks are also often seen along roadsides in April. As the days progress, some insect-eating birds may be here too; phoebe, tree swallows and a couple of woodpeckers: flickers and yellow-bellied sapsuckers. In open waters of rivers, more ducks join mallards and goldeneyes; ring-necked, scaup, bufflehead, wood ducks and teal. Along the shore, wading birds move about; herons and yellowlegs. Often in mornings, we can hear the unusual winnowing flight of a snipe. This sound made by its wings tells of courtship. But as I step out at dusk, it is the flight of its cousin; the woodcock, that I seek.

As shorebirds go, woodcocks are a bit strange. While many have long legs with a thin body, the woodcock has short legs, chubby body and a long flexible bill; used for catching worms. This strangeness may account for its other name; timber doodle. But stranger still is its mating and territorial performance that I was able to watch recently.

About one-half hour after sunset as the darkness continues to creep in, the male woodcock selects an open area, near a wetland to perform this ritual. While blackbirds sing in nearby swamps and ruffed grouse drum in an adjacent woods, woodcocks choose an open arena. The evening is cool and calm; ideal conditions to witness this ritual. I stand still and listen. Sure enough, a strange call sounding like a "peent" emanates from the edge. It is followed by several more of these sounds and then, the bird flies high up in the air. From here, he take a zig-zag pattern back to the ground. Air through the wings creates a twittering noise. Back on earth, he performs again. The woodcocks began this routine sporadically in late March, but now they are more consistent. He may do this show each evening for weeks; often with a repeat in the early morning. A strange mating performance from a strange bird, but it is a rite of spring that I would not want to miss.

April 17, 2021

Wild Leeks Green the Forest Floor

Early April has continued the pattern for most of recent months by being warmer than normal. The mild temperatures of late March carried into the new month and we experienced an ice-out about three weeks before last year. With the snowpack gone, mild temperatures in breezy days made for fire hazards. This was somewhat abated with a few days of rain and cool east winds.

With an early ice-out, it was no surprise to see the local loon arriving on its homesite well before the normal. Here too, are a few more migrant ducks while a kingfisher and heron were along the shore. In the greening yard, I watched a flock of juncos. Three kinds of sparrows were part of this group; song sparrow, fox sparrow and tree sparrow. But it was along the road where I saw a huge flock of juncos; at least two hundred fifty, also hosting some sparrows.

Mid-April is when we often see the next batch of migrant songbirds arriving; flickers, yellow-bellied sapsuckers, phoebes, tree swallows, kinglets and yellow-rumped warblers (the first warbler). With the snow and ice melted, vernal ponds have formed and the trio of early frogs wake and come by to sing; courting and mating. The first that I heard was on April 3; "quacking" sounds of wood frogs. The following day, small chorus frogs and spring peepers chimed in.

I noted these birds and frogs as I walked the woods a few days later, but it was the greening of the forest floor that I was seeking. It is easy to see greening lawns, a bit harder to see green under these trees. Starting small are the abundant mosses. These tiny plants are at the base of nearly every adult tree. Here they were all winter, remaining green, but now in the vernal sunlight, they develop new leaves and spore capsules. The woods greens from the ground up.

As I continue walking, I look for more green leaves. I find leaves of three common flowering plants; pyrola, wintergreen and hepatica. While the first two bloom in summer, hepatica are spring flowers. And so, with mild conditions, it was no real surprise to find some hepatica already in bloom. With leaves already grown, these blue and white blossoms are consistently the first spring woodland flowers. Nearby, I came to a site thick with new green leaves; wild leeks.

Known as wild leeks, wild onions or ramps, these plants emerge rapidly from underground roots at this time. Four days previous to when I wandered here, I found none. Now, they are obvious. As a member of the onion family, their leaves have parallel veins, a bit wider than the domestic onion. Breaking open leaves or taking a bite, we can easily smell or taste the connection with onions.

Plants stay alive buried in the soil in a robust rounded-oval root. From here the shoots grow. Though these leafy plants now carpet the space beneath many deciduous trees, they do not flower until summer's shady days (usually July). Apparently, leeks form green leaves now; catching available sunlight to make food to survive the shade later.

Soon, this same woods will have a plethora of spring wild flowers putting forth new leaves, stems and blossoms; taking advantage of sunlight before the trees shade them. (Tree leafing also appears to be early this year with elderberry already beginning.) But now, we see the prolific wild leeks as they take over the greening of the woods.

April 24, 2021

Leopard Frogs Add to Spring Quartets

Late April is when we reach fourteen hours of daylight; sun rising 6 AM, setting 8 PM. With the pace of spring picking up, there is plenty to see during these hours. Trees continue their spring response. Now red maples flower much like those of silver maple earlier. Forsythia adds yellow blossoms to the yard. A couple of small trees and shrubs begin leafing. I find consistently, the red elderberry is always first to unfold its new green foliage. This is followed by gooseberry and fly honeysuckle bushes with lilac and quaking aspen also quick to turn green.

Woodland wild flowers abound in May, but in late April, we can see early ones. Hepatica opens the floral scene, but shortly thereafter are spring beauties and bloodroots. Before the woods gets shady, we can find many kinds flowering here. But besides all this to see, there is much to hear as well.

Some of the newly arrived migrant birds now settle into territorial nesting sites and proclaim ownership with songs and sounds. Red-winged blackbirds sing in swamps; robins and song sparrows in yards while hermit thrushes, kinglets and winter wrens announce to the woods. Others speak of territories with varying methods. Ruffed grouse and woodpeckers both make drumming sounds; in quite different ways. Turkeys gobble in the mornings while flights of woodcock and snipe sound overhead. Geese and loons call from lakes and sandhill cranes loudly proclaim in fields and marshes. But birds are not the only ones to make mating and territorial noise now.

With the early ice out this year, I saw that vernal ponds were also open. This meant the awaking frogs would soon respond. And yes, the early spring trio of frogs were awake and calling within days of ponds forming. On April 3, I heard the first quack-like "glucking" sound from wood frogs. The following day, both the creaking sounds of chorus frogs and peeping of spring peepers were added to the vernal singers. For a couple of days and nights, they continued their sounds until cooling weather caused them to pause; only to be continued by mid-month. It is interesting to note that we usually do not see these frogs.

Wood frogs, the first to sing are often the first to stop since they have a short breeding season; frequently over by the end of April. Chorus frogs and spring peepers will continue their sounds for a few more weeks. Now in the last week of April, they are often joined by a fourth calling frog; the trio may become a quartet for a while. Not in the vernal ponds; most-likely in nearby swamps, leopard frogs come to the surface and add their calls. Their contribution to the spring vocals sounds like a snore. While wood frogs, chorus frogs and spring peepers all winter on land, leopard frogs go into the bottom of swamps for the cold season. (Of other frogs and toad in the northland; gray treefrogs and American toads winter on land, green and mink frogs stay under water.)

Leopard frogs get their name from the spots on the body. Later in the summer, they may be more on land and more green, but now, they are an olive-green color in the spring wetlands. Males appear to float on the surface as they do their calling. These sounds will continue into next month. But now, in late April, we can expect their snoring calls from swamps; and maybe heard as part of a spring frog quartet.

May 1, 2021

Hermit Thrushes Return to Our Forests

With nearly fourteen and a half hours of daylight, we enter May. No other month gives us happenings of this growing season like those of May. It is a month of abundant spring wild flowers under trees in the open woods. Their lives are quick before leafing trees shade the forest later in the month. Not only is there a floral display of these small ephemerals, but plenty of trees blossom as well. Among the changing branches are many migrant birds. There are new ones here each day; many also grace the scene with songs. It is during these weeks, we welcome back orioles, grosbeaks, wrens, hummingbirds, vireos, flycatchers, thrushes and about two dozen warbler species. Amazing May is a great time for taking woods walks.

Though it is during May that we see most bird migrants; numbers and variety, the migration has been happening for weeks prior. Probably the most notable early arrivals are geese, swans, ducks, loons and pelicans. Hawks and eagles continue their northing flights. Among songbirds, red-winged blackbirds have been at swamps for weeks. Juncos and other sparrows were in yards and along roads for much of April. Others arrive in late month stretching into May. Each walk during the last week of April has been filled with sights and sounds. Yellow-bellied sapsuckers drum continuously in the woods. Tree swallows and phoebe catch insects near waterways. In the yard, the first yellow-rumped warblers consistently arrive now while in the woods, hermit thrushes return quietly.

For the most part, thrushes are not as well-known as some other songbirds. Typically, seven kinds of this family can be found in the region each spring. Some remain and nest, others keep on going further north to breed. Best known of the thrushes are robins; well-known and well loved. Bluebirds with blue-red plumage are also much appreciated. But the other five kinds of thrushes are not as colorful; mostly brown, and not seen as much. Nearly all have brown backs with spots on the underside. Some, like the gray-cheeked, nest in the far north and are only seen in passing through here. The other four kinds may nest in the region. Swainson's thrush in the northern parts while the wood thrush (most spotted of all) is more in the south. The veery (least spotted of all) and hermit thrush are likely to stay and raise a family. All five of these brown thrushes live in forests.

All are migrants, coming back in spring, mostly in May. The first arrivals, usually in late April, are hermit thrushes. Since they winter in southern states, they have a shorter distance to migrate. Others spend the cold season in Central America. Hermit thrushes are also the smallest thrush. While most are about seven inches, hermits are only six. They get their name from living deep in forests; not venturing out much. Like others, hermit thrushes are brown on the back, spotted undersides; but unlike others, they have a reddish-brown tail. This appendage is often raised and lowered when they sit on a branch.

While walking in the woods on a recent late April day, I observed this early arrival. Though staying in the forest, they do produce a rather loud flute-like series of notes to defend their homes. Perhaps that is why this small brown forest bird was chosen as the state bird of Vermont. Not quite like our state bird, but hermit thurshes are still a delight to behold in the springtime woods.

May 8, 2021

Trout-Lilies Join Spring Woods Bouquet

Those of us who observe nature happenings are treated to an annual array of phenomena. Though nearly all are ones that we've seen before, we are willing to see again. Whether it is aurora, rainbows or autumn leaf colors, we are not willing to see them only once. I find that wandering among spring woodland wildflowers in mid-May is such a phenomenon. After snow and cold, we are ready to see a floral show.

Taking advantage of the nearly fifteen hours of sunlight that penetrates to the forest floor before tree leaves shade the scene, opportunistic spring wildflowers flourish; for a short time. Since their blooming time is limited, they are often called ephemerals. Some are true ephemerals, some are not; but all are a delight to behold now as we walk.

Without exception, this annual floral show begins with the white and blue flowers of hepatica. Following shortly are the eight-petal bloodroots and the five pink petals of abundant spring beauties. Wood anemone and wild strawberry are present with their five white petals. Yellow appears in bellworts of the woods and marsh marigolds in swamps. Violets of purple, white or yellow add variety. More white is seen in the four petals of toothwort and scattered coltsfoot. And the strange white of Dutchman's breeches. While the three large petals of trillium are hard to not see, those of wild ginger are easy to miss. Well known too are the trout-lilies.

We are fortunate to have in our region two species of trout-lilies; one white (Erythronium albidum), one yellow (Erythronium americana). A third kind of trout-lily; dwarf trout-lily (Erythronium propullans) grows in a few counties of southeast Minnesota and nowhere else. White and yellow may be separate from each other or side by side. Plants grow up to about six inches tall. The leaves rise from soil and are abundant in the spring woods. Any patch will have hundreds of these leaves. Most are sterile; single leaves with no flowers. Flowers appear on plants of two leaves. There are two explanations of why they are called trout-lilies. Some say that the splotches on the leaves look like that of a trout. Other say that the name comes from an early naturalist who observed that they bloom at about the time trout swim upstream to spawn. They are also called fawn-lily, dog-tooth violet and adder's tongue.

Depending on the species, flowers are either white or yellow. Bent or curled back, they appear to have six petals, but as with other members of the lily family, they are actually three petals and three sepals; all the same color. Trout-lilies are true ephemerals, they don't last long. We need to get out and enjoy them when we can. Most spring wildflowers are best seen in the vernal sunlight. And they change each day. I suggest walking among these spring flora often; do not pick.

As the month progresses and tree leaves provide a canopy, shade tolerant flowers begin to take over. In the second half of May are jack-in-the-pulpit, starflower, baneberry, wild lily-of-the-valley, bunchberry, blue-bead lily (Clintonia), sarsaparilla, blue cohosh, columbine and the yellow and pink ladyslippers. Trees contribute to this floral display with white blossoms of plum, cherry, juneberry and elderberry.

As we walk among this amazing flowering show of May, we can also observe some early fungi and several kinds of fiddleheads sharing the forest floor. May woods walks are outstanding and worth going back for more; even if we see what we have seen before.

May 15, 2021

Fiddleheads Grow on the Forest Floor

Mid-May in the northland is a remarkable time. Spring's pace is so fast that it is hard to follow all that is happening. Within our yards, we see flowers blooming, green grass growing, garden ready for planting and trees that have been bare for so long are now greening new leaves. Yes, May is the greening month. With ample rainfall, we'll see even more. But there is plenty going on in the forest as well.

During a recent woods walk at Jay Cooke State Park, I was surrounded by May happenings. On such a visit to a site like this, I like to wander at a slow pace; seeing as much as I can. I came here to look at spring plant life on the forest floor, but trees get attention too. The small trees of wild plum, pin cherry, juneberry and elderberry are holding their white blossoms. Nearby, large sugar maples are covered with flowers of their own; staminate or pistilate flowers that hang from the branches. Flitting through the trees are recently-returned avian migrants. I note warblers, sparrows and thrushes.

Trees are growing new green leaves and by the end of the month, this woods will be shaded. But as I wander here now, I am surrounded by spring wildflowers that are eager to grow and bloom. During my walk, I find about twenty kinds showing their colorful petals. Whites: bloodroots, trout-lilies and trilliums; yellows: trout-lilies, bellworts and violets; pink/purple: violets, wild ginger and the numerous spring beauties. I frequently stop and look in every direction to see these flora. I'm not alone in finding these colors and pollinating bees are here too. Soon these opportunists will fade; many leaving almost no sign that they were ever here in the coming summer. Among the wildflowers are other plants taking advantage of the present conditions; ferns. And these will persist into the summer.

Ferns are not flowering plants. Though they do grow large and green, their lives are quite different. They thrive in the shady woods of summer, but appear to "die back" in fall; only to reappear in spring. Plants remain alive all winter; underground in a structure called a rhizome. With the warming weather and longer days, ferns respond by growing new leaves. (Leaves on ferns are called fronds.) Instead of growing fronds from buds as seen with flowering plants, ferns unroll new fronds as spring progresses. Growing in this fashion, they are called fiddleheads (looking like a scroll on a violin; "fiddle"). In the woods where I am, about a dozen kinds of ferns can be found on a summer day; some quite large. Though all produce fiddleheads, many are hard to see. During my present walk, I see fiddleheads of three kinds of ferns that will grow tall and flourish later.

Nearly always, the first one to show above the ground in spring is the "hairy" fiddlehead of interrupted fern. This fern will grow to be three or four feet. The name of interrupted refers to a brown growth of sporangia on the green fronds. Tall ostrich fern; four or five feet, has a green fiddlehead, largely devoid of hair. Lady fern, two to three feet, is very common. Their fiddleheads have dark scales on the stems.

This trio of spring fiddleheads all grow to be large ferns and rapidly, they reach their heights. In a couple of weeks, their long fronds will also shade the fading flora. But now, these emerging fiddleheads are part of the delight of a May woods walk (wander).

May 22, 2021

Least Flycatchers Call/Feed in Woods

It's chilly; about thirty degrees, clear and calm as I step out on this May morning. Many birds sing in this early hour; taking advantage of calm conditions. This is migration time and each day, more is happening. As I pass a wetland, I hear the persistent red-winged blackbirds that have taken residence here in late March and continue to sing about it. A swamp sparrow joins with its trill song. Ring-necked ducks and mallards along with a calling pied-billed grebe are out in the water. I expect soon to see the local Canada goose family. At the shore, vocal sandhill cranes sound off. They are joined by weird squelching calls of a bittern and in the aquatic plants, a sora calls; both are easy to hear, hard to see. A pair of loud and large trumpeter swans fly over; hard to not hear or see.

Moving past a field, I watch a pair of tree swallows demonstrating aerial acrobatics as they feed. A morning dove gives it plaintive call while musical songs of robin and rose-breasted grosbeak emanate from nearby trees. A small savannah sparrow chimes in with a song sparrow, to sing at the field's edge. White-throated sparrows sing among the blooming small trees of wild plum, pin cherry and juneberry.

As I approach the woods, I hear gobbling turkeys and drumming ruffed grouse. These large birds are non-migratory and are nesting now; on the forest floor. Most of the avian singing comes from migrants that have been here a while or recent arrivals. Yellow-bellied sapsuckers repeatedly drum on trees. Flickers, another woodpecker, give their whining calls. A couple of vireos repeat their short songs from high in the trees. And there are the warblers. Beginning with yellow-rumped warblers a month ago, others followed. Palm, black and white were next and earlier this month, I listened to the "teacher-teacher-teacher" song of an ovenbird. More warblers are here too and not all sing loudly. Late May is a great time to see a mixture of different kinds coming by; waves. But as I look in the trees for more of these migrants, it is a short song of another that causes me to stop and listen; a least flycatcher.

This tiny bird of about five inches is the smallest member of the flycatchers. We have seven kinds living in the region. These include: kingbirds, phoebes, great-crested flycatchers, olive-sided flycatchers, alder flycatchers, wood pewees and the least. Though some can give loud calls, most are not too vocal and none are very colorful. Living up to their name, flycatchers feed on insects and all are migratory. First to arrive in spring is the phoebe; April, others in May. This is also the time of the arrival of other residents; the new batch of black flies and mosquitos. And flycatchers find plenty to eat.

I always hear the least flycatcher in these woods in May. With its small size and gray color with white undersides, it can be hard to see (if you can get a close view, an eye ring will show up). But as though celebrating their return here, they give a series of two-syllable notes; "che-bek", accentuating the second syllable. This simple phrase is repeated many times. As I listen to this call from the morning woods, I'm sure I'll hear plenty more later in the day and on other days; even if I do not see the songster. One of many sounds on this May morning.

May 29, 2021

Oaks Grow New Leaves and Catkins

Those of us who regularly walk in northland forests find that going out now, in late May, we are surrounded by happenings. Each day while walking I note sights or sounds and think "that wasn't here yesterday". This is a great time to see that there is a new story here every day. And I'm sure that there will be more tomorrow. The green leafing of trees is reaching its end. Soon the woods will have reached a complete green canopy; reminding us of last summer.

Below, on the forest floor, early spring wildflowers that thrived in sunlight are waning and giving way to the next batch of wildflowers; the shade tolerant ones. During recent weeks, these plants have been growing thick under the trees; soon to bloom. But when I came here recently, I discovered a few that already had begun to flower. The seven-petaled white blossoms of starflower are blooming and nearby the tall baneberry, two feet tall, holds its cluster of small white flowers. Soon others of this unique group will join as we exit the month; wild lily-of-the-valley, sarsaparilla, blue-bead lily and bunchberry.

Trees have been producing more than new leaves. We also see their blossoms. This arboreal flora show began with wild plum, but was quickly followed by juneberry, pin cherry, elderberry, crab apple and choke cherry. Later, in June, viburnums and dogwoods also bloom.

But as we now look among tree branches, it is often that we try to see others also present. This is still the time of bird migration. Each day, each walk, will reveal newcomers to the woods. Warblers may be the most varied and abundant newly arrivals. They present a challenge to see and discern. Fortunately, they wear breeding plumages and often sing. Warbler watching is best done with binoculars and patience. But these active little birds are not alone. Other migrants here include orioles, grosbeaks, tanagers, thrushes, sparrows, vireos and hummingbirds. All make use of trees to pause, feed and sing. We look into the newly foliated trees a lot now.

One of the last trees to become fully foliated are the oaks. In our region, northern red oak is most common. Burr oak, pin oak and white oak may be in the outlying areas; west or south of us. These large and powerful trees that make up much of the local deciduous forests are slow to get new leaves. But now, in late May, they join the forest foliation. Leaves are lobed and at first appear a bit reddish. And as we look among their branches, we are likely to see another growth of spring besides leaves; the catkins.

Catkins on several other common trees have been with us for the last couple of months. We saw long "hot dog" growths on alders, willows, aspen and hazel in April. In May, birch had their long descending catkins as well. Now is the time for oak catkins. These grow as a cluster near the end of the twigs. Not as colorful as blossoms, they are the flowers of oaks. Oak catkins hanging down several inches are male (staminate) flowers. The female (pistillate) are small and form at the base of the catkins. It is weeks from now, but the fertilization of these will lead to a new crop of acorns. Like other flora of spring, they will not last long. We'll soon see them falling onto the ground, driveway and deck after they mature. But for now, oak catkins show us another example of the new growth here every day.

June 5, 2021

Flowers Bloom at the Edge of Woods

May has been a month of greening. Now, equipped with new chlorophyll-rich leaves, plants do a terrific amount of growing in June. With sunrise at about 5:15 AM and setting nearly at 9 PM, plants bask in daylight; approaching sixteen hours. These longer days combined with warmth and amble rain (most years) makes this an excellent growing time. We see this in lawns that demand continuous care, garden produce developing and tree branches putting on new lengths. And growth shows up in the woods as well.

Ferns that were new fiddleheads just a couple of weeks ago, now may reach up to our chest. These plants as well as tree leaves overhead have stopped the first group of spring wild flowers; the early ones that thrive in sunlight. It wasn't long ago that we walked in a sunlit forest surrounded by trout-lilies, spring beauties and bloodroots. When they fade in the shade, they were replaced by those that tolerate shade; flowering in the darkened woods. By the end of May, the forest flora was very green with these tolerants; many of which also flowered. On a single walk, as May exited, I noted the blooming of starflower, sarsaparilla, blue-bead lily, jack-in-the-pulpit, wild lily-of-the-valley, baneberry, bunchberry, columbine, nodding trillium and some impressive yellow lady-slipper orchids. These colors add much to the shady woods, but their time is passing and the spring floral progression continues to move on. Later in June, in a couple of weeks, fields and open spaces will fill with colorful flowers of daisy, hawkweed, lupine, clover and buttercup. This bouquet in the open areas is a sign that spring has ended (shortly before the summer solstice; June 20). But before this floral movement reaches the sunlit fields, meadows and roadsides, it passes through another stage.

Easy to overlook are the plants that grow and flower in the edge; between the woods and open spaces. Taking advantage of light and moisture here, a whole new growth of wildflowers bloom now in early June. During a recent walk, I saw several of these flowers that fill this in-between niche. Here, I found meadow-rues, rose twisted-stalks and solomon-seals. The last two have flowers below their leafy stems. Flowers in such sites can be overlooked. But nearby was another of this group that was easy to see; the false solomons-seal.

This plant, also with a green leafy stem, is about two to three feet tall. Unlike the previous that hold flowers beneath the stem, its cluster of white flowers is at the end of the stem. With a name like false Solomon-seal, we may expect it to look much like the true variety; it does not. Plants are also called false spikenard; another misleading label, not looking like the true spikenard. Regardless of the name, false solomons-seal (Maianthemum racemosum) reigns in this limited space and time. Flowers are borne in a plume above the leafy stem. About five to seven inches long, the plume is filled with nearly one hundred tiny white florets of three petals and three sepals each (looking like six petals). And so, they are easy to see in this edge site.

Once fertilized, they form small berries; ripening to become bright red later in summer. Like others of the spring floral progression, this edge group will not last long. Soon we'll see abundant flowering plants in the open, but now false solomon-seal raises its white plume at the edge.

June 12, 2021

Dragonfly Emergence Time

Mid-June is the time of the earliest sunrises of the whole year. Appearing at 5:14 AM (remaining at this time for about ten days), Sol sets shortly after 9 PM; giving nearly sixteen hours of daylight. It is also the time of warm temperatures and frequent rains. The northland flora thrives with these conditions and we see green growth right in front of us. But these conditions are also excellent for the insects that live here.

Anyone spending June in the region is well aware of the six-legged critters that abound at this time. We are likely to think of the lesser-loved mosquitos and black flies that reach their maturity at this time and come to us for a meal of blood; providing needed protein for their reproductive success. But the northland is home for many other insect types. Walking in the yard and the nearby road in recent sunlit days, I found it hard to not see active insects. Two of our largest butterflies are active now; the black-yellow tiger swallowtail and the black and orange monarch. Both frequently take nectar in our yards and gardens. Other butterflies include the orange-checkered fritillaries, yellow sulphurs and cabbage whites. Taking a closer look, we may see tiny blues and skippers. While watching this activity, I also found a tent caterpillar nest in a cherry tree and the frothy mass produced by spittle bugs on roadside plants. Walking this route at night, I noticed the thick bodies of Junebugs and the glows of a new batch of fireflies; always a delightful addition to June.

Visiting a lake, I saw plenty more was happening. This is the time of dragonfly emergence. Several kinds were flying, hunting and basking on this clear morning. Spending youth as predators underwater, they look much different from the flying adults; also, predators. Young, called nymphs (larvae), survived winter in this aquatic site, but in recent weeks, that time has ended as they climbed up out of their water world and became adults. Clinging to shoreline plants, they underwent a change as their exoskeleton split open and the winged adult emerged. This radical event usually happens at night. Now in the day, they stretch out their wings, raising body temperature while basking in sunlight.

Many shoreline plants hold the cast-off exoskeleton that were left here when the step from youth to adulthood took place. Also called exuvia, they tell just how many there are at this lakeshore on this June day.

Now free from water, dragonflies bask on docks, rocks and an inverted canoe. But walking on trails and in the yard, I also see them at other sunny sites. Looking carefully, I find five kinds at this site: dot-tail whitefaces, chalk-fronted corporals, four-spot skimmers, green-eyed emeralds and gomphids.

One of these gomphids, a dusky clubtail, I found of interest. A medium sized dragonfly, it has a yellow line along the back. It was a bit difficult to identify it as a dusky clubtail, but quite easy to note that it was a type of gomphid. Dragonflies all have huge eyes; covering much of their head. These eyes reach entirely around the head touching in the back; except for gomphids. The eyes of this group are smaller and have a posterior space between them. When seen closely with close-focus binoculars or camera lens, this eye arrangement it easy to note. As these June days continue, we have time to see plenty more dragonflies and other insects as the new season of summer begins.

June 19, 2021

Spittlebugs Along the Roadsides

This is the summer solstice; the day of longest sunlight for any day of the year. Sunrise at about 5:15 AM and setting after 9 PM approaches sixteen hours. This is also the turning point. Very slowly starting now, days begin to get shorter; for the next six months. I think summer has already begun. Since early June, wildflowers are more abundant and colorful in open spaces than those of shady woods; the end of spring.

Other signs of season changing happen as well. Baby birds grow from nestlings to fledglings. Bird song continues in the woods, but not as persistent as earlier. In wetlands are families of ducks and mergansers, while young deer, rabbits and squirrels move through the yard. In lakes, summer frogs; mink frogs and green frogs, are doing their calling; continuing for weeks as young spring frogs emerge into tiny adults. Red and silver maples that were flowering a few weeks ago now are dropping new mature seeds.

Days have been quite hot in the afternoon sun. And so, to be able to take a nice slow observational walk, summer walks are in the cool of morning. With or without a dew cover, there is always plenty to see. As I pass the pond, I see irises are blooming along the edge; taking the place of earlier water calla. Out in the water, yellow pond-lilies still abound, but I notice circular leaves of white water-lilies telling of their flowering soon. Much of summer, this pond will be yellow and white.

But it is the roadside wildflowers that demand attention. With a variety of colors, they are hard to not notice; white, yellow, purple, orange and red are all present. The bouquet consists of daisy, yarrow, buttercup, hawkweeds, lupines, vetches and clovers. They quickly take advantage of their niche in the season; growth and changes are rapid. Though I take this walk nearly every day, there is always news happening.

In addition to the flora show, there are myriads of active butterflies, moths, bees, wasps and dragonflies. But there is one insect present that does not move much; the spittlebugs.

They are on the plants and easy to see; many roadside wildflowers. hold a froth of spittle mass on their stems or leaves. Looking more carefully, I do see movement as the critter living within this bubbly material does do a little walking. What I am seeing is the immature; the nymph, of an insect known as a froghopper. The adult is only about one-fourth inch long, but has powerful legs and hops; giving the name. But most of us know this insect from its immature stage; spittlebug.

Eggs are deposited in young stems of plants. When the eggs hatch, the young quickly begin feeding on plant sap. Besides feeding on sap, they take it into their bodies, mix it with bodily fluids and air to form bubbles of a frothy "spittle" mass; and here the immatures live.

Looking remarkedly like spit, this home site tends to get left alone; exactly what the critter wants. Not looking too attractive to us, this spittle material is an adequate protection for the young (usually only one young per spittle mass). This home also provides for moisture and food. As I walk here, I note the spittle masses, but also the plants that they chose. I find spittle on about a dozen kinds. Tansy, yarrow, daisy and hawkweed seem to be the most often selected. This spittle will be here for a few more weeks until the young grows to be a froghopper.

June 26, 2021

The Chestnut-Sided Warbler Nest

The long days of June; often with warm temperatures and ample rainfall are excellent times for growth in the northland. We see this clearly with our lawns, gardens, roadsides and trees. Each, in its own way, will do plenty of growing during this month. The plants that flourished in the spring months are now forming their seeds and fruits. Maple seeds have been falling for a few weeks lately with more to come. The berry season has begun with strawberries, honeysuckles and elderberries; all seemed like they held flowers only a few weeks ago.

Among the animals, we can easily see the new crop of squirrels, rabbits and fawns following their mothers. Frogs that called in spring are now silent as their tadpoles develop in ponds that still hold water. I have come upon both snapping and painted turtles laying eggs in dug out roadside nests in recent weeks. But it is mostly the bird life that takes advantage of the present situation to produce and raise families.

Migrant birds returned to the region in several phases, starting in March and continuing until early this month.

Once settled, they find a good spot for a nest and proceed to deposit eggs, incubate them and feed the nestlings until the young are able to leave the nest; fledglings. Early returnees have completed this process by this time and the fledged young are mingling with the adults.

Many of the birds that feed on insects are not able to return here until later in spring. They begin nesting soon after and their nesting season will go until June. Indeed, for many, it is this month that has the nestlings; July is the month of fledglings. We often see their new nests. It may be a robin or chipping sparrow in the yard; perhaps a hummingbird on a nearby horizontal branch or a phoebe nesting by the garage. We see these nests, but many we do not see. We can infer their presence from the bird behavior.

Breeding birds will continue to sing on their home territory during the family-rearing time. Hearing the bird songs tells us of their presence and breeding during this month. This is the basis for the Breeding Bird Survey; a national project that uses bird songs to tell the presence of breeding; a type of population count.

Several species of birds that nest in the region and almost daily, I hear their songs as I walk in June. One common one, the chestnut-sided warbler is a small; five-inch, bird of a yellow crown, greenish back feathers and a chestnut color on the sides. Birds often nest in shrubby areas along roadsides. They readily sing during breeding times. The song has been paraphrased to say "please please pleased to meetcha".

Recently, I noticed a nest near a trail that I walked often. The nest was constructed in a small dogwood, about three feet above the ground. Once discovered, the nest was easy to see. It was made of stems of various roadside plants and lined with grasses.

At the time of the nest find, it had four eggs and mother was sitting here incubating the clutch. During the next ten days, one after another egg hatched and the nest held four tiny nestlings. It was interesting to watch this progression as I passed by, but with this valuable family now present, I decided to avoid this route; hoping they would develop undisturbed. Many families succumb to predators at this crucial time, I hope these will survive; but I'll not be watching them grow.

Third Quarter

July 3, 2021

Dewberry Adds to Summer Berries

Early July is a time when we see some changes. The first week of July is Aphelion; when the Earth is at its furthest distance from the sun on our annual trip. It is also when sunsets begin to get earlier; slowly moving towards setting before 9 PM. (Sunrises have been getting later since the summer solstice in June.) Days still have plenty of sun and heat, but the daylight is lessening each day.

July is also the time when bird songs are not as intense or frequent as they were a month ago. Fledglings are moving on their own or with adults and there is not the need for regular territorial songs. It may be hard to perceive now, but some birds will start migration by the end this month. It is also the time of abundant fireweeds and milkweeds blooming from wayside sites. Joining them are thistles, evening primroses, sweetclovers and early sunflowers and goldenrods. But it is also the start of berry season.

It seems like recently; many wildflowers and shrubs were in bloom during the month of May. Getting attention of insects, they were pollinated and soon started to grow the products of the season. Each year in the second half of June, I look for the next step after blossoms have passed. I find that consistently, there are four plants that initiate the berry season. These are strawberries, fly honeysuckle, elderberry and dewberry. (Not necessarily in this order.) And yes, despite the heat and dryness of this June, it happened again this year.

Many avid berry pickers consider the start of the berry season with the ripening of the large and delicious domestic strawberries; and rightly so. But their cousins, the wild ones, are also ripe. The wild berries are here, but instead of the size that we see with the domestic strawberries, their wild cousins are tiny; maybe only about as big as the end of our small fingers. Lacking in size, they make up in sweetness. They are quickly discovered and devoured; mostly by small mammals.

Fly honeysuckle; a small shrub, is very early to produce new leaves and open its pair of yellow trumpet-shaped flowers. Early flowers means, early berries; also, in pairs and bright red. This honeysuckle is not to be confused with bush-honeysuckle or the taller Tatarian honeysuckle.

Elderberry, also known as red berry elder, is a small tree that is usually the first to open its leaves in early May. Later, the plant holds clusters of white flowers and now clusters of tiny red berries. They don't last long since small mammals and birds are quick to find them.

Dewberry, also known as dwarf raspberry, is closely related to the ubiquitous roadside raspberry plants. They are also in the family of the larger blackberries and thimbleberries. (Dewberries, raspberries, blackberries and thimbleberries all belong to the same genus of Rubes.) I find dewberries in bloom along trails in May. Though a woody plant, it spreads out, creeping over the ground. In sunlit spring days, dewberry with its three leaves and five white petals was pollinated; forming the berries we see now. Not as tall or as obvious as raspberry, but just as juicy tasting. Several kinds of dewberries live in the region; some are red when ripe, some are darker.

These plants that begin the berry season set the pace for more to come. Raspberry, blueberry, juneberry, thimbleberry, pin and choke cherry, wild plum and even another kind of elderberry will appear as we move though July and August. But the berry season begins now.

July 10, 2021

In a Patch of Milkweeds

July roadsides are full of summer wild flowers. Passing by on any road now will show us a variety of colors as clovers, vetches, fleabanes, trefoils, sweetclovers, black-eyed susans, sunflowers, primroses, dogbane, goldenrods, tansy, thistles, cow parsnips and water hemlocks all add to the scene. Earlier ones; daisy, lupines and hawkweeds have gone to seed. But with all this flora now, I find two kinds that are best examples of July flowers: fireweeds and milkweeds.

Unfortunately, both have "weed" as part of their names, but neither is an alien nor a pest; often desired and enjoyed. Both have clusters of purple flowers. Those of fireweed are a deep purple and stand up on a spike above the rest of the plant. Clusters of milkweeds are light purple (lavender) and grow in a ball-shape cluster; at the sides of the stem. Plants are in groups and once beginning to flower, they last for weeks.

During my daily walks, I have been passing a growth of hundreds of fireweeds. During recent weeks, I watched as they progressed. The buds grew and finally one plant led the way by opening its flowers. Others were soon to follow and within a week of the first to bloom, I noted about two hundred flowering. Blossoms open from the base of the spike and progress to the top. There is a change here every day.

With milkweed (common milkweed, not the swamp milkweed or the brightly colored butterflyweed; both also in the region) buds are slower to open. Once begun, they last through many weeks of summer. But recently, I found a patch of milkweeds that was earlier than the others.

Road work done a couple of years ago formed a barren spot of sandy soil on a dead end. Empty soil sites do not remain that way for long and many plants had taken residence here. I found hawkweeds, yarrow, daisy, fleabane, blueberries and raspberries. In the midst was a large thick thriving patch of milkweeds. The site was south-facing and able to get plenty of sunlight. Under these conditions; ample light, moisture and limited plant competition, the milkweeds flourished. And while most milkweeds in the area were not yet in bloom, this group was in full flower. I stopped for a closer look.

Tall and robust; I estimated about one hundred fifty plants here. Each had at least two ball-shaped clusters of flowers. More than three hundred clusters; each held many florets. As I walked, I quickly noticed that I was not the only one to be amongst them. The site was alive with insects. Large butterflies of tiger swallowtails, great spangled fritillaries and monarch (both, the adults and dozens of caterpillars) as well as tiny skippers fluttering about. Here too were bumble bees and milkweed beetles and the opportunistic dragonflies patrolled.

A delightful odor permeated from the floral clusters; helping to attract attention. Most insects came for nectar, but there is more going on here. The petals of milkweed are arranged in a V shape and at the base, they hold pollen in a "saddle bag" container. The design is that insects would get their feet caught here and when pulling free, they carry the saddle bag of pollen off with them. This scheme works good for large insects, like bumble bees, but can be a trap for some smaller ones. As I wandered among the plants, I saw skippers that got their foot caught and could not escape; their small yellow bodies hung on the clusters. Despite this; milkweeds are a delightful addition to the July flora.

July 17, 2021

Nursery-Web Spiders

July mornings are delightful for walking. Later it may be hot and a bit filled with annoying insects. Usually, dawn is the coolest time of the day. I find that this pleasant temperature is when deer flies and the latest batch of mosquitoes are not as active. Long summer sunlight provides for changes every day and roadside flora shows much with each walk.

Taking advantage of these conditions, I note plenty of wildflowers in the open spaces. Fireweeds abound here and show new blossoms each day. Cow parsnip and water hemlock hold white umbels above the rest. Black-eyed susans are taking over from the waning daisies. Both yellow and white sweetclover stand tall at the road's edge. At this early hour, the yellow petals of evening primrose are still open from their nocturnal blooming. Some hold a moth that visited at night. And of course, I need to go to a couple of milkweed patches along the route. Milkweed may be the most dominant of all these July flora. There are some new ones that just came in bloom recently; tall sunflower, bergamot and the first of the goldenrods. They'll be around for weeks, but it is good to see their arrival. Among all these flowers, I also locate and sample the ripe berries of blueberry, raspberry, juneberry and pin cherry. Their delightful tastes are great additions to breakfast.

There is more here besides the plants. In the dew and occasional fogs of a July morning, I see plenty of spider webs. Some are on the ground; funnel webs. Others are in bushes; sheet webs. And there are the circular orb webs that are mostly in shrubs and trees. I visited a swamp during the fog of a recent walk and was overwhelmed by how many orbs were here. I estimated two hundred that I could see from where I stood without moving. Mid-July is the beginning of the spider-web season; which will continue for about two months. With foggy mornings later in summer, we will see many more webs. But now is also the time of spider eggs and nests.

Spiders lay eggs that are placed in containers called sacs. These are put in a variety of places. Some are left alone; some are carried by the mother and others are guarded. It was the last of these that I recently discovered. During a visit to a patch of milkweeds when I was looking for flowers, I noticed something else. A couple of the plants had bent-over leaves that were coated with webbing material. The folded leaves made for a safe hiding place. I recognized this as the work of nursery-web spiders. These spiders get their name from this. The egg sac is inside the folded leaf and the webbing holds it in place. She then goes down the stem of the plant and stands guard. A little searching among the leaves and stem revealed mother as she guarded.

She stays here as the eggs hatch and, for a while, with the young inside. I looked into the leaf hiding place and saw many tiny spiders (spiderlings). Mother remains nearby until the young are able to move on their own. Finding nursery-webs are a regular part of July phenology. These were on milkweeds, but I have often seen the nests on raspberries, goldenrods and grasses at this time.

Nursery-web spiders are in the same family as dock and fishing spiders that are often seen on or near lakeshores. Once the eggs hatch and the young disperse, they go back to their mostly aquatic lives.

July 24, 2021

The Swallow Staging Site

The late July morning is fairly cool and calm with a forecast of a hot afternoon. It is a pleasant time to walk. Along my usual road route, I pass plenty of wildflowers. Fireweed and milkweed still show blossoms as they did for much of this month; also with purple flowers are the Canada thistles. Their flowering is quicker and they will soon be forming fluffy seeds. Tall sunflowers have joined black-eyed susans to add yellow to the scene. More yellow is here each day as goldenrods are flowering. I see Canada goldenrods holding its yellow cluster above the leafy stem as it joins with a couple of goldenrods earlier. And a real sign of the season moving on; I find the first aster, flattop aster, has opened its white flowers.

The advancing season means fewer bird songs, but as I walk by a woods, I hear some songsters. Song sparrows and yellowthroats continue singing from the brush while a couple of persistent vireos give their short-repeated phrases from the trees. A few other birds are also active. I see goldfinches at the thistle seeds, while cedar waxwings visit small trees in search of berries.

When I reach the pond, I see that wood ducks and hooded mergansers have joined the grebe family that resided here all summer. The resident red-winged blackbirds are active; young are so well grown that it is hard to tell them from the adults. I stop at the nearby swamp. Dead tamaracks and spruces out here provide great places for orb webs of spiders. Looking over the scene; facing the rising sun in the east, I see dozens of these webs. But there is more going on in the trees as well.

The same branches that hold aerial orb webs, are the site of movement of birds. About a dozen small birds are circling and feeding on insects in mid air and then returning to their perches on the trees. I recognize this avian crowd as tree swallows. And I realize that what I am seeing is a staging site. These little birds are congregating in the very early phase of their autumn migration.

The second half of July seems like a long way from autumn and migration also seems far away; but with some birds, it begins early. Tree swallows were the first of the swallows to arrive in spring. Though they had to deal with some cool spring weather, they did find nesting locations early and successfully raised a family before most other birds. By July, young are with plumages of white beneath and dark above; like the adults. And like the adults, they actively feed on the wing.

July days are often hot and summer continues; however, the daylight is getting shorter, sending a message to the birds that south-bound movement is beginning. Fall migration, with large flocks, is later, but it begins now with these family units. The ones that I see here this morning are too many for one family and probably represent members of a couple families that have joined. Here at this staging stie, they will gather to feed and rest. At this swamp, there are plenty of insects to provide food. They'll meet with other groups and form migration flocks that will be heading south.

I'm glad to see the swallows here today, but I don't expect this group to stay. Just as quickly as they arrived, they will be going into the next phase of their south migration. Starting now, they have plenty of time to move on in their flight.

July 31, 2021

Bergamots Add to Roadside Flora

As we exit the month of July, we can look back on a time of heat, haze and dryness. July is our warmest month and so, the heat may be considered normal. However, lack of precipitation here as well as west of us gave way to wildfires; more than usual and accounted for haze that we have been dealing with. Days continue to get shorter and the near-sixteen hours of daylight at the solstice in June has become nearly fifteen hours now. But July gave us much to see among the plant life.

July is a month of berries and the amount of rain that varied greatly in the region affected what we saw in this regard. I happen to live at a site that had a couple of good rains early in the month and many developing berry plants responded. Strawberry season was not long, but did produce. Blueberries, juneberries and pin cherries were limited; red elderberries and raspberries did better. Many of my July morning walks were embellished with handfuls of ripe raspberries; and late in the month, I added blackberries. (On another walk, nearby, I noticed how these berries did not handle the dryness and failed to mature.) In the woods, I have found plenty of red, white and blue on baneberries and blue-bead lilies; results of these spring flora. Some of the berries later to develop may find it difficult as we move further into summer.

Walking in the morning, avoiding the impending heat, I saw much more than berries. I have observed a wonderful progression of roadside flora. There has been a colorful change of flowers growing at this edge site throughout the month. Cow parsnips, black-eyed susans, vetches and clovers early gave way to thistles, fireweeds, milkweeds, evening primroses and st. johnsworts at mid-month. It has been interesting to watch the flowers of fireweeds as they move up the spike at the top of the plants. Flowers forming early gave way to plants now holding many thin seed pods. These will soon open allowing fluffy seeds to scatter. In the wetlands; jewelweeds, water hemlocks, joe pye weeds and arrowheads gave more color, sizes and shapes to the scene. Now, walking here, I find news every day of the flora that will persist through late summer. Sunflowers, asters and goldenrods are making their entry. Only a few sunflowers and asters presently are in bloom. Goldenrods of which we have about a dozen in the region, now have about half in bloom. Unlike many of the other flowers from earlier in the season, these three late summer ones will hold blossoms for weeks.

Another flower that started in about mid-month and continues as July wanes is the bergamot. Also known as Monarda and bee-balm, this member of the mint family grows from two to four feet tall in sunny sites. From the square stem, leaves grow out opposite each other. A rounded cluster of flowers is at the top of the stem. These aromatic clusters of strange-shaped tubular flowers; stick out from the circular terminal growth. Flowers are a pink and pale lilac in color and are often discovered by wandering bees and hummingbirds. Plants may be alone in the roadsides or in groups of dozens. Usually, I see bergamots in clumps of ten to twenty. There's plenty of roadside color now and since bergamots may be the same color as milkweed or thistle, they can be easy to overlook. But they are here and add their flowers to the bouquet of July; despite the heat, haze and arid conditions.

August 7, 2021

Grasshoppers and Locusts Time

Thanks to recent rains in late July (more rain in the last ten days than fell for the whole month previous), there is now plenty going on as we enter the month of August. The trio of fall wildflowers; goldenrods, asters and sunflowers are all emerging and progressing as we reach and pass mid-summer. I have seen in bloom about two-thirds of the dozen kinds of goldenrods that grow in the region; fewer with asters and sunflowers, but more to come. In addition to this trio, there are some excellent growths of joe pye weed, pearly everlasting and thistles. The season is moving on. Chokecherries and hawthorns are getting ripe while acorns and hazelnuts are developing. The garden is doing its part with daily new produce. Tomatoes, lettuce, peas and beans are available. In the yard, day lilies of July are replaced by August phlox.

In the woods, the ground is more moist than a few weeks ago and we have quite a variety of mushrooms and other fungi taking advantage of these conditions. Also, each walk is filled with sightings of the new crop of small frogs and toads. A few green frogs still call at the lake and some gray treefrogs are beginning their late-season calls as well. Much is going on now with insects and spiders as well. This month may be the best time of the year to observe these critters.

During a recent walk in a field, I noted many monarchs and fritillaries taking nectar at wildflowers. Along the edge, were several dark, almost black, butterflies; common wood nymphs. Moths were present too; both adults and caterpillars. At the goldenrods that thrive in the field were many bumble bees and flower flies. Here too were some beetles, wasps, hornets and ants. Predaceous damselflies and dragonflies patrolled; seeking insect meals. Late in the season, the two most common groups of dragonflies are the large darners and the small meadowhawks and I see both. But no insects are more abundant now in the field or roadsides than grasshoppers and locusts.

It seems like each step would cause movements from these insects. Grasshoppers and locusts are both members of the insect order of Orthoptera. This is a highly diverse group, but two kinds dominate the scene during my walk. The grasshoppers; two-striped grasshoppers, are mostly a dark greenish with a pair of yellow stripes that run from the head to wing tips.

When scared up, they are more likely to hop than fly. Larger; about two inches, and brown-gray are locusts (unfortunately, cicadas are sometimes called by this same name). When leaping, they often spread wings and fly; sometimes long distances. The inner wings are used for flight and frequently when in the air, they make a clicking-crackling noise; known as crepitation. When flying, the wings can easily be seen; dark with a light band on the edges. (It is not likely that we will confuse a grasshopper with a butterfly, but when the locust is in flight, their wings can look like that of the mourning cloak butterfly.)

Grasshoppers and locusts thrive in this hot dry summer and I found them frequently as I walked in the last few weeks. Recent rains will not stop them since they are herbivores and feed on the grasses and other plants in these open sites. Other orthoptera that can be seen or heard in this month are crickets and katydids, but their presence is not as obvious as the grasshoppers and locusts now; early in the month.

August 14, 2021

Blue-Stain Boletes Now in Woods

The August silence prevails as I step into the woods. In the open site nearby, I see the late summer wildflowers; goldenrods, asters and sunflowers all in bloom. Fireweeds from July have gone to seed. And I stop at a patch of blackberries. The woods is quiet with no bird songs in late season, but I do hear croaking of a raven and some woodpeckers. Calls from a gray treefrog speak of territory at this time. Silent, but not empty and as I walk on a woods trail, I note many of the new crop of tiny toads that have moved here from a local pond. Along the route, I also see small frogs; spring peepers and larger wood frogs. All this happening on the ground keeps me looking down and I see what is most numerous in the August woods; mushrooms.

This time of late summer is always good for these fungal growths. This year has been dry, but recent rains have allowed them to grow here and there is a variety of fungi on the soil, tree trunks and downed logs. Probably the most colorful is that of sulphur shelf (chicken of the woods). They grow large and bright. I find some yellow and others orange; on trunks or logs of oak. Also on logs are coral fungi; always an early-growing fungus, and new puffballs.

Mushrooms that usually grow in an umbrella shape are here and quite variable. All have stems with a cap on top. Under the cap, there is diversity. Most have lined structures called gills. These gilled mushrooms are most common and I see Russula, Lactarius (milk mushroom), Marasmius, Mycena and Hygrocybe (waxy cap). (Mushrooms are often known by their scientific names.) Most have brown-tan caps, but I see some white, yellow or red. (In the lawn, there are gilled mushrooms of Amanita and Agaricus (meadow mushroom).)

Though most mushrooms have gills beneath the cap, others do not. I find a small golden one with folds of skin under the cap; somewhat resembling gills. This is the often-sought Cantharellus (chanterelle). Frequently in big growths, but I find only a few. Some species of mushrooms have spines or teeth below the cap. Best known of these is Hydnum (hedgehog mushroom). The one I find was alone in the woods. And then there are the boletes.

A rather large group of mushrooms differ from the others by having numerous tiny holes, pores, under the cap. They are common and quite diverse. Collectively they are known as boletes. As I walk in the woods, In find Suillus (slippery jack) near a pine tree and the tough looking Strobilomyces (old man of the woods). But the one that I was most glad to see was Gyroporus (blue-staining bolete). When seen from above, it is not so impressive. The mushroom is only four or five inches tall and light brown-tan in color. But I stop for a closer look and when I do, I'm rewarded with an excellent observation. Like many other mushrooms, this fungus has white flesh beneath the outer skin. However, it is quick to change. Breaking off a piece of the cap exposes the white flesh to air where the cells respond to the oxygen presence and turn blue; within seconds! This explains the name of blue-stain bolete. Other mushrooms can stain blue, but not as much or as quick as this one. I'm glad to see this bolete on the forest floor of August. Over the next couple of weeks, many more mushrooms of various kinds will join this growth.

August 21, 2021

Joe Pye Weed in the Wetlands

The roadside flora goes through a change now in late August. The three dominant wildflowers of July have moved on to the next phase. Canada thistle has its flowers replaced by thick growths of fluffy seeds that now blow about. Fireweeds were a little slower to open their thin seed pods as blossoms progressed up the stem, but now their fluffy seeds also float in the breeze. The third July wildflower, milkweeds, are now growing pods in which, seeds will develop, being released when the pods open in late September or October; and we'll see their drifting parachutes in fields and roadsides. Sweet-clovers that grew tall with either yellow or white flowers in July now hold numerous seeds.

The berry season continues to progress through summer. Raspberry time has passed on and was replaced by lingering blueberries and blackberries. The tart-flavored choke cherry; a small but very common roadside tree in the region, has its ripe dark berries now. The berries of both highbush cranberry and mountain-ash are becoming orange-red and maturing. I've noticed a nut crop with American and beaked hazel at this time. Several red oaks are dropping their new acorns. But roadsides also have plenty of wildflowers too.

I find that the late season trio abounds during August; sunflowers, goldenrods and asters. Each of the three groups has about a dozen kinds in the northland. Sunflowers range from very large plants to small. They include black-eyed susans, coneflowers, cup-plants and Jerusalem artichokes. This group is quite varied, but nearly all of the sunflowers are yellow. (Purple coneflower is an exception.) Goldenrods are also nearly all yellow. (The upland white goldenrod, growing along the lake shore, is the exception.) At first, all the goldenrods may look the same. But when we take a closer look, we see variety in size, leaves and habitat. They may range from about two feet to ten feet tall. They are most common in open fields, but there are goldenrods in bogs, swamps and forests as well. But when it comes to diverse flora of late summer, asters are the most varied.

Not only are asters of different sizes, they also vary in color. Many are white, others purple-blue to magenta. And they remain with us as we move from late summer to fall. Seeing flowering sunflowers, goldenrods and asters at this time, it might be easy to overlook what else is in bloom.

I find two flowers of note in the wetlands; at the edges of swamps, lakes and rivers. One is the white arrowhead rising above the water with white blossoms and big arrow-shaped leaves; some nearly linear. The other is the purple flowers on a plant reaching eight feet tall; the Joe Pye weed. They are often hard to not notice as we pass by. Similar to the sunflowers, goldenrods and asters, Joe Pye weed is also a composite. The lavender-purple cluster of flowers at the top of the stem is made up of many tiny flowers. Leaves are borne on the tall stem in whorled patterns; of three, four, five or six. This large flowering plant is a great addition to the late summer wetlands.

There are several stories of who was Joe Pye, but a common one is that he was a Native American herbalist of the late 1700's. This robust plant was said to be his source of many herbal medicines; and so, the plant continues to bear his name. Using it as an herb or not, it a beauty to behold in the wet areas of late summer.

Aug. 28, 2021

A Strange Visitor to the Screenhouse

The screenhouse was put up in late spring, when the new mosquitoes of the season were arriving. The plan was to give shelter from these insects while still being able to enjoy the mornings and evenings of summer in this shady site. It has lived up to the goals and many summer hours of watching sunrises during the coolest time of day has been spent here; welcoming the new day. Returning in the evening, the screenhouse has been a great place to be as Sol exits. While here, we watched the days of the season pass. We heard songs from various birds in the early morning. Twilight sights and sounds again added to the scene and the darkness was punctuated by owls. But the screenhouse that was meant to be an excluder of insects has also been the host of many of these small critters during the summer.

I'm not sure how they were able to gain access; but many times, as I sat within the walls of screen, I noticed that I had companions. Flies of various kinds seemed to find an opening and enter. Not only the "pesky" ones of warm weather, but also the very long-legged crane flies came in. A dragonfly patrolled for meals. Diverse bees, including a few hard-working bumble bees gained access; not wanting to remain. As the season progressed, different kinds of wasps and hornets appeared here as well. Early in the season, a confused June bug came by; buzzing against the walls. Perhaps even more confused was the carrion beetle that was recently found one morning. All were persuaded to leave.

Not just insects made an entrance, a variety of spiders were here too. An opportunistic fishing spider (Dolomedes) climbed the wall waiting for prey. A brown crab spider (Xysticus) and a wolf spider scurried across the floor. None of these make webs, but a funnel-web spider constructed its web up in one of the corners. More common than any of the spiders were the daddy-long-legs through the season. They wandered by each day; often staying for a while. At about mid-summer, tiny toads began to appear and continue while their cousins, the gray treefrogs call from on or near the screenhouse in late summer.

Maybe the most common insects that got disoriented to be here were the myriads of moths. There are a variety of these nocturnal insects nearby all summer and many showed up in the screenhouse. Where there are moths, there are caterpillars. They were present too; some even making cocoons. And there was a recent surprise.

Though moths abound inside, their cousins, the butterflies, seemed to stay out. I found only one of these critters all summer; but what a one. Not long ago, as I sat here, I noticed fluttering wings along one side. Getting up to see it more closely, I realized that it was a small butterfly. As colors go, this butterfly was more moth-like; except for some black and yellow. It sat with wings closed and I was able to identify this minute butterfly (about one inch) as a harvester; quite a sight. Though not rare, they are unusual. This is our only butterfly that is a predator. While others spend their youthful (caterpillar) days feeding on leaves of various plants as they grow, the larvae of harvesters feed on aphids; especially those on alders. The adults abandon the predacious lives of youth, but still usually stay among alders; not in screenhouses. I was glad to host such an unusual butterfly. This harvester, like everything else that came here, was released undisturbed.

September 4, 2021

A Walk in a Dewy Field

August was warmer than normal; several days hot and dry. Such days were not conducive for what I wanted to do. I waited for a clear night followed by a dew-covered cool morning with patchy fog. And this morning is worth waiting for. I take a walk in a dew-covered field; conditions are right. The field is wet; virtually every plant is coated with dew and so I need to wear waders.

In the dawn, I hear calls from crows, ravens, sandhill cranes and loons. A few warblers are darting about. The field has huge growths of goldenrods of several species. This is goldenrod time and nearly all are in bloom. Most abundant is the tall goldenrod (Solidago atissima). Thick patches of these flowering plants; three to four feet tall, are impressive. Other goldenrods, asters and sunflowers are scattered about the field; all holding dew drops. Later in the day, goldenrods will be buzzing with activity as bees, wasps, hornets, flower flies, beetles, moths, butterflies and predaceous dragonflies will visit the flowers. Now it is quiet. I see some bumble bees that have sought shelter under bent goldenrod plumes and a few dragonflies (meadowhawks) that sit on the flora; coated with dew. They are inactive now, but later when the dew dissipates, they dry and warm their wings and take flight. I'm here mostly to look for and observe spider webs.

Webs from these eight-legged predators abound at this time on most any day, but dew covering allows them to show up better. Walking east; in the new day light, I see plenty of webs. There are four types of webs here. On the ground are funnel webs; looking like a cloth with a hole in the center (where the spider sits). Shrubs hold sheet webs; looking bowl-shaped. On top of many plants, I note irregular webs; cobwebs. All are well represented here, but it is circular orb webs that I seek. I am not disappointed; I find many.

Making up the webs are non-sticky threads (spokes) that go to the center (hub). They are surrounded by sticky spiral threads from the edge to the hub. Insects get caught on these spirals. Typically, the spider sits inverted in the hub waiting to feel prey on the web. Most webs were made at about dusk and remained in this vertical position all night; mostly trying to catch nocturnal insects like moths. As the night cools towards morning, dew condenses on the webs. Not all spiders appreciate the wet and heavy dew coating and though I see many webs, I see few spiders. Some kinds make a retreat, a shelter, by curling over leaves at the edge of the web. Others go along the side and wait until the day warms. A few remain in the hub and get wet.

Typically, these circular webs are stretched between a couple of plants; mostly goldenrods. Four kinds make webs here. Most common are shamrock spiders (Araneus trifolium) and banded garden spiders (Argiope trifasciata). Both are large and make big webs. During my walk, I find more than one hundred webs, but only a few spiders. Some garden spiders remain on the web; one even repairing it. A shamrock spider was wrapping a recently-caught insect. Most webs were empty.

With winds and warmth later in the day, webs will be gone; but not the spiders. After resting in the daylight, they will again make snares for more night feeding. And maybe if conditions are right in the following morning, I will be here to see them again. I'm wet and cool, but the walk here at dawn was worth it.

September 11, 2021

Showy Goldenrod; a fall flower

September to many northlanders is a time of autumn and lots of the happenings of fall are taking place now. Daylight continues to lessen; later sunrises and earlier sunsets. Temperatures, though still warm, begin to slowly descend. We may soon see frosts in the morning. It is also a time of garden produce. Apples, hawthorns and acorns ripen on the trees. September is migration; best noted with raptor movements at Hawk Ridge, but it happens with many others as well. Warbler waves pass through the yard; various sparrows appear here and it is common to see the family units of flickers along the roads; often on the ground. Most days, we see (or hear) migratory flocks of Canada geese. But birds are not the only migrants. We also see movements of green darner dragonflies and monarch butterflies. Not as obvious, snakes perform a migration of their own in fall as they head to their hibernacula for the colder times. And there is the leaf color. It seems like each day, we see more reds in maples, sumacs and dogwoods. Yellows dominate birch, aspen and basswoods. This annual arboreal show is watched each year.

We don't think of this time much for wild flowers. Many of the ones that filled the roadsides with colors in summer now show the product of the season with myriads of seeds; often drifting in the breeze. Others that have flowers will linger through this month. The fall trio: sunflowers, asters and goldenrods continues to give plenty more color to the scene. Sunflowers, typically yellow, range from two feet tall to the robust ones of ten feet. Asters, most diverse in their colors, light up the fields and roadsides with purples, blues and whites. No hurry to begin flowering, some have just begun; they are in no hurry to stop their flowers. Many last into next month. And there are the goldenrods.

About a dozen species of these fall wildflowers bloom in the region. With the exception of upland white goldenrods; fairly common along the lake shore, all are yellow. They range from about two to eight feet tall. Most common in fields and roadsides, goldenrods also can be found in swamps, bogs, woods and cliffs. Nearly all hold plumes of numerous small florets; above leafy stalks. Like sunflowers and asters, they are composites. All belong to the same genus of Solidago.

They begin to bloom in late July with the early goldenrods (Solidago juncea). These first ones of middle summer are quickly joined by more that thrive in August; especially the Canada goldenrods (Solidago canadensis). As August exits, I find that we are in the time of greatest goldenrod presence. Tall goldenrods (Solidago altissima) take over the flowering sites. It seems like in early September every road side and field has massive patches of these delightful flowers. Some goldenrods will not bloom until later; often September.

Consistently, the last species that I find to bloom is the showy goldenrod (Solidago speciosa). Plants live up to their name and put on quite a show in their growing sites. Standing about two to four feet tall, they are branched more than most goldenrods. The stems, that become reddish, hold numerous leaves and yellow florets that form thick clusters. Not so common in the region, I find that where they grow, the plants are hard to not see. Without a doubt, showy goldenrods tend to be the showiest of all. Like other flora of this month, this finale will fade in the frost. But now they are a terrific show to see and walk amongst as we enter autumn.

September 18, 2021

Opportunistic Asters

As we approach the Autumnal Equinox; first day of Fall (September 22), we look forward to cooler temperatures, leaf colors, migration and ripe apples. We can also look back on a summer to remember. Weather statistics tell us that summer of 2021 was the hottest on record. Though few, if any, heat records were set, we did have a near-record number of days of 80 degrees or higher. The summer had other natural happenings of note. Fires here and to the northwest of us gave us much smoke and haze. Drought was prevalent in much of the state and country. Storms in various parts of the country caused devastation; and the following floods. These natural events are hard to appreciate at the time, but they lead to changes and nature's reclamation.

I saw a great example of this on a smaller scale recently when I was driving a local road. To the side, in the midst of a forested growth, was a large patch of wildflowers in bloom. I had driven this route for many years and it wasn't until the last few weeks that I saw this thick growth. I had never seen such a profusion of these wildflowers here before. Stopping, I examined the plants and recognized them as a species of aster; Largeleaf Aster (Eurybia macrophylla). And then I realized what had happened. This was the result of a summer storm.

It was not the summer of 2021, but 2020 in mid-August, when a short-lasting, but strong, wind came through the region. During less than one-half hour, this straight-lined wind hit local forests and downed hundreds of trees. Some, like the woods that I looked at, were hard hit and many trees succumbed; all showing the west to east wind direction. However, most of the surrounding area was not hit as hard and I noted only a few places that showed results like this.

The summer became autumn and winter; the downed trees were salvaged. Spring and summer developed. Along with other growths in the following season, this open site, now devoid of trees, was filled with Largeleaf Asters that now, in late summer, were flowering. Not here before, I wondered where did they come from.

Largeleaf Asters are very common in the northland. Of the approximately dozen aster species that live here, it is the most likely seen in woods. Most asters grow and flower in late summer and fall in open sites. Quite diverse, they are white, blue or purple and grow in roadsides, fields and swamps. But Largeleaf is one that abounds in woods. It also represents an example of a wildflower that most of us are quite familiar with and recognize better by the leaves than the flowers. A woods walker in summer will probably see huge heart-shaped leaves that may cover the forest floor. (Some refer to this plant as woodsman's toilet paper) In the shade of the woods, very few will flower; but all can if the opportunity happens. Plants are able to flower but need to wait for available sunlight. That chance came when the sunlight penetrated here due to the downed trees. Similar things happen after fires and logging. And the patient plants are quick to take advantage of this flowering opportunity. All of the numerous plants flowering at this time had the namesake aster flowers; composites looking "star-like". Their rays ranged from white to purple; disks are often yellow; giving quite a show. Asters often linger well into fall and I expect these will; a follow-up of a storm of summer of 2020.

September 25, 2021

Some Great Mushrooms

Late September is a wonderful time to see the colorful leaves in the northland forests. As I walk on the road, passing the woods, I see plenty even with the dryness of this year. Reds; more common in sunny sites. (Apparently, the red pigment of anthocyanin acts as a "sun screen" within the leaves.) I see bright ones of red maple, sumac, dogwoods pin cherry, American hazel and young red oaks. Yellows outnumber the reds and they shine on birch, aspen, basswood, sugar maple, beaked hazel and ash. These black ashes of the swamps are not usually credited for colors of fall, but today their glow abounds.

As I step away from the road and walk on the trails of the woods, I'm treated to another delight of September; the variety and abundance of mushrooms and other fungi. Until recently, September has been dry, but responding to precipitation has caused a bit of a "'shroom boom". The many mushrooms here are of two types. Most mushrooms stand up from the substrate (ground or logs) with a stem that has a cap on top. Under the cap are many lined structures called gills. This is where the spores are found. Others mushrooms, also common at this time, are on a stem (stalk) with a cap, but instead of gills below the cap, they have numerous tiny holes called pores; that hold spores. These porous mushrooms are collectively called boletes. And this woods walk shows me many gilled and porous mushrooms and non-mushroom fungi.

Among the gilled mushrooms, I find Russula; caps of red, yellow, brown and white. I also find Lactarius (milk mushrooms) and bright red Hygrocybe (waxy cap) on the ground. Tiny Mycena and clusters of Pholiota (scaly-caps) are on logs. With gills, but without stems are large growths of Pleurotus (oysters) scattered on logs and tree trunks. A couple of non-mushroom fungi are on the sides of trees and stand out now; the bright red-orange of Laetiporus (sulphur shelf) and the branching teeth of Hericium (comb tooth). Puffballs of a couple kinds, still not ripe, adorn prostrate logs as well.

Among the many boletes seen in the woods on this September day are some terrific ones. Boletes are often overlooked as mushrooms, but are highly varied and common in the forests at this time. Though I see boletes of several kinds, three stand out. The yellow-capped Suillus (slippery jacks) are growing in good numbers under white pines. These mushrooms are often associated with pines and can be abundant even though they are only inches tall; giving quite a sight. Not as clustered, but still of note are the Leccinums (dark scaber-stalked boletes). They have bright yellow, orange or red, caps above the tell-tale rough dark stalk. But the great discovery of my walk is a group of Boletus edulis (king boletes). I had seen them before but not at this location. Many mushrooms can be passed by, but not king boletes. Living up to the name, they were about eight inches tall and some with caps of nearly eight inches in diameter; quite a mushroom gathering. I noted their presence and photographed them; counting ten in all. Returning to this site two days later, I saw that the number had been cut in half. Apparently, some hungry fungivore also found these mushrooms attractive and walked off with them.

The mushroom woods walk had an encore as I found three more; Coprinus, Amanita and Lepista in the yard. Hopefully, with adequate moisture, we will see many more fungal delights as we go through this new season of autumn.

Fourth Quarter

October 2, 2021

Some Late Warbler Migrants

With a sunrise shortly after 7 AM and setting before 7 PM, early October has more hours of darkness than light. This increases as we go through this autumn month. The arboreal show continues and though many reds are not as vibrant as they were in September, we still have plenty of yellow foliage. Shorter days will trigger more changes; leading towards a massive drop of these photosynthetic organs in a couple of weeks. Now there is color and more. Often while walking the October woods, I find late-season mushrooms; some quite numerous. Apples, crab apples, hawthorns and highbush cranberry all hold ripe fruits. And since many are brightly colored, they catch the eye of hungry animals. Wildflowers have lessened in the shorter amount of daylight, but some hardy asters will defy the frosts and linger for a few more weeks. This is especially true with the late-blooming New England asters. Despite its name, they are fairly common here and the tall plant with purple rays is quite impressive on chilly days. Spider webs are harder to find as are many insects. The ones seen now will either hibernate soon or die in the impending frosts.

Many of the birds show another response to the cold; they migrate. Living where we do, we are able to witness this movement to the south quite readily each fall; north in spring. With hawk ridge so close, we get plenty of views and news of the southbound raptor flight. Except for owls, especially the small saw-whet owls in October, raptors fly in the daytime. They are often large and we can witness the antics of eagles, osprey, turkey vultures and harriers along with several kinds of hawks. Buteos of red-tailed and broad-wings; accipiters: sharp-shinned and Cooper's and falcons: kestrels and merlins, all put on quite a show as they work their way to the south. But they are not alone.

Each day, I see and hear flocks of Canada geese heading south. Swans, mergansers and ducks as well as other water birds move by too; more silently than the geese. They may be joined by sandhill cranes, sometimes also in large groups. And the biggest numbers of birds southing now are the smaller birds.

Songbird migration began about two months ago. Tree swallows set the pace. Later as August led to September, many vireos, warblers, thrushes and flickers could be seen moving through. Louder and larger than most songbirds are blue jays and it has been hard to not notice their presence as they migrate; thousands pass by.

I find that in early October, two groups of songbirds are the most abundant migrants; sparrows and late warblers. To many, all sparrows look alike; small brown birds. But the patient observer may discern ten kinds during this time of early October. (This may be the best time of year to see a variety of sparrows.)

Warblers have been migrating for weeks, but since this group is so diverse, they are still not through. The two that consistently are late in their movement are the yellow-rumped and palm warblers. Both are numerous and readily appear in our yards and parks. Yellow-rumps have yellow at several places on their body, but it is the rump patch that stands out. Palm warblers are more brown with a rufous crown. But I find it is the behavior characteristic that helps identify them. Birds almost continuously flick their tail. As common as they are now, the season changes will soon send them on. But more migrants will be visible through the fall.

October 9, 2021

The Funnels of Fall

Earlier sunsets and later sunrises continue as we get further into October. Days are mild, but nights are cool and this carries over to early mornings. When I go for a walk at dawn,

I'm greeted by the happenings at this time. In the cool temperatures, dew coats roadside plants. In addition to this, there is frequent fog in this cool and moist environment. Later this month, dew and moisture will become frost.

Leaf colors so vibrant in afternoon sunlight are still here in the early morning. As I walk, I note the arboreal glow (mostly yellows) emerging from the surrounding darkness and fog. Reds that were so dazzling in September have been fading. Plenty of bright yellow leaves take their place and I see birch, aspen, basswood, hazel, ironwood, sugar maple, mountain maple, cherry and willow filling the scene. Though some reds still do appear, this is yellow time. We will enjoy these until they drop shortly after mid-month.

During the walk, I pause often to see leaf colors, but also to look at the roadside migrants. Some warblers may be present, but the birds I see are a variety of sparrows; white-throated sparrows appear to be most common. The abundant blue jays with occasional blackbird flocks are here too. Overhead, groups of Canada geese loudly speak of fall travels.

But there is another reason to pause frequently. The route also has many spider webs in the morning dew. With the season moving on, I see fewer of these snares, but I do find each of the four types of webs that spiders build. Cobwebs (irregular threads) as we often see around our house, are common in the tops of grasses or last-year's tansies. Within these threads are the web makers. Small, but hardy, they will last for a few more weeks. In some shrubs and conifers are bowl-shaped sheet webs; also lingering into the fall. The circular orb webs, so abundant a couple of weeks ago in nearby fields, are less common now, but I do see several. Most of these constructions hold dew, but the web makers have gone. However, I do see one willing to get wet.

The fourth kind of web is most common at this time; the funnel webs. So named because these insect-catching snares are composed of numerous threads surrounding an opening. This is where the spider sits in readiness to pounce out to catch a passing insect. This form of a hunting web looks like a funnel. Webs are usually on the ground and may appear to be a flat "cloth shape" appearance. Being low to the ground provides a good site to catch wandering insects. But being close to the ground means that they get wet with dew readily and I see them easily. This is also where the first frosts appear. All types of webs that get a dew coating can also get frosted as we progress into fall, but I find more frosted fall funnels than any other.

Funnel webs were very common all summer and myriads were in our yards and roadsides during the warmer times. The spiders grew, the webs grew. The ones that we see now will last for a couple more weeks into October, but will succumb to the impending chill. Dealing with the cold, some funnel-web spiders will move indoors. It is not unusual to find the funnel webs of these brown spiders in basements and garages as the temperature drops. Some will last into winter, but now they are another seasonal change to watch with our local fauna.

October 16, 2021

Some October Mushrooms

Mid-October is a time of great changes in the northland. The colorful woods of deciduous trees blending reds and yellows in September has shifted to more yellows in the first half of October. Now at the middle of the month, the foliage goes to its next phase. The leaves leave their arboreal home for the last five months and cover the forest floor. Rain, wind and storms can sometimes make this drop very dramatic and quick. Looking into the woods now, we can see much differences than before; often bare trees. However, the yellows of aspens that lasted until recently have their place taken by the yellow-gold of tamaracks. These conifers of the swamps and bogs give a glow that frequently persist for nearly the rest of the month.

This is also a time of migrants. Songbirds now include sparrows; many from the far north, blackbirds of a couple of kinds, robins and the continuous blue jays. And there are a few lingering warblers and tiny kinglets. Among the raptors, we see sharp-shinned hawks, red-tailed hawks, turkey vultures and bald eagles in the daytime while the small saw-whet owls move by at night. Plenty of geese, swans and ducks are seen too as they pause on their southing at lakes and rivers. But there is more going on in the woods of October.

During recent woods walks, I have found an abundance of forest fungi. Most of these were mushrooms that appear to thrive in the present conditions here. The days have been damp enough with mild temperatures; not so chilly. There were several Amanita. I find them with caps of yellow, gray and white; one with cap was eight-inches in diameter. Honey mushrooms (Armillaria) were growing well at the bases of trees and on the walking trail. On nearby tree trunks, I found clusters of the rough-scaly caps of Pholiota. On the trail ifself, there were Russula of several colors, including red. Milk mushrooms (Lactarius) was here too and the colorful waxy caps (Hygrocybe); ranging from yellow to red. I had seen all of these in recent weeks, but as I passed a couple of downed logs, I found others. Hundreds of tiny fuzzy-foot mushrooms (Xeromphalina) cover a log. Though individually, they are only an inch wide, their numbers give the whole log a yellow-gold glow. A large number of puffballs are on logs and trees stumps. Still not mature, they do not yet release their numerous spores, but I expect that soon they will. On another log, I located two terrific growths of a white-body fungus; Hericium.

Not shaped like mushrooms, so common in the woods, and not as robust as the shelf fungi, Hericium stands out. Their growth pattern is one of branches that reach out with numerous spines or teeth. This shape and the white color has given them a variety of common names. This fungus may be called comb tooth, bear-head tooth, bearded fungus and a couple of other perspectives; icicle or waterfall mushroom. Whatever the name, this white branching growth on logs or trunks of trees adds much to the beauty of the October woods. Within these branches and tooth structures, spores are produced.

Going from the woods, and onto a lawn, I find three more of note. Shaggy mane (Coprinus), or inky-caps, stick up above the grass. Two more that often grow in a circular pattern (fairy ring) are here too. The white meadow mushroom (Agaricus) and brown Marasmius are very common now. It may be mid-October, but still, plenty of mushrooms.

October 23, 2021

Ducks at Dusk

Each year at about the middle of October, we make note of a change in the season; a change in the region; hard to not notice. The leaves that have hung onto the local deciduous trees for the last five months (since mid-May), now take leave of their arboreal abode and drop. This was preceded by a magnificent dolor display that makes us forget the greens of summer. From now until the return of the foliage next spring, the deciduous woods around us will be bare. It takes a little while to get used to such a scene. For the first time in months, we can see deeply into the woods. Small mammals such as squirrels and chipmunks along with the migrant songbirds can now be better observed.

Regardless of the temperature, the leaf drop is accompanied by shorter daylight. As we enter this last week of October, we have sun rising at about 7:40 AM and setting near 6:10 PM; nearly ten and a half hours of daylight. Cooler than a month ago, we may be seeing frost and maybe the first ice. Wildlife prepares to deal with the impending cold in one of four ways. Some lay eggs and die (mostly insects), others hibernate (some mammals and herps), a large number will migrate (usually birds) and there are those that will adapt and stay active. Bird migrants are now part of the daily scene. I have been watching some every evening.

I began going to a nearby swamp at dusk in September. The goal was to observe the large insects; giant water bugs, that live in the shallow water here in summer. As the days get shorter and cooler, they will fly from this site and head for a deeper aquatic home for winter. With a body up to two inches long and robust, they are quite impressive insects. The predacious big brown bats come out at this time too; trying to snatch a mid-air meal. The bats and bugs put on quite a show. But as I watched these aerial battles, I noticed other happenings here too.

In the nearby woods, I saw robins and various sparrows. Ravens and bald eagles flew over. As the darkness expanded, I watched the resident beaver making its rounds. And there were the sounds of dusk. As the sun sunk, I heard from a nearby gray treefrog, a barred owl called and the distant coyotes spoke up. But the most abundant critters were the flight of ducks; what I called "ducks at dusk".

Some Canada geese and sandhill cranes passed over; loudly going south. The ducks that I watched were mostly silent. Nearly every evening, the pattern was repeated. The ducks came in small groups; normally less than ten. They flew from the northwest, passing over and going to the east. Though the groups were never large, the total number of ducks at dusk was about fifty. Ducks ranged from a dozen to, one night, more than a hundred. There was a little variety, but nearly all were wood ducks. Though they are often known to squeal in flight, these were silent. They began the twilight trip about fifteen minutes after sunset and ended within a half hour.

What was happening? It appears as though these migrant ducks are now forming flocks. They spend the daylight hours at one location to feed, but as darkness moves in, they go to another more protected site for the night. The ducks at dusk has made for interesting fall watching, but soon the cold will send them more to the south.

October 30, 2021

Whirligig Beetles Moving to Shore

Now, as we exit the October, we can see fall advancing towards the impending colder temperature and changes. The days have less sunlight; ten hours, and we regularly note many of the happenings associated with late autumn. Chilly with frequent frosts and often showing the presence of ice. When freeze-up of lakes is still weeks away, puddles and ponds may start wearing the cold coats now. The snowfall of October 2020 was impressive; but light snows are more regular and expected. Usually, we do not get a lasting snow cover until a couple of weeks into November. These are the days of AutWin; after the leaves have fallen from the trees and before a lasting snow cover. A few trees, like silver maples and weeping willows, retain leaves into early November and some yellow-gold tamaracks will linger late. But nearly completely, the woods is bare.

Animals deal with the coming cold in four ways; migration, hibernation, lay eggs and die or adapt and remain active. Recently, as I sat on the deck, enjoying the October sunlight, I watched insects that demonstrated three of these four tactics. Small meadowhawk dragonflies and yellowjacket hornets were active and like me, they basked in the autumn sunlight. But their fate is one of succumbing to the chill. A butterfly; a Compton tortoise-shell, flew by the house seeking a site on the siding, a crack, where it would have protection enough to hibernate. And some ladybugs came by. They migrate from earlier locations to where they can congregate and hibernate; often choosing our buildings.

Out in the aquatic setting, similar preparations are taking place. The insects living under water, not usually seen by us, will often remain active (but slowed) for the winter. But while I was here at the bay, I was watching ones that were on the surface; the whirligig beetles.

These oval-shaped and dark-colored insects; a little less than one-half inch long, are residents of the water's surface. Here they spend the warmer months. They prey on smaller aquatic critters; both, above the water and beneath. The whirligig beetle gets its strange name from its unusual swimming skills. Insects live in large groups, maybe in the hundreds, forming a rather close-knit raft as they float. There is safety in numbers. When disturbed by us paddling by or other possible danger, they go through a frenzy-like swimming motion; circling in all directions. They are harder to catch when doing such gyrations. (Their scientific name is Gyrinidae.) This self defense can cause problems for them as well. The motion may get the attention from other possible predators that live below them. And so, these strange insects are even more strange by having four eyes. Not only can the look above them as they swim, but also see beneath; above and below simultaneously.

Their oval shape makes them well adapted for swimming. Like other aquatic insects, they use hind legs to swim with, but unlike others living in the water, their front legs are longer the hind ones. These frontal appendages are used to grasp prey. Their uniqueness continues. As the cold moves in, so do the whirligig beetles. In the warm weather, I watched them far out from shore. But now in the chill, they move into the shallows. Here, they go right up to the land to find sheltered sites, in mud and under debris to hibernate. On the water surface for weeks, they now go to shore; before the ice moves in. Next spring, they will emerge to lay eggs and continue their never-ending gyrating swimming.

November 6, 2021

Red Leaves Persisting in Fall

Early November is a time of AutWin; after the leaves have dropped from the trees and before we have a snowfall that covers these same leaves. This autumn interlude varies in how long it will last, but nearly always early November is part of this seasonal gap. This is also a time of late migrants in the region. Some of these; redpolls, pine grosbeaks, crossbills and snow buntings, are late to arrive here, but may be staying for weeks; perhaps even for the entire winter. Among the raptors; bald eagles, rough-legged hawks and goshawks are now passing through. The leaf drop allows us to see this movement better; as well as other nature happenings.

Though the bulk of the leaves from deciduous trees has fallen in October, there still are those that linger into this month. Most notably are the yellow-gold needles of tamaracks, out in the swamps and bogs. Their needles are falling and soon these conifers will be as bare as the deciduous trees; but in early November some still hold the gold. Also, a few other trees continue to be with leaves. In driving in the region lately, I saw plenty of yellow leaves on aspens and willows in the swamps. In yards, domestic poplars, weeping willows and silver maples held leaves. Non-native plants, such as mountain-ash, apples, lilacs, forsythia, Siberian-pea and buckthorn are still green. Along roadsides, yellow was apparent in reed canary grasses and asparagus. Some late-blooming wild flowers; aster, tansy, sow-thistle, fleabane, sweetclover and yarrow were seen at these sunlit sites.

Within the woods of AutWin, much more can be found. This is the time to note the greens of mosses, clubmosses, ferns and lichens before the forest floor will be covered by the impending snowfalls. Also, plenty of fungi; puffballs and shelf fungi are visible too on logs and tree trunks. But as I wandered among these green plants and gray fungi, I noticed that there were reds in the woods as well.

Though the colors were bright, this foliage was easy to overlook since most of the plants were small. I found about a dozen kinds with red leaves during this AutWin walk. Only arrowwoods, dogwoods, hazels and sumacs were taller than me; most of these plants were less than a few feet. Very young red oaks and red maples held red leaves on their one-foot frames. Bunchberry and strawberry, even smaller, were also red. At the woods edge, raspberry, blackberry, bush-honeysuckle and roses all blushed with scarlet foliage. But it was the red-leafed blueberries that were the most numerous.

We are all familiar with blueberries in the northland. As small woody plants, they survive the winter and in spring open their bell-shaped white flowers. After pollination, they develop the berries that many wildlife, including us, find so attractive in mid-summer. With the passing of the tasty berries, we mostly forget these low plants. But now, after the taller trees have shed leaves, sunlight penetrates on these clear and often sunlit days. And these small plants develop their red leaves of autumn. The anthocyanin pigments within the leaves serve to protect other leaf cells from excessive sunlight.

As I walked the woods, I was amazed at how many blueberry plants were here; all with red leaves. I don't remember seeing that many green plants at this site in the summer. I plan to remember these locations. Most of the autumn leaves and leaf colors are gone, but blueberries and some other small plants wait until AutWin to show.

November 13, 2021

With Green Leaves on the Forest Floor

Mid-November is frequently seen as a gray time of year. The colorful leaves have fallen, we usually have no snow cover and clouds often prevail. Until a snow cover remains, these are still the days of AutWin (the interlude after leaf fall and a snow cover). Despite looking like a bland scene and uninteresting walks in the woods, I find the opposite in my wanderings. Highbush cranberry, hawthorn and crab apple all hold their berries and fruits; often red, garnering attention from blue jays, woodpeckers (including pileated), grouse and the local small mammals. By this date, most insects are not to be seen, but the brown late-season moths and crane flies are still active. In the afternoon sunlight, we can see myriads of threads made by spiders as they move through the leafless tree branches. Best seen by looking towards and below the sun.

Not all trees of this woods have dropped their leaves. The obvious and common conifers still hold green needles. And I find a trio of unrelated trees with brown leaves still present. Some red oaks (pin oaks to the west and south of here), some sugar maples and many ironwoods will persist through the winter filled with their curled brown foliage. On the tree trunks and logs, there are many kinds of fungi; puffballs and shelf fungi that do very well at this time of year. Continuing the look on to the forest floor, I find several green-leaf plants growing here too.

As I walk, I find about a dozen kinds of plants with green leaves in this November woods. Some of these plants like raspberry, largeleaf aster, pale vetchling, bedstraw and strawberry may be green, but they appear to be just late plants that will fade soon. Others, such as mosses (probably the most abundant green plant on the forest floor of AutWin), clubmosses (lycopodium; princess-pine) and wood ferns will retain their green under the snow. (Wood fern does fade later in the winter, but another fern; rock-cap fern, is a true evergreen).

Mosses, clubmosses and ferns are non-flowering plants, but with some searching, I find several flowering plants that are holding green leaves now; and will continue for the entire winter. I find six kinds. In the mixed woods, twinflower, pipsissewa and goldthread are remaining green. Wandering in the deciduous woods, I find three more plants with green leaves among the fallen brown leaves on the ground. Hepatica, pyrola and wintergreen are quite easy to see here and, in some sites, they abound. It is interesting to note that these plants are not related to each other. All have flowers, but bloom at different times. Hepatica flowers in spring (usually the first in the April woods). Goldthread will also bloom in spring. Twinflower, pipsissewa, pyrola and wintergreen flower in the shade of summer. All form berries or seeds after flowering, but only wintergreen shows its berry at this time.

Next to the oval pointed shiny green leaves of wintergreen are the bright red berries. And red berries on the forest floor are easy to see now. Many critters, including some human berry pickers, will sample these half-inch berries. Wintergreen should not be confused with winterberry holly of the swamps; also, with red berries. Wintergreen (Gaultheria) has white bell-shaped flowers, like that of blueberries, that open in early summer. We may not see the bent down flowers at that time of year, but now the bright red berries among the green leaves in a mostly brown and bland November woods are a delight to see.

November 20, 2021

Milkweeds Again Get Our Attention from the Roadsides

Once we get to the last third of November, we settle down to see the happenings with weather and the impending cold season. November changes are nearly daily for a while as we witness ice forming on ponds and swamps one day, gone the next only to return. Once this fluctuating scene has become permanent, lakes will join the freeze-up. In like manor, snowfalls move in. Typically, the first snowfalls cover our yards and leaves of the forest floor. Usually, it will melt quickly, but the snow season has begun and soon, it will remain.

Changes appear elsewhere too; shorter amount of daylight has brought in the late-season migrants. Among these arrivals are; redpolls, crossbills, grosbeaks, waxwings and snow buntings. Unlike earlier migrants, many of these avians will spend the winter. For them, our region is their wintering site. Such migrations vary in different years, but this year the flight of redpolls has been abundant. After few last year, it would be good to see these small hardy birds at feeders again.

Tree colors and leaf drop so common in September and October has not entirely stopped in this month. During the last week of October, I took a drive in the region. As many local routes go, I passed a large number of swamps and bogs. The majority of these wetlands held tamaracks with needles. Though some were fading from the bright yellow-gold, others glowed. This was similar with the nearby swamp willows and their yellow leaves. Things changed and as I drove again a week later, early November, I noted that the tamaracks had dropped their leaves (needles) as had the swamp willows. Now, at about the halfway time of this month, the only trees still with green leaves are the non-natives; lilacs, weeping willows, apples and buckthorns.

Going from the trees, I shifted my observing to the roadside plants. Here, I could see an abundance of plants that gave much color to the scene in summer; goldenrods, asters, fireweeds and milkweeds. Then, they held blossoms of various colors that were hard to not see. Now, they hold the product of their pollinated flowers; the fluffy seeds. Not as bright as they appeared earlier, but just as obvious are the ones of today. Goldenrods and asters both bloomed late in the season and received much attention. They now have stems with fluffy seeds trying to take advantage of the autumn and winter breezes to disperse their products. Not as numerous as goldenrods and asters are fireweeds and milkweeds. Both of these native plants bloomed with purple flowers in mid-summer. Each day, at that time as I walked, I noted new florets opening. Fireweed flowers climbed the stalks and finished blooming before the milkweeds. Many fireweeds opened their thin pods in August, some lingering until now. Milkweeds were slower.

The ball-shaped pink umbels of milkweeds formed long green carpel pods in late summer; not ripening until autumn. Though many gray-brown milkweed pods do open in October, I find that it is not until about early to mid-November that the pods are fully open. Driving along roads now, I see patches of milkweeds with their clusters of white fluffy seeds; often just as obvious as the flowers were. Within the pods, small brown seeds are attached to white threads, forming sort of a parachute; allowing them to drift in the winds. Pods are late to open; but thanks to breezes, they quickly empty. Now, with plenty of fluffy seeds, milkweeds add much to the bland November scene.

November 27, 2021

A Couple of Flocks of November

The day is a "typical" gray November day. We have thick clouds, a temperature in the twenties and as the day has progresses, so have the winds. By the time that I step out for a walk, hard-hitting northwest winds are carrying light snow. The day feels colder than what the thermometer says. Such a day may not seem like a good time for a walk, but this is late November, a time of change, and there is always more to see as autumn begins to prepare for winter.

During a morning walk, I saw movement on the roadside. Here, in a growth of tansies was a flock of redpolls. Many of these small birds have been reported in the region recently, but this gathering of about twenty is the first that I've seen. They were feeding on tansy seeds, but nearby are alders and birches also with seeds. (Usually, they are late to arrive at bird feeders.) Moving on pass the redpolls, I heard and saw two flocks of Canada geese flying over; heading south. Neither flock was large, but it was great to see them passing over at this time of November; later than normal.

As I walked, I noted the swamp and the nearby pond were both wearing coats of ice and a subsequent dusting of snow. Snow on ice allows for it to be seen well. The adjacent lake is still without ice, even along the edges, but I think the freeze-up; a regular phenomenon of late November, is beginning and it won't be long before the lake will follow ponds and swamps with an ice cover. (With moving waters, river freezing will wait a while; usually in December.)

During the afternoon walk, I see a few chickadees and a couple of woodpeckers, but it is wind that provides the sounds; until I hear a flock. From high overhead comes the guttural calls of a large group of birds. I recognize these sounds as coming from sandhill cranes. I pause to look up high in the sky. The flock of these long-legged birds circles and moves towards the south; I estimate eighty to one hundred birds. They are here every year and some nest in the region. But seeing flocks like this in autumn is quite unusual. I listen and look until this large flock of large birds is far off to the south. Quite a surprise on such a raw November day, I continue my walk.

The route takes me into a woods where I stop to check the ice cover on another pond. I'm standing here when I hear more sounds of note. Looking northwest, I peer through the trees towards where the sound emanates. And I see another loud flock passing over. This one is in a V-shape. With white bodies, these large birds are identified as tundra swans; I count sixty. Nesting in the far north, they now are heading to a resting site along the Mississippi River before continuing east and wintering at Chesapeake Bay. Spring flights may rest in the northland, but in fall, they only pass over. I am fortunate to see this flock. A few days ago, I saw their cousins; three trumpeter swans, as well.

Late November is often chilly with periods of snow as we head for deeper cold and snow. It is a time of clouds and freeze-up. But as I see during my walk, it is also a time to see flocks of migrating birds. Whether these birds continue or stay, they make for great watching.

December 4, 2021

Rough-Legged Hawks of Late Fall

During November, we saw many changes as we got deeper into the season. It almost appeared as though the weather could not decide what to do during some of the days this month. The nights froze, the days thawed. Snow came, complete with plenty of tracks from wandering critters; only to then melt. Ponds and swamps took on a coat of ice and opened again. But once we reached the second half of the month, the cold seemed to settle in to last. When I noted ice on ponds and swamps during my morning walk on the fifteenth of November with a temperature well below freezing, I suspected this cold cover was to stay. About a week later, the nearby lake followed this pattern. An interesting progression happened at about this time. I enjoyed sitting on the dock in sunlight of the twentieth, surrounded by the lake's open water. The next day, the bay held some ice. The following day, the entire lake was covered.

And the month continued to host shorter days; sunrises later and sunsets earlier. Darkness and cold impacted the late-season migrants. I noted flocks of geese, swans, mergansers, ducks and cranes. Wetlands freezing was driving these birds south. Other southing birds during this time were the smaller ones; various songbirds. Bohemian waxwings, crossbills, grosbeaks, snow buntings, shrikes and literally thousands of redpolls have been flying by each day. Many of these birds can and do winter with us. I expect, even if we have not yet seen it, that they will appear at our feeders. I always wait to put out suet until late in the month and it was quickly discovered by downy, hairy, and red-bellied woodpeckers, black-capped chickadees and nuthatches; white breasted and red breasted. And there were the day-flying raptors.

With hawk ridge nearby, we get great views and constant updates as these migrants fly by. The large variety of raptors of September, lessened a bit in October and became only late ones in November. But these November raptors were quite consistent. Most common were the large bald eagles; coming over each day, sometimes in the dozens. Others included golden eagles, northern goshawks and a couple of buteos: red-tailed hawks and rough-legged hawks. Red-tailed hawks are common in the region during migration and many also nest here. But the rough-legged hawks are not as familiar.

Rough-legged hawks are a buteo like the red-tailed and broad-winged hawks. Larger than the latter, they are about equal the former. Bodies are mostly brown above with a banded white tail. When seen from under, they reveal a pattern of brown, white or dark. (Usually, some dark on the belly.) The name of rough-legged refers to the feathers going all the way down the legs to the talons. This is an adaptation to life in the far north; where they nest. Nesting in the tree-less tundra, they move south late in the season for a wintering site. Since they hunt in the open tundra, they are likely to winter also in open sites. Fields, swamps and marshes to the south of us are usually their goal. Here they carry on their hunting; frequently hovering in mid-air.

With all the forests here, we will mostly see rough-legged hawks as they pass by. Some will winter in selected sites in the region; but they are a regular migrant during November. We don't see them much during the other months. As usual, November this year gave us many opportunities to see these large buteos in flight.

December 11, 2021

Snowshoe Hares Need Snow

November of 2021 continued the trend of most of the year; being above normal temperature and lower with precipitation. It appears that the drought talked about so much this year is still going on. With virtually no snowfall in October and limited snows in November, we are far behind in that category as well. A landscape during the last days of November with almost no snow on the ground is not unheard of here, but not what is expected.

Two years ago, 2019, the first of December gave us something to remember as about twenty inches of snow fell. This, added to snow fallen earlier in the season, gave a snowpack that would remain for the whole winter. Snows of this amount make us change or adjust our lives. Local wildlife need also to cope with such conditions. Some would have a hard time with this new snow. I noticed more birds at the feeder than what we had earlier. Tracks along the road told of how foxes, coyotes and deer were using this route for their travel. Eventually, the deer made their own trails through this snowpack. Such trails were used by plenty of others in following weeks.

But that was two years ago. This year, snow seems to be slow to arrive. According to the National Weather Service in Duluth, as of December 1, only five and a half inches of snow has fallen; and mostly melted. I found that walking in the woods is fine with such a small amount of snow on the ground. I had plenty of opportunity to see much happening; plants, animals and animal signs. The only sites where a small covering of snow persisted was on downed logs in the woods and frozen surfaces on some ponds and swamps. Walking in the woods, I scared up several ruffed grouse; easier to see than normal. Out on the ice where light snow was present, I found a few tracks of meadow voles and snowshoe hare. These reminded me that little or no snow has advantages for some, but others are depending on a snow cover.

All three of these critters; grouse, voles and hare can survive without a snowpack, but snow helps them. Ruffed grouse will frequently bury themselves in an ample snowpack where they find shelter and relatively warm conditions; but without food. Meadow voles make a long series of tunnels and runways under the snow where they will move about throughout the winter; with both shelter and food. And then there is the snowshoe hare.

Their dependency on snow is mostly for protection. Squatting in their winter white coat, only slightly under the snow in wooded sites, usually conifers, they become hard to see. I have found that though their tracks abound in winter, sightings of the critters themselves are uncommon. They blend in well with the snowpack. But what if there is no snow?

The white coat usually forms in November in synchrony with a snow cover. As expected, they suddenly become hard to see. But if the snows are late to arrive, they will have a different situation, as happened this year. The cryptic white coat does not protect them, but instead makes them easier to see. They have a hard time hiding until the snow cover.

I have had late autumn ramblings in a snowless scene where I have readily seen several hares that would have been passed by in a usual setting. We may not always appreciate early winter snowfalls, but some of wildlife do and even depend on it.

December 18, 2021

Quick Arrivals in New Snow

The forecasted snow started after midnight and when we rose at dawn, we had an estimated five or six inches covering the bare ground that was here yesterday. With a temperature in the upper twenties, the snow was a dry powder and easy to sweep off the porch and deck near the house. There was some letting up at times in the afternoon, but the snow continued; often light, until well after dark. When finally finished falling, the total amount in my location was about seven inches. And so, December's first week is above normal for snowfall. Though we had some snows earlier this season, those were light coverings that melted rather quickly. This snow that fell when the temperature was in the twenties and with a forecast of dropping to single digits and subzero, appears as though this blanket will persist. Not waiting until the snow would stop, I went out while it was still falling for a woods wandering walk and some early-season skiing.

The ground is frozen beneath the snow and I'm able to glide through the powder with ease. As I go on and off of a couple of woodland trails, I look around and see that I'm not the first to be here. Tracks along the road, driveway and trails told of squirrel, deer and coyote movements. The deer were digging into the leaves below in search of acorns while several squirrels were going into their buried caches. A fox wandered the length of the trail; no doubt, also looking for a meal.

Back further in the woods, I saw where a couple of members of the weasel family hopped through the snow with the agility of this group. The large tracks of a fisher leapt a couple of feet with each movement, while its smaller cousin; the long-tailed weasel, left similar, but smaller marks in its travels. Both are predators and though usually expected to be nocturnal, they were out in this daytime snow; probably hungry.

I continue skiing on another trail and in another section of woods I see more happenings. The turkeys that have been wintering and roosting here have also been rummaging through the snow for food. There are several in this group. Further along, I see where a porcupine has waddled and slowly moved from one tree to another despite the falling snow. Smaller critters have also been active and I see several sites where shrews energetically pushed through the new snow. These tiny predators don't let a snowfall stop them in their hunting. Tracks going over the snow were made deer mice (white-footed mice); going from one downed log to another. Though many wintering mammals hop, these little mice are the only ones that leave tail marks and footprints.

I have been out here for only about an hour. I didn't go far during this falling snow, but I have seen that this new snow has not stopped many local wildlife. With the exception of the squirrels, I did not see any of the track makers, but thanks to the messages that they left, I can tell that they were active during this snow falling.

The light snow continued to fall in the late afternoon and even after dark. By the time that I returned to these locations the next day, all their tracks had been buried; new ones were appearing. Due to the snow cover that we get regularly, we will be able to follow the seasonal progress of our wandering winter wildlife in coming weeks.

December 25, 2021

Natural Lights in a Dark Month

Starting on December 7 and continuing for the next eight days, up to and including December 14, we had the earliest sunsets of the entire year; 4:20 PM. Beginning with December 15, the sunsets are later. (Some say that this is the first tiny step towards spring.) In the mornings, sunrises continue to be later and from December 29 until January 4, Sol's rising will be the latest of the year. In between these times, we experience the winter solstice; December 21. Besides being the first day of astronomical winter, it is also the day of least amount of daylight for the year; sunrise at 7:51 AM, setting at 4:23 PM. (The Weather Service calls meteorological winter starting with the first of December. Some phenologist acknowledge rivers freezing as the start of winter.) With these early sunsets and late sunrises with short periods of daylight, this time has been called the dark week; in a dark month. I find it a bit ironic that it is a good time to see various natural lights.

The full moon this month happened about the time of the solstice. Long dark nights are lighted by Luna's reflected light. But this reflection goes beyond the usual. With a snow cover, light from the moon is reflected again off the snow.

Like water and ice, snow has a high albedo; making nights bright. Despite the cold, such nights are conducive to winter walks. But there are more lights of note.

Three planets brighten the sunset time by glowing in the southwest sky fairly soon after sunset: Venus, Saturn and Jupiter. During the phase of the waxing crescent moon on December 6, Venus and Luna formed an impressive conjunction shortly after sunset. Each year, shortly before the middle of the month, we have the Geminid meteor shower; a time when we can see more meteors per hour than normal. And another light was present this year as Comet Leonard appeared in the early morning of December 12 in the east and returned on the evening of December 18. I found that even though we need optics to see it well, the "nearness" to Venus helped us to see this comet better.

Even without all these glowing objects, a clear night sky at this time gives us superb stargazing; allowing us to appreciate the darkness that is often not appreciated. Aurora may appear at times as well; giving more colors to the night. And this year of December 15, we had an unusual display of December lightning.

I note that the sunrises and sunsets in winter are also a lighted show. With the angle of the winter sun being low, the light of Sol's rising and setting tend to linger and remain longer in view. With some searching, we may be able to see nearly the entire spectrum. Such light shows are present in both the rising and setting; I find they are more spectacular in the setting. The sun's low angle allows for this spectacle and also the light tends to scatter both to the south and north; making for a "wrap-around" sunset.

Though not one of light, we have another astronomical event at this time. On January 4, Earth is at perihelion. During the annual trip around the sun, this is the time when we are closest to Sol. It is a good time to start a new year; just happens to nearly coincide with January 1. It may be dark, but we get plenty of natural lights and happenings in winter.

Average Temperature: 38.7° F

Highest Temperature (June 20): 94° F

Lowest Temperature (January 1): -23° F

Total Precipitation: 34.06 Inches

Total Snowfall: 125.6 Inches

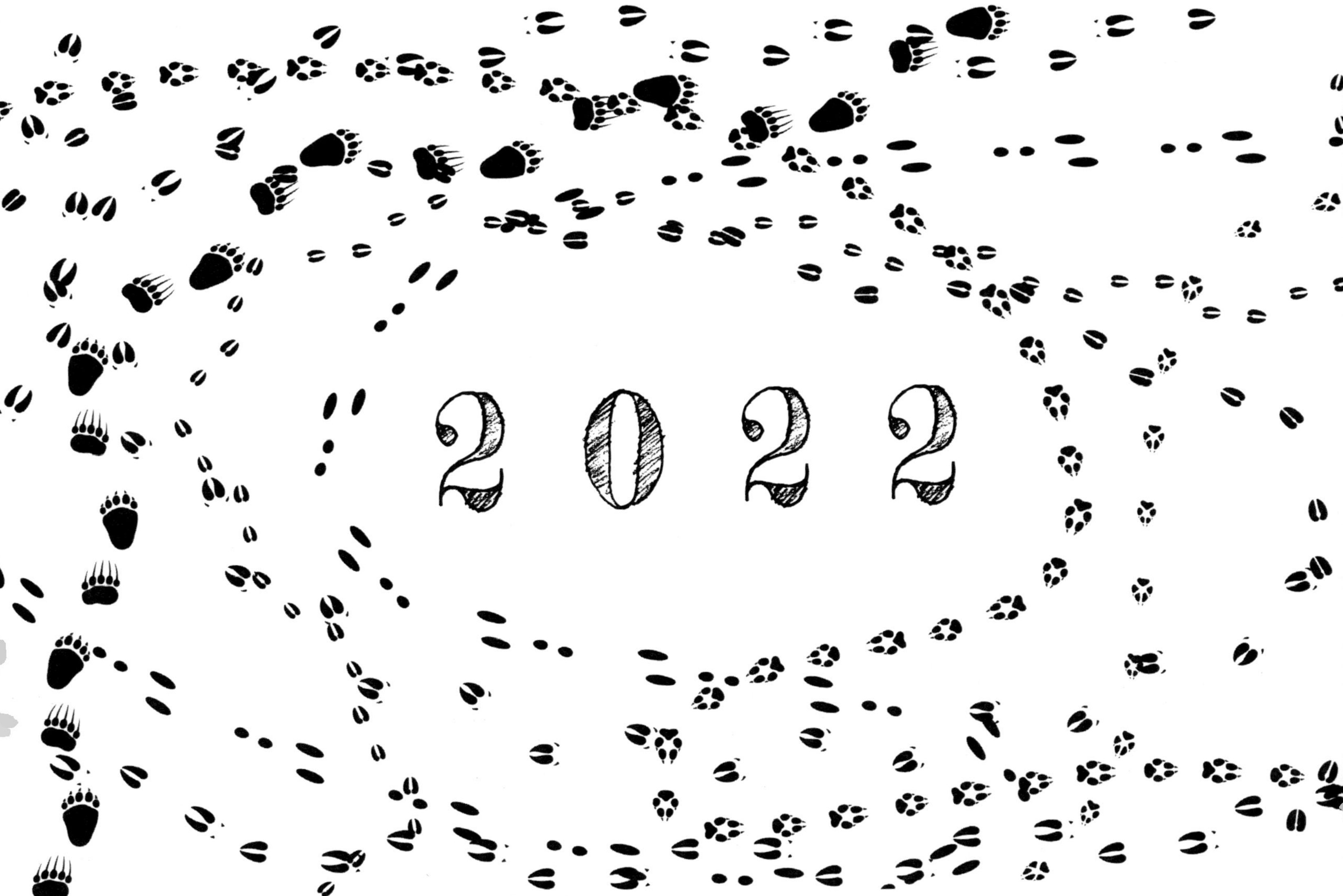
2022

First Quarter

January 1, 2022

A Surprise at the Bird Feeder

Like many in the northland, I maintain bird feeders near the house for winter. From about mid-October until April, not a day goes by that we don't have avian visitors come by for a meal. Sunflower and thistle seeds along with suet are kept available. I try to put out fresh food each day. And the local birds respond by feeding here regularly.

Last fall, some of the arrivals were migrants, but now in winter, they have settled into the regulars; here every day. (During unusually mild times, they are less likely to arrive; apparently finding meals on their own elsewhere.) Each day, I see black-capped chickadees, white and red breasted nuthatches, downy, hairy, red-bellied woodpeckers and blue jays. Often a half dozen to a dozen turkeys walk out of the woods to dine at the feeders as well. Though the chickadees may be as many as ten, the other birds are usually in pairs.

I find that watching birds on winter days is not boring. They adapt to the weather conditions with fluffed feathers or eating more. Chickadees, nuthatches and blue jays go for the seeds while woodpeckers devour suet; often with the help of chickadees and nuthatches. This animal fat is high in energy that is needed to cope with the cold. The birds are a delight to watch and though they do not really need our handouts, we might need them through the winter.

I have seen various finches; pine grosbeaks, pine siskins and redpolls in the region and pileated woodpeckers call in the nearby woods often, but they have not yet chosen to come by our feeders. I hoping that will change now in January.

Nearly every year, especially in December, we have a visit from some unusual bird at the feeder; normally lasting only a short time, but still arriving. A few years ago, we watched as a house finch and a starling showed up during a snowstorm. Another time, it was a cardinal. None stayed very long. These birds are common at some bird feeders in the area, they are not present at ours. Two years ago, a varied thrush; a relative of the robin, a bird more common in the Pacific Northwest, came to the feeding site, again for only a day. And recently, we were surprised to see a flicker joining others at the feeder.

Flickers are a species of woodpecker. Larger than the three kinds that have been at the feeder lately, they reach about one foot long. While the other woodpeckers are mostly black and white, flickers are largely brown with black spots on the undersides. Red markings on the head, often with a black "mustache" makes for an interesting appearance. Two other colors of note help to recognize the bird. Feathers have yellow shafts and when wings or tail are spread, this color is easy to see. When in flight, a white patch on the rump shows up.

Flickers are a common resident of the northland in summer. Being as large as they are, we see them regularly. Traveling in small groups that often go to the ground, flickers are easy to see in fall migration; especially in September. A few may be seen in later months, but in December at our latitude, they are rare. Like the other unexpected bird sights, this one did not persist.

The flicker and the other feeder surprises, despite their short show, still add much to feeder watching. We have plenty of winter to go; and lots more to see at feeders in coming weeks.

January 8, 2022

Cloquet-Carlton CBC

Each year as we reach mid-December, we go through many happenings in our lives. This is the time of the holidays and winter solstice. Not quite as well know, but just as regular of a feature to the year's end, is the Christmas Bird Count (CBC). Though Christmas is part of the name, it does not have any other connection to this winter holiday. The name is a reference to this time of year when the count is conducted. It can take place any day from December 14 until January 5; a twenty-three-day period. Begun about the year 1900, the counts have spread out to include all of North America; hundreds of counts. During a chosen day, volunteers look for and count the species of birds seen within an area and how many; results are compiled. The area surveyed is a circle with a fifteen-mile diameter; nearly one hundred eighty square miles. The local Cloquet-Carlton CBC done entirely within Carlton County was begun in the 1980's; continuing for more than thirty years.

I see this count as a way of finding out what kinds of birds are present with us at this time of winter. The counters select a part of the given area and canvas it either by driving or on foot. In addition, birds are observed and tallied by staying at home and watching feeders. Getting out before sunrise or after sunset, owls are also listened for. The three days prior to count day and the three days after are designated as count week and birds seen on these days can also be included. The totals of this counting gives us a good idea of the birds here in winter. Birds present are likely to be those that live with us all year (permanent residents) or those arriving and staying here for winter (winter visitors).

The Cloquet-Carlton Christmas Bird Count was held on December 30, 2021. The day was delightful for winter birding. Temperatures ranged from a low of minus ten to a high of fifteen degrees. Clouds prevailed all day and winds were calm. These conditions make for good hearing of active birds. The snowpack was about ten inches; new snow. Limited walking could be done in woods, but we were able to move about by walking roads, skiing and snowshoeing. Much of the new snow of a foot to a foot and a half was hanging on conifers; making for a beautiful scene as well. When the dozen counters tallied results late in the day, a total of thirty-five species, thousands of individuals, were recorded.

These included: wild turkeys 84, ruffed grouse 2, bald eagles 14, rough-legged hawks 2, rock pigeon s130, mourning doves 49, red-bellied woodpeckers 9, downy woodpeckers 33, hairy woodpeckers 35, pileated woodpeckers 19, northern shrikes 5, brown creeper 1, blue jays 127, crows 66, ravens 80, black-capped chickadees 528, red-breasted nuthatches 68, white-breasted nuthatches 30, starlings 203, house sparrows 25, robins 2, varied thrush 1, Bohemian waxwings 203, cedar waxwings 3, pine grosbeaks 570, house finches 14, pine siskin 69, common redpolls 527, goldfinches 71, white-winged crossbills 241, cardinals 7, snow buntings 7, juncos 36, song sparrow 1, horned larks 2.

Most of these birds are regulars in winter and the numbers are about normal. But the number of pine grosbeaks, common redpolls and white-winged crossbills were far beyond the usual. Varied thrush, song sparrow and horned lark were unexpected wintering birds. We have much of winter ahead of us, but thanks to the CBC, it is nice to know we have plenty of avian company.

January 15, 2022

Crab Apples in Winter

Mid-January is upon us. As expected, chilly temperatures with an ample snow cover are what we deal with each day. When temperatures drop to subzero or when a foot of snow falls over the scene, we may have some difficulties going about our usual lives, but with some planning, shoveling and help from friendly neighbors we get through these tough times. Many of us, being well fed and sheltered, find these conditions as being benign and we participate in much outdoor winter recreation.

But much of the wildlife surviving winter here with us needs to struggle to get by. I notice tracks each day that tell of deer, mice, squirrels and rabbits; all seeking sheltered meals. Tracks and trails of weasels, foxes and coyotes who are looking for any available prey that they can find are also seen. There is a daily struggle during the dark and cold season.

Besides these mammals that winter here, there are many birds present as well. These are permanent residents; ones that live with us all year and remain active in winter: chickadees, nuthatches, woodpeckers and blue jays with maybe some robins and goldfinches. Other birds are winter visitors; those that breed in the far north, but come to us as a place to spend the cold season. These are often finches: redpolls, pine siskins, pine grosbeaks and crossbills with some juncos. Many of these birds can be seen at feeders and it is easy to think that they would not survive winter without our handouts. But there is plenty of food available away from the feeders. This could be seeds of roadside plants like tansy, but also fruits and berries of trees.

Last spring, we noted the flowering of small trees in May; plums, cherries, juneberries, elderberries, mountain-ashes, highbush cranberries, hawthorns and crab apples as they bloomed on the roadsides. These delightful blossoms were discovered by pollinating insects and they developed into fruits and berries in the summer and fall. I remember walking last September among the ripe products of plums, chokecherries, mountain-ashes, highbush cranberries, hawthorns and crab apples. Most were red after the leaves departed from the trees, they showed up clearly. Birds, small mammals and bears were quick to locate them and the fruits and berries were rapidly gone; some lasting longer than others. As we advanced to winter, I noted that highbush cranberries, mountain-ashes and crab apples seemed to be the only ones still on the trees.

But with plenty of hungry birds and following a hot dry summer, fewer of these arboreal foods were to be found. I took a November walk to visit a few crab apples that I was familiar with, only to find bare trees. I continued the search until I did find a grove of trees with many holding crab apples; not looking as delicious as they did a few months ago.

Crab apples are essentially just like little apples. They are closely related to the domestic apples and can be both wild and tame. I was not the only one to find them. Starlings, robins, Bohemian waxwings and pine grosbeaks discovered them too. Now, in mid-winter, fewer fruits are present, but the ones here even if partially eaten and frozen will still be found. The crab apples present on the trees now are dry and shriveled, but still contain some nutrition and wintering birds will go for them. We have weeks of winter to go, the pickings may be slim, but winter crab apples are still present.

January 22, 2022

Ironwoods Keep Leaves All Winter

It was a little over three months ago, mid-October, that the vast majority of leaves fell from the local deciduous trees. The outstanding colors; reds in September, mixed with the dominant yellows that gave way to nearly all yellows in early October, preceded this arboreal event of the leaf drop. We experience this each autumn and after a few days of wind and rain, the leaves that have been with us since last May and given so much color in fall, depart from the trees. Suddenly, the yards and forest floors are covered with the fallen leaves.

As often happens in nature; the event does not take place with all the trees at once. Within our native forests, it is unlikely that we'll see leaves staying on branches past October. But many of the non-natives that thrive in the region, along with some late natives, will continue to hold leaves until early November. I find this most with silver maples, small swamp willows, large weeping willows and others of the yards and parks such as lilacs, forsythias and buckthorns. And out in the wetlands, the second half of October is lit up by the tamaracks; our only conifer to drop all its needles in preparation for winter. No matter; native or not, by the time we reach the end of November, the deciduous trees are bare; mostly.

Now, with a snow cover in January, it is easy to see as we pass by the winter woods that some trees are still holding leaves; though they are brown, curled and dead. They are present on the tree branches. A closer look reveals three species of trees that continue to carry dead leaves throughout the winter; a condition known as marcescent (also called "everciduous"): sugar maple, red oak and ironwood. While it is only some sugar maples and red oaks; usually the smaller or younger ones, that hold leaves all winter, this condition is more widespread with ironwoods. (In some places, mostly to the south and east of our region, pin oaks also are marcescent. Further east, beach trees exhibit it too.)

Ironwood (Ostrya virginiana) is a small to medium-sized tree that grows well in the shade of the larger forest deciduous trees. Toothed leaves are much like that of elms and the wood is hard. Male catkins also stay on trees in winter; much like what is seen on birches. Catkins develop in spring to pollinate the female and produce a scaly nut; known as a hop. (Ironwood is also called eastern hophornbeam.) The hops drop off in fall and if it were not for the long-lasting leaves in winter, we would never realize how common these trees are in the area forests.

The main reason that deciduous trees drop their leaves in fall is an adaptation to winter. In the arid air of winter, broad leaves would lose moisture and cause desiccation. Such dryness could harm the trees; best to drop the food-producing leaves for the cold season and grow new ones in spring. Also, such leaves would be dangerously burdened by the weight of snow on the branches. One of the reasons proposed as to why ironwood keeps leaves all the way to the new growth in spring, is that dead leaves can also help from drying. Another reason may be that dead leaves can discourage browsers from eating the small buds. Or maybe, it is just a genetic variation. Whatever the reason, ironwoods let us know how common they are by keeping leaves all winter.

January 29, 2022

Coyote Crossing Active Now

With a snowpack of about a foot, most of my winter trekking has been on the road or trails. The walking is much easier along such routes and though occasional traffic can take away from critter watching, I can still see what is going on in nature on these winter days; there is daily news.

January had given us both; the bitter cold and several mild days (January thaw), and the local wildlife respond. At the feeders, more birds seem to make use of available food in the cold; often staying away on mild days. Conversely, reading the daily tracks along my routes tells me that many of the woods wildlife that winter with us, react in another way; more active in the warmer times and taking shelter, less moving, during very cold.

My routes go through woods, but also past swamps, ponds, lakes and fields; good sites that reveal various activities. Many of the tracks that I find are from wandering wildlife that frequently cross these routes. They leave word of their movements; past and present (plenty of daily tracks, but I usually do not see the track makers). Deer and squirrels are the most common tracks that I find. The large deer walk on hoofs while the small squirrels have a hopping gait. Local canines are also active and I regularly find tracks of fox, coyote and maybe even a wolf. In recent light snow cover, I noted where cottontail rabbits and their cousin, the snowshoe hare, had come by. Small deer mice go hopping over the snow surface while the tiny shrews are typically beneath; leaving trails of where they crossed the path where I now go. Members of the weasel family continue their energetic lives in winter and at several sites, I find the hopping styles of weasels (ermine) and their larger cousin, the fisher, as they cross and recross the road and trails in their pursuit of prey. Near the swamp that I go by, I see where an otter (maybe more than one) has made its sliding trail from the swamp to the lake. During a mild day, I found where a waking skunk had wandered about. The three-toed footprints of birds are often seen too. Turkeys, wintering in the woods, come out in search of food and the smaller grouse tracks reveal their activity. The ever-present crows and ravens gather on the roadsides as well.

Besides telling me who is present, tracks also tell of happenings. Squirrels have been visiting caches made last fall while turkeys and deer dig under for acorns. At one site, I see where a barred owl swooped down to catch a deer mouse that hopped over the snow. The owl left telltale wing and tail marks.

But besides the feeding, late January, with nine and a half hours of daylight; growing more rapidly, is a time of breeding among the canines. I have noticed this mostly along the road that I walk daily; especially with coyotes. Ranging through their territories, they regularly cross the road. I have named one site as "coyote crossing". With a field on one side and a pond on the other, the local coyotes pass through a small woods between. Their world is very active now with the breeding season happening; territorial routes need to get maintained with regular travels and scent markings. With a gestation of about two months, the pups are born in spring. Despite the snowpack and the cold, coyotes remain very active; especially at this designated "coyote crossing" and we'll see more as we go into next month.

February 5, 2022

Redpolls Arrive at the Feeder

Half way between the winter solstice of December 21 and the vernal equinox on March 20 is the first week of February. Putting this in different words, when we get to early February, we are half way through winter; according to the calendar. Anyone who has spent the entire cold season in the northland is well aware that the season doesn't quite follow this timeline. We will be getting plenty more snow and cold in the coming weeks; however, there are happenings that will change the conditions of the season in the second half.

The nine and a half hours of daylight that we experienced at the end of January is quickly growing to be ten hours by February 8. Earlier sunrises; later sunsets each day changes the photoperiod of winter. And the local wildlife responds to such lengthening light, even more than the rising temperatures. We can see some of these responses.

In February, the squirrels that came to the feeders all winter, now seem to be interested in more than just eating. They chase each other about in a form of dominance; leading to pre-mating behavior I notice crows and ravens flying now in pairs; plenty of flight and calling. Woodpeckers have been in the yard all winter, but now many are drumming on tree trunks and branches; proclaiming territories. And there are changes with the birds that have been at the feeder for the last several weeks.

I have been hosting what I call the "same seven" species of birds since early December. The black-capped chickadees, white and red-breasted nuthatches, blue jays and three kinds of woodpeckers; downy, hairy and red-bellied, arrive each day. Occasionally, a few turkeys move in from the woods to make eight kinds. But that changed recently.

Redpolls that breed in the far north spend most winters in our region. This year was no exception. They began showing up locally in November. Feeding on seeds of alders and birches, that both abound here, they did quite well. In addition, I have observed a few small flocks that were eating tansy seeds; also, common here. Even though the Duluth Christmas Bird Count recorded nearly four thousand redpolls, they were mostly not at feeders. Though I wanted them to be present at my feeders, I had to wait. I have noted in previous winters that they are slow to go to feeders; usually not before January. Apparently, they find the other seeds to be just fine in early winter.

January came, but no redpolls. Finally, when I looked out on January 20 in the late morning, I saw a lone redpoll on the feeders. Before the day was over, there were three. This grew to four the next day; then six, eight, fifteen and on January 26: twenty. I expect that this number will continue to rise. Some winters, they can be in the hundreds.

Well-loved and a delight to watch, redpolls are tiny finches, but very hardy birds. A streaked body, with white undersides and a black face with a red forehead (why they are called redpolls). Both males and females have red on the head, but with the males, the red extends down to the chest. The antics of these energetic flocks; feeding on thistle seeds, add much to the days of February and beyond; usually they depart in April. Besides some "wheezy" calls, they are quiet; becoming louder and restless as we move into late winter. It's been a wait, but when redpolls arrive, the winter changes.

Feb. 12, 2022

Woodpecker Drumming in February

The month of February, with twenty-eight days, is our shortest month. Ironically, for some who may be winter weary, this month can feel like the longest. We are still in winter and spring can look like it is far out on the horizon; several weeks away. This month can give quite a variety of temperatures. It could be very cold (as seen in the record-setting days of February of 2021), but can also give us mild days with readings in the forties or fifties. Not only our shortest month, February is also our driest month. We have had some snowstorms at this time, but usually snows during these weeks are not like other winter months. Among many of us, the days may feel like they are slow moving; not leaving mid-winter in a hurry. However, in another way, the month of February is a month of quick changes.

We began the month with nine and a half hour of daylight and by the eighth, it had become ten hours. As we exit the month, this will lengthen to be eleven hours. Subzero temperatures can and often do persist until the end, but with longer times of sunlight, things are happening. I notice changes with our wintering birds.

On a recent morning, I looked out at the bird feeder and watched a large breakfast celebration of at least fifty redpolls in the cold. With fluffed-up feathers, chickadees, nuthatches and blue jays were here too. I stepped out for my morning walk in minus ten degrees; clear and calm. A colorful lingering sunrise prevailed in the southeast. In these pleasant winter conditions, I walked on my usual road route. I take this same trek nearly every day but there is always more news to observe. This morning was no exception.

The ever-present crows and ravens were calling as though the temperature was irrelevant. These large black birds were joined by their smaller cousin; the blue jays. A white-breasted nuthatch added its grunting call from the nearby woods. But one of the loudest in this chilly morning was not a call, but a different sound coming from other wintering birds.

From sites scattered in the woods that I walk by; I hear the drumming of woodpeckers. Drumming is when these birds take their powerful bills and hit it rapidly against a tree trunk or branches to make a "drumming" sound. Drumming is a woodpecker's way of proclaiming territorial ownership; a pre-mating behavior at this time. With some searching, I found the bird; a hairy woodpecker, as the noise maker. Larger than its look-alike, the downy woodpecker, the hairy is also black and white and about ten inches long. Birds are permanent residents and frequently come to suet at the feeder. Males with a red spot on the back of the head, are the ones to do their drumming. I began hearing drumming of hairy woodpeckers in January; almost always on cold clear calm mornings. (A few years ago, I heard and watched one drumming on a morning of minus forty.)

As I continued my walk, I listened to another drumming coming from deeper in the woods. This one was louder and more deeply resonating; a pileated woodpecker. These huge woodpeckers, about seventeen inches long, also begin their drumming now. This was the first that I heard from the pileated this season. It may be mid-winter, weeks before spring, but these woodpeckers that do not migrate are using their bills to prepare for the breeding season in their way. They drum on cold clear mornings, a step towards spring.

February 19, 2022

Irises: Then and Now

During the second half of February, we are still in winter, but with the longer hours of daylight, it may feel like we are further along in the season than we are. Days rapidly get longer; Feb. 8: ten hours, Feb. 18: ten and a half hours, Feb. 27: eleven hours. And for the first time in months, we have a sunrise before 7 AM. Even if the temperatures and snowfalls tell us winter it is, the longer days can get us to think about other seasons; past and future.

While taking my daily road walks , I see plenty of tracks that tell of critters that are wintering with us and remain active. The mammals continuously leave their markings of where they have been and where they are going. Among the birds; sounds of crows and ravens are still with us and are now being joined by calls from blue jays, nuthatches and woodpecker drumming. But there is more here to note.

The roadsides also hold an abundance of the plants from last summer. Without the colors of that time, they are still easy to recognize by their shapes. Standing above the persistent snowpack of the last couple of months, are goldenrods, asters, sunflowers, tansies, evening primroses, mulleins, sweetclovers, milkweeds, fireweeds and bergamots. Despite the lack of petals and leaves, many are still with seeds. Those of goldenrods and asters are fluffy while those of primrose and bergamot are not. The milkweeds and fireweeds that dominated this scene last summer now hold empty pods where their seeds have all dispersed in the wind. All of these plants tell of other seasons; past and future.

Today, I add a little variety to my route and walk through a nearby swamp. The ice here is covered with several inches of snow, but the walking is fairly easy. Deer and coyote have been using this route as their own recently, as seen in their numerous tracks. But in this winter wetland, many plants also rise above the snowpack. At the edge of the swamp are the small trees of alder and willow while tamarack and black spruce are right out in the swamp. Smaller plants, but still above the snow, are the abundant leatherleaf and Labrador tea. Both of these wetland plants continue to hold leaves for the entire winter. Sedges and cattails dominate much of the view. Despite the season, there is plenty to see. And along the shoreline, I find a plant sticking up with several dark pods. A closer look reveals it as an iris.

One of the delights of early summer is looking out at the swamp and seeing the blue-purple flowers of iris (Iris versicolor); also called blue flag iris. Most of the petals and sepals are this bluish color, but a look inside shows other colors, including yellow. The plant is beautiful, but growing at the edge of the wetlands, it can get overlooked.

Pollinating insects do not pass by these flowers of June and after pollinated, they develop the product of the flowering time; seed pods. These growths are usually between two to three inches long and about one-half inch wide. The green color of last summer is now dark. Unlike the pods of milkweed, the iris pods do not open to disperse in the wind. The iris pods are still closed, now in February. They will open by summer and help to prolong the growth of irises at the swamp. This is an iris of then and now; past, present and future.

February 26, 2022

Awakening Skunks

As we approach the end of February, we are also moving in to the final days of meteorological winter. The National Weather Service defines winter as the months of December, January and February. With more daylight and the vernal equinox only three weeks away, we can see that the season is progressing. We can expect more cold and snow after we exit the short month of February, but the pace is towards spring.

Looking back at these three months, we see weather of winter. December was a few degrees above normal and also several inches beyond the usual for snowfall. January's temperature dropped and mostly remained cold. The northland recorded an average temperature of more than six degrees below the norm; twenty days had subzero readings. Snowfall was about equal as to what was expected. The first half of February continued this trend set in January and we again had temperatures considerably less than normal by about eight degrees. Snows, though not heavy, were enough to maintain a snowpack of about a foot for several weeks.

During my regular walks through these days, I found plenty of activity in the form of tracks from the local wintering wildlife. Deer and squirrels were so common that I don't think a day went by without their tracks being present. Foxes, coyotes and an occasional wolf prevailed in these months. While voles and shrews went under the snow, deer mice hopped over. Also leaving hopping tracks were members of the weasel family; ermines, pine martens and fishers. And, of course, the rabbits and hares were here. Crows, ravens, along with some turkeys and grouse were seen too. Except for extreme cold, all remained active.

Though the temperatures have been cold in January and February, we did have a few mild days; in the thirties: January 18, February 8, 9 and 20. Mild winter days always get a response. I usually see fewer birds using the feeders on such days. And other wildlife are more mobile during the thaws. Taking a walk on a warming day in January, I added a new track to the list. Along the edge of my route, I noted the gait of a striped skunk. It was only that day, not more. A few weeks later in early February, at the same site, I again found that the skunk was active.

Skunks, like raccoons, deal with winter by sleeping; not hibernating. They enter a dormant phase, often called torpor, while in the shelter of a burrow or under logs. Is such a state, they cope with the coldest times. When rising temperature happens in January, they go out to wander; usually at night. As omnivores, they eat anything. Hungry, they locate what they can get at this time; seeds, berries or maybe some grubs under the leaves and snow cover. And then go back to sleep.

But seeing tracks (or maybe smelling their odor) of active skunks in February often means more. The awakening skunks during this month of late winter are seeking more than food. Males will travel about trying to locate mates at this time; their breeding season. With a gestation period of about two months, the young will be born in spring.

Both times that I found skunk tracks this winter, the weather was mild and returned to cold. But as we enter the month of March, skunks will become more active and we may see their tracks, smell them or see the skunks themselves in yards, driveways or streets; moving into spring.

March 5, 2022

Despite Snow; Early Spring Things

The last week of February gave us something to remember. February 21 and 22 was an almost continuous snowfall and with strong winds, poor visibility kept many of us at home (maybe the best place to be). The total amount of snow varied much in the region, but many recorded at least a foot. Cold temperatures kept this coating from being wet and sticky. The dry powder was easy to blow about. I saw that spruces were able to hold snow in their branches, but most other trees not able. Low horizontal branches and downed logs collected much of this recent addition; good measuring gauges.

Both January and February were considerably colder than normal and so the snow; seventeen inches in January and nineteen in February, has remained mostly dry powder; not as much moisture content as we might expect. For many years, February was called the dry month and huge snowstorms at this time were unlikely. This is changing and February now often records more snow than March. Yet, with recent weather that gave us much snow and cold, the season is moving on.

Despite ending the month with a two-day snowstorm, a snowpack of nearly two feet and several subzero times, days continue to get longer. Beginning the month with nine and a half hours of daylight, February extended that to eleven hours by the end. The vernal equinox (the first day of astronomical spring) is only two weeks away (March 20). We begin daylight savings time next week (March 13). Because of the lengthening days, "spring things" are happening.

It is not unusual to see the opening of fuzzy buds on willows and quaking aspens as March begins. During some searching, I found only a few openings. But there is more. Among the swamp willows, many had red or yellow stems. And I located a few bright red patches of the small tree: red-osier dogwood; all parts above the ground are red. Also, more is happening at the base of deciduous trees. Sunlight absorbed by the bark warms the nearby snow to form little circles. And among the birds, there are some very early migrants.

Driving on clear days, before and after the snowstorm, I did see several flocks of small birds along the road. With the present snowpack, many birds will come to the edge of the road to feed on seeds of nearby plants. Most of these birds appeared to be wintering redpolls; letting me know that they do not all go to feeders. But one group was snow buntings. Sometimes these white and brown birds will winter here, but usually they keep on going south. Ones seen now are probably very early migrants; feeding and resting as they move further north. Out in a field, I saw a bald eagle; also, maybe an early migrant. Ravens and crows were gathering. The ravens were wintering, but some of the crow flocks had probably moved in from further south.

Not migration, but still an interesting sign of the time, I found many tracks of snowshoe hare as they scampered over the new and deep snowpack. Using large feet, they are able to move freely. This gathering tells of nocturnal mating behavior; another spring thing.

Much will happen in this month of March and by the end, we will most likely have a lighter snow cover and we may be seeing migrant songbirds in our yard and perhaps geese, swans and ducks in open waters of rivers while red-winged blackbirds call at swamps. We have plenty of cold and snow, but spring things are happening.

March 12, 2022

Squirrels Chewing Maple Bark

Both January and February were colder than normal. January's 4.7 degrees was 6.5 below the normal of 11.2 F. This impressive deviation was less than what we experienced in the following month. February recorded 5.9 degrees. This was quite beyond the normal of 15.4 F; 9.5 degrees less than expected. Both months had twenty days of subzero readings and both had more snowfall than the usual. But the winter is not done despite the longer days. As we entered March; historically the time of the greatest snowpack, we had about twenty inches of snow on the ground. Wildlife that wintered with us through these conditions, can have a tough time finding enough food. Add to that the fact that with many this is their mating season and they need to remain active. They are hungry; late winter can be a hard time to survive.

During my winter wanderings in the last few weeks, I have noticed signs of this. Deer seem to be moving wherever they can; often following trails of others. The smaller critters of mice, squirrels, hare and ermine are able to go over the snow; and in some wind-packed drifts, so have foxes and coyotes. While the fisher hopped through the deep snow, otters slid and a hungry arboreal porcupine waddled from tree to tree. I saw where a muskrat and beaver left the safety of their aquatic world and climbed over the ice to find more food along the shore. Even the crows and ravens walked along the roadsides searching. And at two sites, I found where ruffed grouse buried themselves in the snow.

I have also noticed differences in the behavior of the local squirrels. All winter, they have been arriving before the birds at the feeders in the mornings. They still do arrive, but there appears to be fewer. And while going on the woods trails, I have seen that many squirrels' tracks lead to their caches. Seeds and nuts that were buried under fallen leaves of last fall; and now are beneath the snow. These stashed foods are now gathered as needed food in late winter.

In the last couple of weeks, I have found young trees in the woods that have had their branches stripped of bark. All were sugar maples only a couple of inches in diameter. A closer look revealed the tracks of squirrels at the base. Apparently, squirrels hopped over the snow to these trees and then climbed up; chewing and removing the bark. (As often happens when finding animal signs, we usually do not see the critter making the sign. But one morning, I came by and actually saw a dark-phase gray squirrel as it was working on the tree bark.)

What is going on here? I have seen this before in the forest during the late winter. The outer bark was chewed off, but not too deep. I noted few strips of bark in the surrounding snow; evidence that the squirrels were either eating the bark or taking it for their nest. I think that this is another sign that shows squirrels are hungry at this time of year. They choose young trees that do not have thick resistant bark. They chew through this outer bark and get into the cambium layer beneath. This growing region contains nutrients and sweet sap; now starting to rise. Wanting more of this good taste, they continue with the bark stripping and expose large parts of branches on these small trees. If you see such stripped sugar maples, you see a sign of hungry squirrels of late winter.

March 19, 2022

A Moth at a Window in March

With an average temperature of about twenty-six degrees, March is certainly not a warm month. Usually, we have the ground covered with snow for all or much of these thirty-one days; and subzero readings can happen. However, as we reach and pass the vernal equinox, longer daylight will prevail. The mercury will frequently climb to the forties and fifties. It is an unusual March when we do not get these numbers.

With light more than dark, nature responds and we see plenty of happenings during these weeks. Skunks and raccoons move about now mostly in search of mates and meals. The little striped chipmunks are in the yard again; leaving the safety of the den. A few early migrants arrive. Open water will likely host geese, swans, mergansers and ducks. And soon, we'll be looking for robins on lawns and red-winged blackbirds at swamps. The first crocuses and dandelions are up and give a sight that many of us are glad to see. But there is more.

Even with these spring things, it seems too early to be seeing insects, but they are here and active. During my woods walks of late winter, I have several times seen insects on the snow.

Most abundant are the tiny hopping snow fleas (springtails) that abound on the surface during mild days. Looking like grains of pepper, they move on the snow using a tail appendage to jump. Larger, and looking like mosquitoes, are winter crane flies; some with wings, some not. Near moving water of streams may be the site of stoneflies and caddisflies that recently emerged.

Sap is rising in maples and some waking butterflies take advantage of it. A group of butterflies, called anglewings, hibernate as adults. Now awake, they go to trees to bask in the vernal sunlight and feed on the oozing sweetness. Bearing names of mourning cloak, comma, question mark, Compton and Milbert's tortoiseshells, they appear each early spring. Spread-wing, they are easy to see, often colorful, but when closing their wings, they blend in with the tree bark.

Not as common or as obvious as butterflies, a few kinds of moths are about at this time as well. A little dark one with white wing spots, known as the infant, is a delight to see on these early spring days. With brightly colored orange underwings and flying in the day time, it is easy to mistake it for a butterfly. I usually see them on a mild afternoon after the middle of the month. But it was at night of a mild day in March, that I saw another moth. The moth was about an inch long, mostly gray, and fluttered at the window; attracted by indoor lighting. A closer look revealed long antennae and lighter blotches along wing's edges. I was able to identify this early spring night visitor as a type of pinion moth.

It is not uncommon to see moths fluttering at windows; as we sit inside. Sometimes they are expected in cool weather, but not in March. Last fall; late October, a couple of gray and light brown moths; linden looper and spanworm, came here too. But these late-season moths do not feed; only breed on cool fall nights. The pinion moth that I observed had wintered as an adult and now in early spring emerged to mate and feed; mostly on sap. Coming to the window was only a diversion and it did not stay long. But I was glad to see another early spring insect.

March 26, 2022

A Goshawk Goes Hunting in a Barn

The thermometer says twenty degrees above zero this morning; far beyond the minus twenty yesterday. Overnight, we had a light snowfall of about one-half inch; falling before midnight. And when I step outside onto the porch this morning, I quickly see that I am not the first to be here. Apparently, during the wee hours, after the snow fell, a skunk came by. It visited every site it could on the porch, but as I learned by following the tracks, it also went through the yard. Going on the driveway, it wandered on the road for about a mile. Newly awaken skunks are well known to do much travel; seeking mates and meals. I think this particular one was very hungry. (It is not likely to find a mate on my porch.) I never did see or smell the wandering skunk. A few days ago, I also found raccoon tracks. Like the skunk, raccoons sleep in the coldest weather, rising now to find companions and food. Squirrels coming to the feeder all winter are now eating suet that they avoided before. I have also seen their tracks in the woods leading to caches and young sugar maples where they stripped and chewed bark recently. All of these speak of hungry wildlife this month. Some people have called March and April; "the hunger Moons".

Besides these mammals demonstrating food searches, I also saw this at the feeder with a couple of predator birds. A few days ago, in mid-day, a shrike arrived here. It even sat on a platform that had earlier held plenty of sunflower seeds. The smaller birds scattered quickly and the shrike departed. This gray-white bird about the size of a blue jay, did not come to eat seeds, but was pursuing the seed eaters. Though classified as a songbird, they act like raptors; complete with hooked beak. Wintering here, they feed on small birds and mammals. At about the same day, a barred owl came to the feeder too. Birds feed in daytime, the owl came at night. Probably, it came by since I also feed nocturnal flying squirrels. These were two more examples of hunger.

But another interesting story of predator hunger at this time was told to me by a land owner in the area. When approaching his barn recently, the owner saw that a large bird was in the building; coming in by way of open doors. Upon closer inspection, it was seen feeding on pigeons that lived in the barn. The owner was able to take a photo of this predaceous bird as it sat inside. Later, it was identified as a goshawk.

Goshawks are well known in the northland. A member of the accipiters, this largest one in that group, is a bird mostly of the forests; often quite remote, and not likely to be seen in barns. Apparently, the bird (I could tell from the photo that it was an adult) was so hungry that it sought pigeons; even following them through the barn doors to get inside. In the wild, they are predators of ruffed grouse and other forest birds and small mammals. With a little persuasion, the goshawk was willing to leave after feeding on a few pigeons.

A few days later, the temperature rose to the forties and during my walk, I heard Canada geese. The season is changing, but it can still be difficult for some wildlife to find food. The days are getting longer and warmer and the goshawk will probably do fine outside the barn.

Second Quarter

Apr 2, 2022

Red-Wing Blackbird: Harbinger of Spring

By the time we reach April, the new season of Spring is getting well established. We may have some cold and snow (sometimes substantial), but the longer daylight; thirteen hours in the first week, continues to lengthen through the month. Those of us who spent the winter here are likely to look for various spring things at this time.

Crows and ravens take pair-bonding flights. The redpolls that have been at the feeders for the last two months, now are restless and giving "wheezy" calls. Bald eagles have been northing regularly in the region. And out in open water sites, recent arrivals of geese, swans, mergansers and ducks are resting and feeding. Other sights of springing are in "hot spots" in our yards. South sides of buildings or hillsides are great places to see early crocuses and dandelions blooming in the green grass. Awakened chipmunks and butterflies may be here too. A couple of trees are forming flowers as well. In wetlands, alders are developing ripe pollen in their catkins while large silver maples are opening their staminate or pistillate flowers. Added to these sights are spring sounds.

Crows and ravens now do more territory calls. Woodpeckers are going from the beak drumming to calling now. And it seems like every walk I take at this time, has loud honking calls from Canada geese added. We may not appreciate these birds later, but now their calling is good to hear. Recently, a few trumpeter swans contributed blasting sounds. And on a cool windy morning a few days ago, I heard the guttural calls of sandhill cranes as they circled overhead. Soon the wing drumming of ruffed grouse will emanate from a downed log in the woods. There will be more sounds soon. But to me the greatest sound at this time is from the harbinger of spring: red-winged blackbirds.

Red-winged blackbirds are about nine inches long. Birds are well named. Males have a body of black feathers with red patches of the top of wings; shoulders or epaulets. This red, blended with yellow, is often bright enough to be seen as we pass by. Birds nest in cattail swamps and wetlands. They are very common and widespread. My daily walks take me by a couple of swamps where they have nested for years.

Due to the large population of these birds, the males need to return early from their wintering in southern states to sing and claim ownership to these nesting sites. Typically, I will hear and see the male in the last week of March. Hearing, more likely than seeing, these blackbirds have a song quite diagnostic. The song of "konk-a-lee" that is loud and often repeated is not to be confused with others. The returning males sing quickly upon their arrival. Females; with streaked bodies, "sparrow-like", usually do not arrive for about another month. Male songs of these weeks are aimed at other males to tell of territorial ownership. And they persist. Their songs will continue long after the females return. I have heard their songs as late as July. They may continue to defend the territory; often flying at any intruders.

These early swamp red-winged blackbirds are later joined by the females, but also by large flocks of various blackbirds. Here red-wings may be joined by other species such as grackles, rusty blackbirds, Brewer's blackbirds and cowbirds. Such flocks may be in the hundreds and can be quite loud with their springtime calling. But now, the red-winged blackbirds do a great job as being harbingers of spring.

April 9, 2022

Hooded Mergansers Join the Migrants

Though not as obvious, March followed January and February with an average temperature of less than normal. We had some mild days (55 degrees on March 20), but chilly times too (minus 13 on March 12). Snowfall was considerably below the usual; despite snows in the final days. Precipitation also was less than expected.

It was interesting to see the bird responses. During mild days, birds that had been coming to the feeders stayed away; only a few sporadic chickadees, nuthatches and woodpeckers here. But when the day became cold, snow and wind, they returned. One day, I noted about one hundred fifty redpolls; more than any other day for the whole winter. The weather appears to have affected bird migration (and non-migrants). A few robins and mourning doves have been observed in the area, and though the red-winged blackbirds have alluded me, they have occasionally been seen by others. Their songs, usually heard during the waning days of March were absent this year. Also, I have not yet heard the drumming of ruffed grouse in the woods or the woodcock's performance in the wetlands. I expect that to change soon.

During morning walks about two weeks ago, I heard a tom turkey gobbling from back in the forest. A few days later my silent walk was interrupted by loud guttural calls as three sandhill cranes flew over. Their delightful sounds are hard to not hear. Bird news was happening here a bit slowly, but to see more migrants both in numbers and in variety, I went to visit the St. Louis River.

The ice cover here persisted through the cold times, but now with temperatures above freezing and movement of the river, the site held large stretches of open water next to remaining ice. It must have been quite chilly out there, especially in the wind, but the newly arrived water birds were here. And I saw many.

The most common of these early waterfowl were Canada geese. Wintering further north than most, they don't have a long flight. The four that I saw on the first day of open water eventually led to dozens more in following days. Several large white trumpeter swans came by a few days later. These two species were joined by two others often associated with cold water; goldeneye ducks and common mergansers. And after about another week, the smaller hooded mergansers arrived here too. (Some bald eagles watched as they sat on the ice.)

Hooded mergansers get that name from the puffy rounded crest above the head. Males have black surrounding a large white crest patch. They also have a white chest with dark feathers on their back. Females are mostly brown. Hooded mergansers are the smallest of the three kinds of mergansers in the northland. The other two, common and red-breasted, are more likely seen in larger lakes. All mergansers have rough, tooth-like bills (sawbills); not seen with ducks.

I was glad to see the pairs of hooded mergansers in this early spring open water. While many of the other water birds here at this time will leave to breed in lakes to the north, some of these birds will stay local. I have seen their families for years when they breed in regional woodland ponds. These wetlands are chosen since they nest in hollows in trees (like wood ducks). Their home ponds may still be covered with ice, but it is good to see these mergansers back in the region. And I expect to watch them later in the season.

April 16, 2022

Spring Snows Help Vernal Ponds

The sports news this morning is of the beginning of the baseball season; with some local games scheduled. However, when I step outside, I'm greeted by four inches of new snow. Canada geese are calling as they have been doing every day since mid-March. These wandering geese are joined by some trumpeter swans and the distant sandhill cranes (two of the loudest birds in the state). The usual crows, ravens and woodpeckers add sounds too on this spring morning.

With a temperature of thirty-two degrees, the snow that fell is very wet. It is heavy and hard to shovel. Fortunately, the temperature rise today will melt much of this snow from the deck and driveway. Springtime snows tend to be wet and sticky while those of a couple of months ago fell in colder temperatures and were light powder; easy to shovel or sweep. (Four inches of snow in April may hold about one-half inch of moisture. Four inches in January maybe only one-tenth.)

I put out more thistle and sunflower seeds on the feeders that I was planning to discontinue. Redpolls that have been here for more than two months are quick to find them. Along with these two dozen small streaked birds, I see a new arrival; a purple finch. The bright colored male is very easy to see. Though some purple finches will winter here, I consider this to be a migrant. Spring migration has been happening, but not so quickly. I have noted robins and mourning doves along my walks and one day a red-winged blackbird sang from the swamp. In the open waters of a nearby river, I observed a pair of hooded mergansers. Usually, I expect more migrants by this time. Among the plants, I have found crocuses and dandelions in bloom. Sliver maples hold male or female flowers while the alder catkins have matured with pollen.

As we began April, we had a seasonal snowfall total of seventy-five inches and a diminishing snowpack. It looked like the snow season was waning. Mother Nature had other plans. It varied greatly in the northland, but during the first five days of April, the Weather Service in Duluth had recorded more snow than all of March. Being wet, hard to handle and late in the season, spring snows are often not appreciated.

But I have found some values in the snow at this time. It is a great time to see animal tracks. Wet snow tends to give good impressions of footprints; neat and clear. In dry powder, it is often difficult to see clear footprints. Also with milder temperatures, more wildlife is active now. During recent walks, I have located clear footprints of deer, fox, coyote, bobcat, squirrel, hare, weasel, fisher, skunk and raccoon (still no bear).

Spring wet snow is of value for what is to come. Unlike a rain of equal moisture content in which much of the water might run off on the still frozen ground, the wet snow keeps the precipitation here. And as it melts, it goes on to low sites; replenishing the vernal ponds that will soon be appearing. I looked at these pond sites a few weeks ago and noticed that they held snow, but could use more. The snows of April are giving that moisture to the ponds and maybe helping the frogs and other critters that call these small ponds home. These replenished ponds will come alive in coming weeks with sights and sounds of frogs; thanks to late-season snows.

April 23, 2022

Early Season Butterflies

In late April, we witness several spring happenings that have expected and anticipated; even though we've seen them before. Thawing ice in wetlands; small ponds are first to escape from the winter covering, but they are quickly followed by swamps and usually late in the month, lakes will undergo ice-out. (This varies greatly in different years.) We have experienced these in previous years, but worth seeing again.

Our list of desired repeats in the spring continues. With the greening of grasses, I also delight in seeing the first dandelions and crocuses in bloom. In the woods, green growth of leeks (ramps) followed by early spring wildflowers; always a welcome sight. But there is much more.

Several times in recent weeks, I visited the St. Louis River as the opening water expanded. Here were plenty of waterfowl. Geese, swans, mergansers and ducks were a delight to observe. Calls of sandhill cranes and red-winged blackbirds came from the shore where herons hunted. In a nearby open space, woodcocks performed their ritual flights at dusk. None of these were new sights or sounds, but each spring they keep us coming back. As the month continues, I'll search for phoebes, thrushes, swallows, sapsuckers, sparrows and warblers in yards and hearing frog calls from newly open vernal ponds.

Recently, I found a flock of robins in a field and juncos took over the yard. And I noted the anticipated flock of white pelicans at the river. These large white birds huddled against the cool winds had a black-necked cormorant in their midst. I've seen all of these bird news before, but worth seeing them all again.

I also walked a trail in the nearby woods. Here, I scared up a butterfly that was basking in the springtime sunlight. Orange and black wings with spots of white, identified this as a Compton tortoiseshell. This butterfly with a colorful wingspan of about two and one-half inches is a member of a group called anglewings. Each year (I have never had an exception) it is an anglewing that is the first butterfly to be seen in spring. The reason for this is that, unlike most other butterflies, they hibernate as adults and are quick to wake and fly on warming days. Other members of anglewings include: Milbert's tortoiseshell, mourning cloak, comma and question mark. The last two are named after markings on wing undersides. In addition to being winter hibernators, they have camouflage undersides of wings. Startled while basking on a tree trunk, they close wings and blend in with the bark.

When it comes to dealing with winter, butterflies run the gamut. Many overwinter as eggs, some as larvae. Others will spend the cold in the pupa stage (chrysalis for butterflies, cocoon for moths). The anglewings hibernate as adults. (Hibernation with insects is often called diapause.) And there are those that migrate; best known is the monarch.

Anglewings choose a site behind bark or beneath boards to winter. (On a fall day once, I watched as a Compton tortoiseshell flew onto the porch and slipped into a crack; not to come out until spring.) Waking early; March, April or maybe even May, they do not have many flowers to visit for nectar. And so, they feed of sap oozing from maples, rotten fruits, animal droppings and maybe pollen from tree catkins. Later in spring, they mate. The next generation grows up feeding on leaves of birch, willow or aspen and are adults for summer and fall; hibernating later. Like many other spring things, I've seen these early season butterflies before, but they are a joy to see again.

April 30, 2022

Return of the Insect-Eating Phoebe

Like many in the Northland, I feed birds near the house during the winter. Looking out at the activities of chickadees, nuthatches, woodpeckers and jays nearly every day adds much to the cold season. About mid-January, this winter dining became more crowded with the addition of redpolls. As the winter days passed, the birds continued, but during mild days, I noticed fewer. And so, as January became February and March, I planned to stop feeding in April. But when April showers became snow hours, I decided to continue and the birds responded.

Some of the largest numbers of birds that I hosted for the entire season happened as the spring unfolded. Not only did some winter birds return for more snacks, but also many migrants paused to eat on their northing route. Redpolls that maybe are gone by April remained and often filled the feeders. They were joined by the black and white juncos (a type of sparrow) feeding on seeds on the ground. Scattered among this group reaching two hundred on some days, were a few bright red purple finches and yellow goldfinches. Other sparrows; song, tree and fox sparrows appeared as well. The fox sparrows were a delight to watch. Larger than the others, they have a reddish-brown plumage and their feeding habits on the ground are done with ambitious scratching.

Despite the slow-moving season advancing, I have seen other migrants. Bald eagles were on the river ice while geese, swans, mergansers, ducks, pelicans and cormorants were in the open sites. During my walks, I also noted red-winged blackbirds, mourning doves and robins. I observed woodcocks performing their strange dance and flight while ruffed grouse drummed and turkeys gobbled. Spring is happening.

And so, about a week ago, I took a walk to look for plants. I had seen crocus and dandelions bloom, maybe I'd see more in the woods. I went to a site where many ramps (wild leek) are quick to green the forest floor in spring and maybe, I'll also see hepatica. Despite mild conditions and plenty of sunlight on this day, I found neither. As I was getting ready to go, I noticed a bird fly into the woods, alighting on a branch. A closer look revealed that it was about seven inches and nearly all gray; lighter on the undersides. As it sat, it pumped the tail up and down. I was watching a phoebe.

Phoebes are common in the region, often seen in our yards since they readily accept porches and garages as sites to build nests. They get their name from their two-syllable "fee-be" call; frequently repeated. Phoebes belong to a group of birds known as flycatchers; they feed almost completely on insects. The woods where I saw it has plenty of insects; even in spring.

The day after I saw the phoebe, we received several inches of snow with chilly temperatures. I wondered how it survived. We have another six kinds of flycatchers in the region; least, alder, great crested, olive-sided flycatchers; wood peewee and kingbird. Only the phoebe is an early migrant. Returning early in spring has the advantage of a bird claiming an available site to nest; chilly temperatures and snow can make finding insects a bit difficult. But the phoebes will survive. They can and do eat seeds and berries when needed and they may do their bug collecting near open water or along roads; both of these locations are a bit warmer and attract insects. Yes, the phoebe was a welcome sight of an early spring insect-eating bird; there will be more.

May 7, 2022

Red Maples Bloom a Bit Late

Following the patterns of January, February and March; April's temperature this year was several degrees below normal. The thawing month remained frozen with ice-out being a couple of weeks later than expected. However, the days continue to get longer and warm in May.

During a couple of recent walks, I noticed plenty of the migrating birds that showed up in the region in April. Here they rest and feed before moving on. Along the roads, have been flocks of juncos mixed with other sparrows; white-throated, fox, tree and song. In the woods was a large group of robins and also among these trees, I saw the camouflage brown creepers, energetic ruby-crowned kinglets, yellow-rumped warblers and a patient phoebe and hermit thrush. Yellow-bellied sapsuckers joined resident woodpeckers to add drumming to the springtime woods. I would have expected that the redpolls would be gone by this time, but I did see a few. Also, despite the days being chilly and cool in the sunlight I found a mourning cloak butterfly (another late arrival to the spring scene). And a waking chipmunk scamped by.

A year ago, a walk in the woods in early May would have also included a few more kinds of warblers and sparrows. Besides these birds, last year, I noted many kinds of spring wild flowers in bloom. In a single walk, I found hepaticas, spring beauties, bloodroots, marsh marigolds, trout-lilies, violets, bellworts and trilliums; even the first fiddleheads were up. Not so this year; I had to search to find a single hepatica flowering.

Not as obvious as last year's birds and wild flowers, but this late spring is happening. I find that a good place to look for spring is in the trees. Here the buds that were in the winter weather for months are opening; also, later than normal. The furry buds of willow and aspen that dared to open in March have now grown into longer catkins. These structures, rich with pollen hang from alders in the wetland; nearly a month late. The tiny hazel flowers are showing now too. Instead of seeing the first green leaves growing on trees (usually elderberry) in early May, we are seeing the colorful flowers of red maples. Normally, I find these small delightful flowers on the large trees in late April. This year, it is May.

When it comes to flowers on trees, maples reveal quite a variety. The red maples are a lot like those of the early silver maples. With both of these, the female flowers (pistillate) and the male flowers (staminate) are borne on separate trees (usually). The female flowers of red maple live up to the name and are a bright red color. Unlike tree blossoms that we'll see later, they are small and without petals. Male flowers are on threads (filaments) where pollen forms in capsules called anthers.

Later this month, the strange flowers of sugar maples and boxelders will develop. Both hold male flowers hanging on long stalks so that the pollen can blow from here to the female flowers; also on stalks, but shorter. Both are green. Not until June, do the white spike flowers of mountain maple form. The non-native Norway maples have their yellow-green flora in clusters among the leaves.

We had to wait a bit longer than normal this year, but now in May, we can see the numerous small red female flowers of red maples; male trees nearby. Looking at these trees, we see that spring things may be are late, but still happening.

May 14, 2022

May Walks; Dawn, Daytime, Dusk

I find that these spring days, after snow and ice have receded and before warmth and mosquitoes move in, are excellent for taking leisurely walks; noting what is happening in nature. And these wanderings are never disappointing; three times a day.

Dawn. It's cool, in the thirties, clear and calm when I walk. The show of Jupiter, Venus, Mars and Saturn is lost in the rising sun, but much more is going on. In the yard, I hear drumming of sapsuckers that found maples with dripping sap. Here too are songs of robin, phoebe, song sparrow and mourning dove. Ruffed grouse drum in the woods and a loon calls from the nearby lake; finally free of ice. My route takes me past a swamp and a pond. Without ice, there is plenty of bird activity; some to rest, others to nest. On the surface are mallards, wood ducks, buffleheads, hooded mergansers; and a group of about thirty ring-necked ducks. A pair of Canada geese are beginning a nest along the shore. Also at the edge, red-winged blackbird males are singing; after a month, females will soon join. In the distance, I hear loud calls of sandhill cranes. A new May day has begun.

Daytime. Temperatures have climbed to the fifties when I return for the mid-day walk. Once again, pleasant conditions prevail; making for a slow movement through the woods. No pesky bugs, but I do see a couple of insects of note. At one sunny site, I am greeted by two basking butterflies; a Compton tortoiseshell and a mourning cloak; both are awakened anglewings. Some arriving migrant birds are seen too. A group of juncos feed on the forest floor. Tree and white-throated sparrows join them. A brown creeper works its way up a tree trunk while small birds flit in the trees. I recognize a yellow-rumped warbler and two of the smallest birds of the northland; a ruby-crowned kinglet and a winter wren. There's also a silent hermit thrush here and a loud-calling flicker. The nearby vernal ponds that I pass abound with calls from wood and chorus frogs (first heard on April 28). Scanning the forest floor for spring wildflowers, I locate only hepatica in bloom; a bit later than normal, others will follow. Here too, are the abundant green shoots of wild leek (ramps). The trees tell more. The minute purple flowers of hazel are opening near their catkins. Red maple buds are numerous with their show of color. And the large buds of elderberry speak of leaves to come soon.

Dusk. The evening is clear, a waxing crescent moon in the west and a cooling temperature in the forties. It's another great time for a walk. Before I leave the porch, I hear a sound that I have been waiting for recently. From overhead is the winnowing sound of the Wilson's snipe. Snipe are shorebirds that feed along the edges of wetlands; putting their long bills into the damp soil in search of small prey. Mostly brown, they are easy to pass by unnoticed. But now, when the male is trying to get the attention of the female, he does so by movement of wings and tail in flight; causing the air to flow and produce a whirling "hu-hu-hu" noise, known as winnowing; a regular part of dusk and dawn sounds. Walking past a vernal pond, I hear that wood and chorus frogs have been joined by a third kind; spring peepers. A couple of barred owls call. Canada geese and sandhill cranes are flying and calling. A wonderful May day is passing into darkness; there will be more.

May 21, 2022

Red Cup Fungus with Spring Flowers

Taking woods walks at this time of May is wandering through constant happenings. I've learned to go back and forth in looking between the surrounding trees to note the newly-arrived migrant birds and keep an eye on the forest floor where I walk to observe the vernal spring wildflowers. Both abound during May and the walks are filled with plenty of sightings.

While the birds give sounds and quick movements to follow, the spring wild flowers do not. Calls and songs from orioles, grosbeaks, tanagers, flycatchers, thrushes and vireos can keep us looking among the branches for visual confirmation. Warblers are much more varied and if we are at the right place at the right time, we may be able to make note of ten to fifteen kinds. It seems like most of the warblers, despite their abundance, can be a challenge to observe. They are small; they often move among the branches and despite the name of warbler, do not usually sing loudly.

Seeing the wild flowers that now are opening their colorful petals in these weeks are less of a challenge to see. Their timing is critical in May as they grow leaves, buds and flowers rapidly. Before the leaf canopy develops overhead and they ae shaded, the forest floor flora needs to get the sunlight that penetrates through the trees for their development. Soon this woods will be shaded. When conditions are right, they take over these sunlit sites. Walking among all this color is a delight and we can see at least a dozen kinds on these woods walks. Beginning with hepatica that is soon joined by spring beauty, bloodroot and anemones. Trout-lilies, toothworts, wild ginger, violets, bellworts and trilliums are also all regulars to be seen now. Each has colored petals and open for a short flowering season. On a sunlit day, they cover the forest floor with color; coming back the next day shows even more. They invite us to keep looking down as we walk. With all of this thick forest floor flora, it would seem as though there is little else that can grow here. But there is plenty more.

The wild flowers are mostly white and yellow among the leafy greens. And there is more green. Unrolling here too are the thick new growths of ferns. Due to this shape, they are frequently called fiddleheads. Fern stems are underground all winter and now in spring, these new leaves (fronds) reach above the ground and unroll for the new season. Unlike spring wild flowers, ferns thrive in the shade formed by the impending arboreal leaf growth.

But as I walk among these flowers and fiddleheads recently; yellows, whites and greens, I paused when I saw a growth that was bright red. Taking a closer look, I discovered that a cup-shaped fungus was growing among these plants. Like many fungi, this one, a scarlet cup fungus (Sarcoscypha sp.), on the ground was feeding on rotting matter. The cup of the fungus was about two inches across and circular shaped. Bright red in the cup, white beneath. Scarlet cup belongs to a group called sac fungi. Unlike mushrooms, spores develop in tiny sacs; being released when ripe. With this fungus, spores are in the cup. Perhaps the most unique feature of scarlet cup is that it grows in spring. May fungi are unusual and except for an occasional morel or false morel, we are not likely to see any. But this bright red fungus is a delight to see.

May 28, 2022

Jack-in-the-Pulpit; Unusual Flower

By the time that we get to late May, we are in a different environment than the beginning of the month. Trees that had been bare at the start, presently are growing green leaves. The forest floor that may even have had a snow cover, now has another coating; this being green foliage and white and yellow florals; abundant spring wild flowers. These perennials that we never tire of seeing each spring began with hepaticas, but was quickly followed by spring beauties, bloodroots, anemones, Dutchman's breeches, trout-lilies, violets, bellworts, marsh marigolds and trilliums. Each plant grows rapidly to form new leaves and flowers in the available vernal sunlight; before shade moves in.

But the shade does come. Elderberries, aspens and willows begin this arboreal greening; quickly spreading to ironwoods, birches and poplars. In the midst of this foliage, some open buds form blossoms of white petals. Wild plums, pin cherries and juneberries add color above to go with that below. The forest greening comes to a fruition with large trees forming leaves; maples, basswoods and oaks.

In the shade created by such canopies, a whole new set of wild flowers develop. Not as well-known as the earlier ones: baneberries, starflowers, sarsaparillas, wild lily-of-the-valleys (Canada Mayflowers), bunchberries (Canada dogwood), Clintonia (corn-lily) and columbines are able to tolerate the shade. Except for columbines that glow with bright red petals and yellow Clintonia, most are white.

However, there is a flower, mostly green, that stands up in the woods at this time. Besides the predominant color being green, it also has a unique shape flower with large leaves. This latter half of May is when the jack-in-the-pulpit will bloom.

No petals or sepals are visible on the plant, instead it stands with a cylindrical growth from the stem that holds a part sticking up. This part is known as the spadix; the "jack" of jack-in-the-pulpit. Over the spadix is a leafy growth that is called a spathe. Together, they reveal an unusual flower, what some call a person on a pulpit with a canopy overhead; jack-in-the-pulpit. I find that they are quick to form the leaves and spadix and spathe and later they will grow taller.

The large leaves also grow from the stem divide into two big leaves with three leaflets. Stems rise from an underground corm. (This underground growth is very bitter; making us wonder about another name for the plant is "Indian turnip".) Plants can grow to be a couple of feet tall and are likely seen in damp woods. Plants are either male or female; the reproductive structures are found beneath the spadix, in the lower part of the cylindrical floral growth. Not being very colorful, mostly green, (they often have purple on some parts), they get pollinated by insects attracted by odor. When pollinated, the female plants will grow a cluster of red-orange berries in summer; ripe in fall.

It is interesting to note that a plant that was male one year may be female the next year; and a female one year may be a male the following. Apparently, the success of the reproduction can determine this. Yes, "jack-in-the-pulpit" may become "jill-in-the-pulpit". And like most of the spring wild flowers that we see each year, they are native plants and perennials.

Though an unusual plant, jack-in-the-pulpit belongs to the Arum family which has two other northland plants as members; water calla and skunk cabbage. I always find the discovery all of these plants to be delightful parts of the spring flora of late May.

June 4, 2022

The Arrival of the Monarchs

The ice out was later than normal (about two weeks). The growth of the spring wild flowers, though quite prolific, was delayed more than a week due to the melting to the snowpack and thawing ground. Cooler temperatures also slowed the greening of trees in May. Our waiting was worth it as the month of May was winding down, we had plenty of wild flowers with trees blossoming and leafing. Warming temperatures and moisture gave the spring that we were waiting for.

The bird migration was a bit slow in the northland and the ice cover on rivers and lakes postponed the arrival of geese, swans, ducks and mergansers. Others, such as red-winged blackbirds and woodcocks, were also noted at a later date. Songbird migration in April was less than expected; the first warbler (yellow-rumped), phoebe, tree swallows, sparrows and hermit thrushes, all a bit late. And then we moved into May.

Instead of a month with temperatures considerably below the norm, they proved to be about normal; a blend of chill and warmth with plenty of precipitation. The rest of the spring migrant songbirds made their appearance. During the weeks of May, we saw the return of the colorful and well-known rose-breasted grosbeaks, Baltimore orioles, scarlet tanagers and ruby-throated hummingbirds. And those not as well-known: thrushes, flycatchers, vireos, wrens and a huge variety of warblers. It is interesting to note that most of these migrants came back at about the time expected. They did not appear to be delayed by the late arrival of spring. The reason for this is that many May migrants winter in the tropics. Wintering there, they did not deal with our colder-than-normal winter and late spring. And so, with the increasing length of daylight, they flew north. This timing is important to these insect-eating birds. They need to be here when the insects emerge and caterpillars feed on the newly-opening leaves. Warblers are often hard to see, but with the slow leafing, I saw many; fifteen kinds in one day.

Now as their arrival lessens, we look for another migrant; the monarch butterfly. Probably the best known (and loved) butterfly, their migration is often referred to. Spending summer in the northland, they lay eggs on milkweeds and this next generation; maturing late in the season, will be the ones to fly about 1200 miles to the wintering site in the Transvolcanic Mountains of Mexico.

This south-bound flight is done by the grandchildren of the ones arriving here in spring. After hanging onto branches in a mountain forest, they leave in late winter to go north. Getting to the southern states, they locate new growth of milkweeds where they lay eggs and subsequently die. These young grow up on the milkweeds and as adults go north to our region; arriving usually in early June. (I have seen some years when they are here before May 20; others are near mid-June.)

Monarchs are large and mostly orange; rather easy to discern from other butterflies at this time. Also called milkweed butterflies since they lay eggs on this plant. Young caterpillars grow up feeding on milkweeds. (The name of monarch is believed to have been given to them in honor of King William III of England; the Prince of Orange.)

Though some local butterflies hibernate for winter, most of the variety seen in June, hatch from eggs or emerge out of chrysalis. But the one that we look forward to seeing is a migrant. Once arrived, we will monitor the progress and populations of these summer monarchs.

June 11, 2022

Yellow Warblers: Residents

May has lived up to one of the names applied to this month; the greening month. Beginning as bare woods; ending fully green. Shrubs and small trees began this change with; larger trees being late. Once foliated, the woods that was so open and filled with sunlight became one of shade. Another attribute to this time, spring wild flowers, have waned. Though there are several species that are tolerant of shade and continue to flower, the time of spring beauties, trout-lilies and trilliums is a memory. And the forest floor now holds an abundance of ferns. Not only do these plants thrive in shade, they also grow quickly in June's moisture. At the woods' edge are small trees blooming. The trio of plum, juneberry and pin cherry that began with white flowers was followed by elderberry, crab apple and chokecherry with apple and lilac in our yards. The May's flowering has moved, but still here in June.

Another happening that is so much part of May is the migration of songbirds into the northland from southern wintering. Migrants began arriving in earlier months with flights of raptors followed by many water birds. In April, some songbirds began to return. During thirty-one days of May, we saw the arrival of many more: thrushes, flycatchers, vireos, orioles, grosbeaks, tanagers, wrens and hummingbirds. But the most diverse group of spring migrants are warblers.

Each May, twenty-six species of these small birds move through the northland. They arrive at about the same time as the emergence of insects and caterpillars among the newly-formed leaves. They feed wherever they appear. Not with much singing, but with plenty of movement, they flit through the branches. As long as the trees are not filled with new leaves, we are able to see them. With a pair of binoculars (and patience), we can discern many. (Warbler identification can be difficult, but just watching their activity in the trees is a fine way to get acquainted with these migrants.)

About half of this group will remain to nest while others continue to journey further north where they breed in boreal forests. One that I look for each year not only as a migrant, but also a resident, is the yellow warbler. While May is the month of migrant songbirds, June is the month of breeding songbirds. Yellow warblers are both. These small birds are not the only warbler to have this color. Plenty of yellow can be seen in about a dozen others. A few of these also have yellow in their names; yellow-rumped warbler and yellowthroat (not to be confused with a yellow-throated warbler; further south). Others, such as Wilson's, Nashville and mourning warblers have bodies that are largely yellow. Yellow warblers continue to add color and song to the scene.

Birds are about five inches long. Males have yellow feathers, but also red streaks on the undersides while females are completely yellow. They seek areas of small trees and shrubs for nests. During my walks in June, I regularly pass a swamp that has a growth of alders and willows along the edge. As I search for their bright yellow bodies, I also hear males sing territorial songs at these nesting sites. The song has been given the memory phrase of "sweet, sweet, I am so sweet". Like many other local breeding songbirds, the song is repeated daily through June and early July; best heard in the early morning. Singing and raising young will continue until the fledglings have moved on. But in June, they add much color and melodies to the days.

June18, 2022

Flowers in the Shady Forests

The woods is shady as I walk on this June day. I'm quickly greeted by hordes of local mosquitoes. But the walk is lovely and worth putting up with these companions. I'm not alone and I hear songs of red-eyed and yellow-throated vireos in the branches while ovenbirds and veeries sing and call from near the ground. It seems like that they only recently returned from wintering sites, but now they are nesting. Raven calls remind me that they have new families as well.

Despite the shade, the forest floor is filled with leaves of green plants. Apparently, these plants do quite well with the less sunlight than what was here weeks ago. Most obvious are the ferns, some of which are up to my waist. The three tallest kinds are ostrich, interrupted and lady ferns. All appear to be thriving in the present conditions. With some looking, I also see oak, northern beech and sensitive ferns with a few maidenhairs. Mixed with them are new growths of their cousins; the horsetails. Lush and green as these plants are, they do not produce flowers. But flowering plants are here and I find many on this mild day.

Gone are the ephemerals of spring beauties, bloodroots and trout-lilies, but as I walk, I find their replacements. Some of the June forest floor flora are easy to see and grow tall. Baneberry with its white cluster flowers stands up a couple of feet. Sarsaparilla has ball floral groupings under the purplish spread leaves. The bent over plants of Solomon's-seal and rose twisted-stalk have flowers below the curved stems. Nodding trillium, a lesser-known trillium, also has its three-petal white flower beneath three leaves. Starflower with its seven petals and bunchberry are close to the ground. At two separated sites, I locate a couple of lady-slipper orchids; yellow and pink. Finding these plants is a true delight in the woods. But two others are the most abundant at this time; littering the forest floor. Often, it is hard to step without seeing or stepping on the Clintonia and Canada mayflowers.

Clintonia (Clintonia borealis) is also known as blue-bead lily (later in the summer, the plant holds blue berries). Large lily-like leaves grow from the ground as does the stalk holding yellow flowers. (And it is sometimes called corn-lily.) But it is the Canada mayflower (Maianthemum canadense), a small plant reaching only a few inches above the ground, that is most numerous in the June woods.

Also known as wild lily-of-the-valley, Canada mayflower has oval leaves on nearly every available spot of the northland forest floor. Some have flowers, but most do not. It is common with many of the forest flowers that they are sterile; not producing blossoms. If the leaf is alone, it does not have a flower, but if a second leaf (occasionally, a third) grows on the stalk, there will be a spike of white flowers. Only a couple of inches of white, but adding quite a lot to the shaded woods.

Though they are often called wild or false lily-of-the valley, I don't think there is much of a resemblance to the domestic plant of yards and gardens. It does; however, have a look-alike. The three-leaf false Solomon's-seal can be confused with Canada mayflower. But this plant has three leaves and is a resident of swampy bog sites. Canada mayflower produces green berries after flowering; later developing into reddish fruits by fall. Forest wild flowers of June will not last long and soon the colorful flora of this month will be seen in the fields and roadsides, but for now, they add much to a shady woods walk.

June 25, 2022

The Moving Otter Family

The last week of June; the summer solstice has come and gone. Sunrises and sunsets continue to be later each day and very slowly, the daylight starts to get shorter. This is the time roadsides and fields show a diversity of wild flowers. Spring is over when the flowering of open sites outnumbers the woods' florals. Daisies, hawkweeds, buttercups, vetches, yarrows and clovers all add their colors to this summer bouquet. And I'm glad to see irises along the edge of the pond that I walk by are in bloom; adding blue to the yellows of pond-lilies floating further out. Chokecherries that had teamed with lilacs for arboreal blooms, have faded and are being replaced by viburnums, dogwoods and mountain-maples; while red maples form new seeds. The growing month continues with plants, but we see plenty with wildlife as well.

Bird songs continue each day. The singing males proclaim territorial ownership to home sites for raising the young. Besides songs of these birds, sounds of chipping nestlings also come from the trees. Young crows, ravens and owls can be heard each day; often following the parents. Babies of geese, ducks and mergansers also stay with the adults in local ponds and swamps while the chicks of sandhill cranes explore fields; with supervision. Turtles use these days to travel up from the water to find a proper site to deposit eggs while the summer frogs; mink and green, add their calls to the persistent gray treefrogs at the lakes. At numerous wetlands, dragonflies of several species climb out of their aquatic youth and take wing as adults. Among all the flora, we can see a variety of butterflies daily. Along with the mosquitoes at night, this is the time of large moths; Luna, Cecropia and Polyphemus with breeding fireflies contributing bioluminescence to the scene.

Often, we'll see young mammals of the year (or last year); sometimes without us searching for them. I have noted a young beaver that moved into a pond recently where there was none last year. In a similar way, a muskrat appeared in a swamp. They show signs of dispersal from their families. And as I sat in the yard a few days ago, a young bear came by to explore. Finding this site already occupied, it decided to wander off. However, the local chipmunks and squirrels continue to stay. It has been interesting to watch the activities of adult squirrels as they leap through the trees; followed by the young. Parents perform some daring jumps between trees; to find more food, or to escape the young. In the roadsides, young rabbits pilfer while a couple of spotted fawns follow the doe off into the woods.

I should not have been surprised as I walked between two swamps one morning when I saw an otter family. Looking ahead on my road route, I observed a critter cross from one swamp to the other. I was able to recognize it as an otter. It was carrying something in its mouth. I suspected prey. When it returned, I realized that it was not prey, but she was coming back for another young to be taken. It took three trips to transplant the family from one wetland home to another; across a road. She was able to avoid the dangerous traffic. And when I got closer, I watched as the family swam off in their new territory; most-likely completely oblivious of me. Yes, June continues to be a growing time for local flora and fauna.

Third Quarter

July 2, 2022

The Patient Pied-billed Grebe

My daily walks take me by a pond close to the road allowing for very good viewing. As we went through the weeks of spring, this wetland provided exceptional watching seasonal changes with birds. It began before ice out when in late March, the first red-winged blackbird arrived back on territory. The bird immediately sang its "konk-a-lee" song; causing me to stop, look and listen. (The females do not return to this site for another month, and so these songs were aimed at other males, letting them know that this place was taken.)

As the days slowly warmed, I heard the flight sounds of snipes and guttural calls of sandhill cranes. In anticipation of the coming thaw, a couple of Canada geese settled onto the ice to wait for open water. Once this melting event occurred, they were joined by other geese and the large loud trumpeter swans. They remained for the duration of the ice out, but then departed for elsewhere. But the arrival of water birds continued. In the next weeks, I watched as mallards, wood ducks, ring-necked ducks, buffleheads and shovelers came by. These ducks that seemed in no hurry to leave did so slowly until only a few ring-necked ducks remained. Since these were all males and still on the water as spring turned into summer, I suspected that they were non-breeding ones that found this pond as a safe place to be for the warm season.

Among other birds that live near the wetland, I observed the insect-catcher habits of phoebes and kingbirds. Catching insects in another way were the tree swallows that regularly flew low over the water. A few birds that did not live here, but came by for a visit included great blue heron and the smaller green heron. I was surprised one day to see a sora rail among the aquatic vegetation. But two others (non-ducks) stayed and added much to the season at the pond; hooded mergansers and pied-billed grebe.

The merganser pair was early to arrive. A white patch on the male's head made it easy to see. However, when he left, their time here seemed to be over. But one June day, she was seen paddling with a close-knit group of seven young right behind. She will stay and attempt to raise the family here; with enough food and shelter. The nest of the hooded merganser is in hollow trees and it explains why I did not see her until the precocial young hatched and went to the pond.

The story of the pied-billed grebe was a bit different. For a few weeks, I saw the grebe in the shallows. Each day that I came by, I would see this small gray-brown bird with black markings on the bill. Occasionally diving for a fish snack, it returned, never going far from this shallow-water site. I realized what was going on. This was the male and he was waiting and watching as the female stayed on a nearby nest. The grebe chose a site where a patch of leatherleaf, cattails, irises and reeds emerged from under water; providing shelter for the semi-floating nest. He remained among the floating leaves of water-lilies as the days of incubation passed. Finally, one day in early summer, he was gone; and so was the whole family. The hidden site was fine for a nest, but they needed more room to raise the young. In the protection of the pre-dawn, they departed. My summertime walks here will be different now, but still much to see as we go through these months.

July 9, 2022

Berry Season Begins

July is usually considered our month of greatest summer. The hottest times normally happen now and thunderstorms are common during these thirty-one days. Passing the summer solstice, the daylight slowly decreases; sunrises get later, sunsets earlier. But it is also the time when we see the results of earlier growths. The nestlings of June become the fledglings of July. A whole new batch of wildflowers bloom along the roadsides. Each day, there are more fireweeds, milkweeds and evening primroses; keeping every walk interesting. A few goldenrods, asters and sunflowers are with them. In the woods, among the decaying leaves and logs, mushrooms make their quick appearance; few at first, but becoming more common later. And it is the beginning of the seed, berry and fruit season.

The ripe seeds of woody plants began in late May with the fluffy material that drifted throughout the region. Within this cottony stuff were the tiny seeds of aspens and willows. They were being dispersed by the wind. These were followed by the samaras of red and silver maples. Their winged seeds spun in helicopter fashion in a dispersal of their own; again, relying on the wind for spreading the seeds.

Looking back to May and early June, we might remember the blossoms of small trees that added colors to the roadsides. With petals and aroma, they attracted attention of insects and were pollinated. Though we no longer saw the obvious flowers after they received pollen, their berries and fruits have been developing. Now, we can see these results.

During a recent woods walk, I noticed some red among the green leaves. Stopping for a closer look, I found a pair of fused berries on the branch of a small plant. This plant; fly honeysuckle (Lonicera canadensis) was one of the first shrubs to flower in spring and now, it is the first one to produce berries. Flowers were borne in close-knit pairs and now, the berries show this same arrangement. Sighting this plant told me that the berry season had begun in the northland. A day later, I discovered and devoured the first wild strawberry. Tiny when compared to the domestic type, it was still delicious and told of more to come. And July tends to be full of wild berries.

The berries of fly honeysuckle and wild strawberry are followed by dewberry (dwarf blackberry) and red elderberry (usually the first tree to leaf out in spring, is quick to form its red berries). Juneberry (serviceberry) and pin cherry; small trees that flowered in the roadsides of May, are next. A few smaller plants of the woods; baneberry and blue-bead lily produce theirs too; red, white and blue. Most, not all, of the earlier berries are edible, preparing us for raspberries, blueberries and thimbleberries. And there are plenty of domestic ones too.

Berries vary in their shapes, colors and sizes but they all have seeds on or within. These berries are another example of plants being able to disperse their seeds. Berries (also could be called fruits) will not drift in the breeze and so another method of spreading seeds needs to work. Plants make use of the mobile animals. Being bright colored and tasty, the berries are quick to be discovered and consumed by birds and small mammals (and bears). Following this eating, undigested seeds are deposited at sites away from the start. We berry pickers during this season, also play a role in dispersing seeds; not quite like birds and other mammals. And we enjoy the products of July.

July 16, 2022

A Few Flowers Bloom in Shady Woods

The days of July provide a constant look at the diverse roadside botany. While day lilies count off the days of summer in the yard, a myriad of wildflowers gives us a continuous daily glow from the roadsides. Taking a walk on the same route each day may sound like a boring thing to do, but I find that the flora here have a variety. Each walk has more to see.

Some of these plants that were so common in June may still be with us and it is not unusual to find daisies, hawkweeds, trefoils, vetches and yarrows lingering into this month. And we get a peak at what is to come next month as early goldenrods, asters and sunflowers blend with the flora of July. But July flowers, those of mid-summer, demand attention.

I find a trio that dominate the scene at this time. Purple flowers of fireweeds and milkweeds continue to unfold new florets each day. Though they both have the suffix of "weed", they are each native. Fireweed and milkweed patches are great to observe, but there is more. Evening primrose, the third of the trio, produces four large yellow petals as daylight fades. Other flowers present in the open spaces; native and non-native, include thistles, cow parsnip, mullein, tansy, bergamot, st. johnswort, butter and eggs, wood lily, black-eyed susan and sweetclover. Milkweeds even provide more variety with swamp milkweed in the wetlands and the orange butterfly weed in the fields. All these flora thrive in the sunny open areas, but some growth also happens in the shade of the nearby woods.

A woods walk at this time will be amongst a plethora of emerging mushrooms and other fungi. Though highly diverse, most do not grow tall or last long, but not so with the ferns. These leafy plants do well in the shade and it is not unusual to find ostrich and interrupted ferns and maybe lady and cinnamon ferns that have grown up to our shoulders. And among the fungi and ferns, there are a few flowers here too.

The strange Indian-pipe plant has no chlorophyll and so looks white. It does not need sunlight and is common in the shady forests of summer. But I also find one that does have green leaves with its ample flowers of white or pink growing under the arboreal canopy; shinleaf (Pyrola).

Since they grow in the non-sunny forests and since they are usually less than a foot tall, shinleaf is not well known. There are sites where several grow, but they do not have the clusters that we might see with the flora of the open. But once discovered, they cause the woods walker to pause and see them more clearly. Plants unfold a rosette of oval leaves that are only slightly above the forest floor. Different species of shinleaf have different leaves as well as flowers. From the center grows a straight stem with many flowers surrounding. Most of the five-petaled plants are white, one kind is pink. The delightful colored petals have a long pistil extending from them.

These beautiful plants do very well in the shade of the woods; often without being seen by us. They are able to grow in this lesser lit site because their green leaves remain on the plant all winter and are able to make use of the early spring sunlight; providing needed resources to survive in the shade. Yes, there is plenty of roadside botany in July, but much to see in the forest as well.

July 23, 2022

Indigo Buntings Sing Throughout July

A regular happening with songbirds in spring is that they will live up to their names and sing when arriving back from migration. May is when most of these migrants that nest in the northland come back from wintering sites. Once settled into a proclaimed territory, the males will produce unique sounds that we call singing. It is often very easy to identify the singer just by listening to his notes; most are diagnostic and species specific. His reasons for producing these vocals is twofold. He is getting the attention of available females. (Many songbirds have already mated by the time they have arrived back north.) Once the couple moves into a home territory, he continues to sing; letting others of his kind know that this place is taken.

Within this chosen site, the songbirds go on to the next phase of their lives together; nest building, laying eggs and incubating them. While May was the month of migration, June is nesting and incubation time. In the midst of this, the local male continues his singing; a daily reminder to others that this home is not to trespassed on. These proclamations each day, usually starting in the early dawn when it is quiet and calm and continue throughout the day and month. When the hatched young are fed by the adults such singing is not stopped. June is nestling time blended with bird songs. Any walk at this time is one of hearing our local avians in song. And then the young birds grow up.

While June is nestlings; July is fledglings. Too big for the nest, they leave; often staying fed by the adults and moving around with them. But things have changed. With the family raised, the vocal proclamations of territory are no longer needed. As we proceed through July, bird songs become less and less. By now, late in the month, only a few are still singing.

During a recent walk, I noted four kinds of birds that had persisted with songs at this late date. Near the yard, I heard a song sparrow. At the swamp, a yellowthroat sang. And the most persistent of all, the red-eyed vireos were singing from high branches. The fourth bird nests at the woods edge and has a brilliant blue plumage; the indigo bunting.

Indigo buntings, birds of about five inches long get this name from the nearly all blue body feathers of the male. A close look may reveal wings are nearly black, but it is the blue that is so obvious as the bird sings from shrubs and small trees. Not only does the male have a color that is noticeable, so is his song. The repeated phrases of "sweet-sweet chew-chew sweet-sweet"; lasting two to four seconds is easy to hear. He sings it regularly from the time of arrival in spring; many times of the day. (I expect to see and hear indigo buntings by about June 1.) And he continues to sing this memorable song well into July; maybe in August.

In a great example of sexual dimorphism, while he is blue, she is brown and "sparrow-like". Indigo buntings are in the same family as cardinals and rose-breasted grosbeaks; also showing sexual dimorphism of male and female colors. (Of note, snow buntings, are in a different family.)

When we think that bird songs of earlier weeks are gone during late July, we can still hear songs of indigo bunting along with a few others; even though we may not know why they sing.

July 30, 2022

Fritillaries Flit Through Summer

Butterflies have been with us for months; from March on. With the longer and warmer days of early spring, the hibernating anglewing butterflies emerge and take wing; often on clear mild March days. Typically, the first to be seen is the dark mourning cloaks, but other hibernators; tortoise-shells and commas are quick to rise too. With few flowers at this time, they frequently go to dripping sap.

From early May on, we see a variety of butterflies that come out of chrysalis (similar to cocoon) as adults and fly; going to the spring flowers. This pace picks up in June. And though there has been a variety and good populations of these colorful insects all summer, I think that July stands out as being the month of butterflies.

During walks at this time, we can see tiny azures (blues), coppers and skippers of several kinds all active among the roadside botany of July. Here too are the mid-sized whites, sulphurs and painted ladies feeding with small orange-black crescents and checkerspots. Red-striped red admirals and white-striped white admirals may be seen basking and taking minerals on the soil. The larger monarchs and tiger swallowtails are taking nectar and laying eggs on specific plants.

We tend to think of butterflies as being colorful, and while most are, some species active now are brown, almost black. While tan common ringlets visit flowers in the open, brown little wood satyrs and northern pearly-eyes stay in the woods. Not likely to go to flowers here, they feed on decaying fruits and droppings. And darkest of all, the mid-sized common wood nymph appears at the edges of forests and fields.

But maybe the most diverse group in species and habitats are the fritillaries. These checkered butterflies carry patterns of orange and black on their upper wings. Some have similar markings on the undersides, while others hold large bright spots. Much of their diversity can be seen in their sizes. Wingspans range from small (inch and a half) to middle (two and a half) to large (three and a half). Their black and orange colors make them easy to see regardless of the chosen habitat; fields, roadsides, marshes, swamps, bogs and open woods.

Among the large one in the area are the great-spangled and Aphrodite fritillaries. Both can regularly be seen on the July flowers such as milkweed and dogbane. Each one have orange-black above with large bright spots below. (When photographing butterflies, it is best to show both the upper and lower wings.) Mid-sized atlantis and silver-bordered fritillaries are common. They share a size and dark bands along the edges of the upper wings. They frequent various flowers, but are often on dogbanes. The small members include meadow and bog fritillaries that usually live up to their names of where to see them.

No matter where they live, fritillaries show their checkered patters of orange and black wings and can be rather easy to see. Flying in the open and in the daylight, they readily take nectar from a variety of flowers; basking here too, what is expected of butterflies. But fritillaries show two stages of their life cycle that differ from others. Caterpillars feed mostly on violets; spring wild flowers of the forests and they do so at night. And over wintering is not as eggs, chrysalis, hibernating or migrating (all done by some butterflies), but as caterpillars.

Apparently, the unique life style of their youth has been successful and we now see the adult fritillaries as they flit through summer.

August 6, 2022

Daddy Long-Legs are Abundant Now

According to the calendar, early August is halfway from the summer solstice of June to the autumnal equinox of September. Though the daylight is getting shorter, more than an hour less than late June, we still have plenty of summer weather. Late summer wild flowers of asters, goldenrods and sunflowers have taken over the roadsides and open spaces and will continue to bloom for weeks. Others that flowered earlier are now gone to seed and we see plenty of plant happenings while walking now. And where there are flowering plants, there are also myriad of insects; much in early August.

Butterflies, moths, dragonflies, damselflies, bees, wasps, flies, beetles, grasshoppers, locusts and katydids are now in large numbers and diversity. Growing through the earlier weeks of June and July, many have now reached maturity and it is hard to not see the actions of these six-legged critters. And where there are insects, there are various predators. These may be other insects and spiders. After June being the dragonfly month and July being the butterfly month, I like to think of August being the spider month.

These eight-legged critters use various ways to catch insects. While jumping, wolf and crab spiders pursue food in their own ways; without making webs, many others construct snares to catch bug meals. Though there are several kinds oi webs, it is the large circular orb webs that we are most likely to see now; often coated with morning dew. Whether in fields, wetlands, woods or yards, these spiders appear to feed on the abundant insects. But there is more to see now.

Recently, as I walked past my garage, I noted movement on the walls. I stopped to take a closer look and saw many daddy long legs on these vertical sites. Continuing to look, I found more. I decided to count them, but after 150, I stopped.

Daddy long legs, also known as harvestmen, are cousins of spiders, belonging to the same group: arachnids. (This group also includes ticks and mites.) They have eight legs as spiders do, but they are not spiders. There are several differences between spiders and daddy long legs. Legs are much longer with the latter. Spiders have eight eyes and two body parts; daddy long legs have two eyes and one body part. Spiders are predators with venom and fangs, daddy long legs are omnivores; usually feeding on dead or decay material of animals and plants and so do not have or need fangs or venom.

The name of harvestmen comes from the fact that their maturation in summer corresponds with the harvesting time. The females lay eggs in fall in the soil; hatching in spring and growing in the warm months. This soil egg-laying is another difference between spiders and daddy long legs. And behaviorally, there is one more obvious deviation. I found several congregations of daddy long legs on the walls of the garage. Such would not happen with spiders since they are extreme loners.

Due to some confusion in terminology, a spider that today is called the cellar spider was formerly known as the daddy-long-legs spider since it has very long legs. These spiders are very common, often indoors, and in webs. Daddy long legs do not make webs. Victims of confusion, stories and terminology, they remain common and easy to see at this time. They are harmless and just interesting to watch. I'll leave them on the garage and watch what they do during the weeks of late summer. And I'm sure to see them at many sites besides garage walls.

August 13, 2022

Jewelweeds Glow at Wet Sites

With a sunrise at about 6 AM and setting at nearly 8:30 PM, the present daylight of fourteen and one-half hours is much less than the sixteen hours at the summer solstice. But we are still in summer; late summer. As we move on, so the flora of roadsides changes. The trio that dominated July's scene; milkweeds, fireweeds and evening primroses can still be found in bloom, but most have been forming seed pods as well. Other wildflowers of July are also seen in seed production. Thistle down blows through these days; often getting caught in the ever-increasing numbers of spider webs; and being selected by goldfinches for their late-season nesting. The tall plants of cow parsnip and water hemlock now stand with clusters of seeds. Dogbanes with the long-lasting white flowers now hold long pods of seeds.

But as the flora of July passes, they are replaced by those of August. I find that these days of late summer are again dominated by a trio; sunflowers, goldenrods and asters. Sunflowers frequently tall with composites rays mostly of yellow. Goldenrods, also composites, have small florets of yellow on long branches. They may be from two to eight feet tall. Asters show more of a variety in their colors; ranging from white and light purple to dark purple and blue. Asters may last the longest of the three; often going beyond the impending frosts. Despite their long season of flowering, all begin to bloom in late July.

But these are far from the full list of present late summer flora. When the sunflowers, goldenrods and asters abound in the roadsides and fields, other plants put on quite a show in the wetlands. While paddling in the shallows recently, I saw the large leaves and white flowers of arrowheads rising out of the water close to yellows of loosestrife, both tufted and yellow (swamp candles). Nearby was the white flowering boneset with its fused leaves, a growth of light purple joe pye weeds while bell-shaped blue harebells were further on land. Only about two to three feet tall are the orange flowers of spotted jewelweed.

Spotted jewelweed (Impatiens capensis), also called touch-me-not is common in the damp sites at this time. Unlike many of the local wildflowers, jewelweeds are annuals; replanting each year. Plants may grow more than three feet tall, but I usually find smaller ones. Stems and leaves are green and succulent; much liquid inside. Squeezing the stems can bring out this watery substance. Some say that this can be applied to help with poison ivy rashes.

Flowers are horn-shaped and orange; spotted mostly on the undersides. Open on one end, they have a long spur on the other. Hummingbirds and bumbles bees take nectar and are the likely pollinators. The name of jewelweed has two possible explanations. Some say that the hanging flowers look like ear rings while others note that rain and dew drops bead up on the plant; looking like jewels. The name of touch-me-not is a reference to the seed pods. Plants are self-dispersing. The one-inch pod will expel seeds in "explosion" when bumped; touch-me-not. However, watching the seed pods sending out the new crop of seeds often invites us to want to touch them.

Jewelweed in our area is orange and tends to be in wet sites. Further to the south and east is a larger yellow jewelweed (Impatiens pallida); growing in more varied sites. The orange one here may be smaller, but it is a delightful color and growth addition to the late season flora.

August 20, 2022

Nighthawks Migrate in Late August

When we get into late August, the changes of the season speed up somewhat. As we approach fourteen hours of daylight, down from the fifteen at the month's beginning, we note a later sunrise, earlier sunset. Mornings are cool with dew and fog quite common. (I find this is an excellent time to observe the abundance of spider webs in the region.) But days can still be warm: plenty of late summer is happening.

In addition to spiders at this time, we also see myriads of grasshoppers and their larger cousins; the locusts. Predatory dragonflies; small meadowhawks and large darners along with thin damselflies, are active now. This is also the time of late summer when we see the roadside trio of sunflowers, goldenrods and asters. Chokecherries and blackberries are ripe and among a few shrubs and small trees, we may see some leaf color already appearing. And it is a time of migration; monarch butterflies and several kinds of birds.

We tend to think of autumn migration as being confined to the months of September and October. But among many birds, it began before this and is happening now. Tree swallows and shorebirds (sandpipers, etc.) seem to set the pace with movements towards the south already in July. Among the swallows, it began as family units lined up in staging areas; trees, but also utility wires, until they get restless and move on. Shorebirds gather at edges of lakes to feed as they begin to go.

During August, this trend continues as the warblers; resident families that mix with others, pass through our woods and yards forming groups called warbler waves. These waves can get rather large and with several species, they head to the south. In true warbler styles, they are quick and without spring plumage or songs, may be hard to recognize.

Raptor flight over Hawk Ridge is also happening during the latter days of August. Beginning rather slowly, without the big numbers as seen in September, the hawks fly over. Sharp-shinned hawks are early ones, but they may be joined by turkey vultures, red-tailed hawks, ospreys and maybe eagles. Not the same as some flocks of raptors, but flocking migrants can also be seen now with the nighthawks.

Though going by the suffix of "hawk", these insect-eating birds are not hawks. Without either talons or hooked beaks, they use wide mouths to catch insects in mid-air flights. Instead of being raptors, nighthawks belong to a group known as nightjars; cousins of the well-known whip-poor-wills, more common south of here. Birds are about ten inches long, mostly gray-brown with thin white bands below, white under the beak and white on the tail. But as they pass over, it is the white bars towards the tips of the pointed wings that helps in recognizing them. Sometimes, even during migration, they give a nasal "peent" call.

Nighthawks breed throughout our region and are usually alone during this time. They do not really build a nest; instead placing their eggs right on the ground, rocks or tops of buildings. Young grow up quickly and soon take wing to join adults in feeding. And during migration, they can form flocks that may number in the hundreds. Feeding like other insect-catching birds, they go through dives and turns while maneuvering for meals. August migrants are usually seen in late afternoon and evening in feeding flocks. Such active flocks are worth us stopping and watching. These flights do not last long and by September, most are further south. Late August is the best time to see this aerial display.

August 27, 2022

Patches of Goldenrods Abound

Late August is a remarkable time in the northland. The days are filled with various seasonal happenings. Bird migration can be seen with raptors at Hawk Ridge, geese in the lakes and warblers in the woods. With ample rainfall, lawns and forest floors respond with a plethora of mushrooms of many kinds, sizes and colors. Also, there is probably no better time to observe the abundance of spider webs in the roadsides, fields and wetlands. All our types of webs: cobwebs, sheet webs, funnel webs and orb webs abound now; but it is the orbs that hold the droplets of dew and fog on these cooling mornings. For anyone willing to get wet, trekking here is well worth the effort; being able to see and photograph dozens of these snares created by our eight-legged neighbors at this time.

As with the roadside botany of the whole summer, the ones in bloom now reveal quite a boquet of colors and species. Walking by, I see several kinds flowering including Joe Pye weed, bergamot, thistle, sweetclover, bindweed, hyssop and white clematis. But most common are the late-season trio of asters, sunflowers and goldenrods. A diligent search may turn up about a dozen kinds of each of these in the region; nearly all of which are native.

During a recent bit of local driving, I noted an almost a continuous yellow along the roadsides. These included the ubiquitous tansy and sow-thistles. Both are non-native and not always appreciated, but produce yellow colors, often with fluffy seeds. In addition to these yellows, there were glowing sunflowers; some high above the others, and large uniform patches of goldenrods. These yellows were mixed with some whites and purples of asters.

While walking among goldenrods at this time, I pause to look and listen. Buzzing sounds tell of insects as well as their movements; very active among these flowers. Goldenrods are a terrific source for anyone wanting to see the activities of bees, wasps, flies, crickets, grasshoppers, locusts, beetles, butterflies, moths, dragonflies, damselflies and spiders. These critters remain active all day and often into the nights.

Though most grow in the open locations of fields and roadsides, goldenrods can also be found in rocky sites, swamps and woods. They range is size from about two feet tall to nearly eight feet. Their season begins with the flowering of early goldenrods at about mid-July and continues throughout the following weeks with late and showy goldenrods do not start to flower until well into September. Plants have leafy stems and branches with numerous small yellow composites florets. Many grow alone, but others form large clumps of clones. Nearly all are yellow, but a white goldenrod grows along the shores of Lake Superior. And all are native.

Perhaps the two species that stand out the most now are the Canada goldenrod (Solidago canadensis) and tall goldenrod (Solidago altissima). Each of these flowers form thick cloning patches of blooming plants. Maybe three to five feet tall, it is hard to not see these hundreds of yellow flowers as we pass by. And it seems like nearly every plant holds a variety of insects with its present flora.

Goldenrods are often blamed for causing hay fever. Pollen from these yellow flowers is too heavy to drift in the wind and needs to be carried by insects; not likely to be breathed in. The real culprit is ragweed. Don't let this time of late summer pass without pausing to look and listen passing a patch of goldenrods.

September 3, 2022

Forest Fungi After August Rains

This time of late summer continues to be very active. Patches of goldenrods, asters and sunflowers that abound in the fields and roadsides are buzzing with insects in the afternoon sunlight. Walking here in the dew-covered early mornings reveals a plethora of orb webs; made by spiders during the previous evenings and being coated with dew and fog droplets in the cooling pre-dawn. The woods trees hold acorns, berries and fruits; ripe or ripening. And some trees also hold leaves changing into colored autumn attire. Among the branches, migrant warblers, often in flocks of mixed species, move on their fall flights. But the woods is also the home to a huge variety of mushrooms and other fungi; recently popped up after August rains.

The first half of August was below normal in precipitation; but once the second half began, showers and thunderstorms came. The amount varied greatly in the region. Though we did not get the downpours as seen in some locations, we did get enough rain to bring about a very good growth of forest fungi of many kinds.

During a walk about two days after the rainfall, I was able to find nearly twenty kinds of these growths. Mushrooms typically stick up above the substrate of soil or logs in an "umbrella" shape. A stem (stipe) holds up a cap (pileus). Under the cap is where the mushroom produces the reproductive spores. They are usually growing between thin structures called gills. But not all mushrooms have this arrangement. While most of the ones that I found had gills, others had tiny holes (pores) beneath the cap. Collectively, these are called boletes. During my walk, I found many boletes, but one stood out as unique. It was a rough and dry looking gray-black one called Strobilomyces (old man of the woods). A few kinds appear to have gills, but instead have folds of skin below the cap. This was apparent in a patch of yellow-gold Cantharellus (chanterelles). And I found one with spines (teeth) under the cap. Hydnum (hedgehog mushroom) has a brownish cap above the white spines. By far most mushrooms were gilled.

Among these abundant gilled mushrooms, I found Russula with caps of many colors: white, brown, gray, yellow and red. Lactarius (milk mushrooms) were here too; oozing white latex. Tiny Marasmius (pin wheels) grew from pine needles. Hygrocybe (waxy caps) brightened the forest floor with caps and stems of red and yellow. Amanita with either yellow or white caps were in the nearby lawns. Wet rotting logs held plenty as well. With pointed caps, Mycena were quite common. Taller and with scaly-looking caps was a growth of Pholiota also on the log. But none were as numerous as the tiny Xerophalina (fuzzy foot) that literally covered a dead log with hundreds of these minute mushrooms; each with a yellowish cap of about one-half inch.

Not just mushrooms were in the woods. On a downed oak log was the bright orange-yellow growth of Laetiporus (sulfur shelf; chicken-of-the-woods). Coral fungi of tan colors adorned a log while golden ones were on the soil nearby. But the one that I enjoyed finding was a growth of Leotia (jelly babies). These small yellow-gold growths rose up from the ground in shapes looking a lot like miniature mushrooms; complete with caps and stems. They are; however, of another type of fungi and not even related to mushrooms. Small and easy to overlook, I don't find them every year and it was great to see them growing in this woods. In a late summer wet woods, forest fungi are doing well.

September 10, 2022

Noisy Acorns

Migration and leaf colors along with cooling temperatures tell us of September happenings. Mushrooms may proliferate in the woods and spider webs abound in yards, roadsides, fields and wetlands. Sun rises now at 6:40 AM setting about 7:30 PM; giving shorter daylight and soon, we will experience the autumnal equinox; daylight and darkness equal. The days, weeks and months following will have more time of darkness than light. But we also see the production of the summer.

Late summer wild flowers of goldenrods, asters and sunflowers are still easy to see as we drive by; and they'll be with us for the rest of the month. Garden produce is plentiful with many changes from what we saw earlier. The products of the garden are only some of the results of warmer days that we see now. Woodland plants, shrubs, and trees are showing what they have produced as well.

Walking in the woods now, I find the red or white berries of baneberry and blues of Clintonia. These spring flowers of May now are with their maturity. The larger shrubs of raspberries may still hold a few red berries while blackberries are with drupes of dark colors. The wild roses that gave such beautiful pink flowers earlier in the season, now hold red berries; known as rose hips. Other small trees and shrubs respond too and I see the dark fruits of chokecherry and black cherry and reds of sumac and honeysuckle. White berries hang from the red-osier dogwoods while pagoda dogwood's ones are dark. Highbush cranberry has red; arrow-woods are dark. Both are species of Viburnum. Even the vine Virginia creeper has dark berries among the twining leaves and stems. Wild plums and crab apples ripened to join the list. And of course; the domestic apples brighten these days.

But northland trees show other types of production. Looking into sugar and mountain maples, we see clusters of different types of seeds; the winged samaras. Not quite as flat, but a similar type is that of ashes. A couple form hardened seeds; we call nuts. Hazelnuts are plentiful, but it is difficult to find ripe ones when squirrels and bears are in the region. And there are the acorns of oaks.

This is the home to two kinds of oaks; northern red oaks and bur oaks. (White oaks and pin oaks may be to the south and west of here.) Finding acorns of bur oaks is quite unusual, but red oaks with acorns is common. At this latitude, the crop is formed every two years. A year ago, most of the trees in my yard and woods held small partially developed acorns. After this past season, they now have clusters of developed acorns; green turning brown. Their nut crop have seeds protected by a smooth outer cover and a rough-looking "cap". It is the small stem on the cap that attaches to the tree branches; until something makes it fall.

It appears as though the local squirrels have learned that these acorns, often still green, can provide food for their ever-growing cold-weather caches. And so, they bite the top of the acorns causing them to drop. The yard and driveway is littered with acorns. It appears to be just another critter preparing for the coming cold. But some oaks grow next to the garage with its metal roof and when the acorns fall on this surface, they send a reverberating sound that tells of their harvesting. Often squirrels are early risers and pounding sounds on the roof welcome the dawn. This will pass, but the noisy acorns tell us of the changing season.

Sept. 17, 2022

Funnel Webs Abundant at Roadsides

The morning is cool; low 50's, when I step out for a walk at dawn. Winds are calm and patches of fog hang in the lowlands. Roadsides and field plants are coated with dew that formed a couple of hours ago. At this time of year, before the frosts prevail, a morning like this is a splendid time for a walk among the spider webs. Their snares will be here if there were no dew, but droplets on their threads of silk allow them to be seen better. It proves to be a delightful, but wet, web walk.

Before I leave the yard, I note that the orb web on the garage last night is still present in the morning. These circular webs are the biggest webs and are the most photogenic. There are four types of spider webs common now; orbs, sheet, irregular and funnels. And I expect to find all four. I pass a swamp that has many dead tamaracks and it appears that most of these branches hold an orb web or two. With the swamp being east of the road, I get great backlit views and many photos of these webs. Some of these orbs are quite large; maybe two feet in diameter. Nearly all are vertical to catch night-flying insects.

A nearby bog that has a thick growth of leatherleaf is home to a plethora of small sheet webs. These bowl-shaped snares are also seen among the needles of roadside red pines.

As common as the orbs and sheet webs are in the wetlands, it is the roadsides that hold the most abundance of webs. Grasses that stick up with a spread of their earlier growth now are littered with threads. Though looking haphazard these irregular webs are home to tiny spiders. Without appearance of order, the spiders stay for weeks; gathering ample food. Such webs are also called cobwebs.

But it is the funnel webs that are most numerous. Nearly all are on the grasses, near the ground. Looking like cloths dropped here, the dew alights on their threads; making them easy to see. As I walk this section of road, I see hundreds of these webs; frequently near each other. Funnel webs are also in a neighbor's field that was recently mowed. Each web is about six to twelve inches long. Some are circular, some are oval, but they all have an opening among the flat-laying threads. This opening is why they are known as funnel webs. And in this site is where the spider hides. Looking closely as I pass by, I sometimes see the brown owner of the web.

Web-making spiders typically are slow moving and may have poor eyesight. Not so with these spiders. Since the threads of the web are not sticky, any insect that hits the web could quickly be gone. The spider sees this potential prey and pounces from its hiding funnel to go after and subdue it. Also differing from many other spiders, females and males are about the same size (with many kinds, females are much larger than males).

Webs remain common and easy to see now in the morning dew, but when dew becomes frost, these web hunters will frequently move indoors. We might see them is basements, garages or outbuildings where they remain active as long as possible; maybe all winter.

My slow walk was only about a mile. The sunlight is causing the dew to dissipate from the roadsides, but I had plenty of great looks at the insect-catching nets of these eight-legged neighbors; especially funnels.

September 24, 2022

Seeing Jack Again

Late September is a time in which it is hard to not notice the colors in the landscape. Leaf tones of trees are delightful. Breaking up of the green chlorophyll allows the ever-present yellow xanthophyll to show up. And most trees in the woods now take on this color that was present, but overshadowed by green, all summer. Along the edges of the woods, in more sunlight, trees are holding leaves of red pigments; anthocyanin. While yellows show in the absence of chlorophyll, trees use excess leaf sugars to produce the red pigment. Being in the sunlight, this acts as a kind of "sun screen" for leaf cells.

It appears that each year, it is the same kinds of trees that are more likely to have red leaves in late September. It begins with a couple of small trees; sumac and cherry, turning this bright color. This color phase was quickly continued by three more small trees; dogwood, highbush cranberry and American hazel. (Interesting to note that while American hazel is red, the very similar beaked hazel is yellow.) The vine Virginia creeper (woodbine) is red with its leaves of five as is poison ivy with leaves of three. The brightest of any large tree is that of red maple, but many red oaks also carry similar foliage. Looking lower among the bushes and shrubs, we see that rose, raspberry, blackberry and even some blueberries have red leaves as well.

But red on plants is not limited to leaves at this time. Ripening apples bring more than good taste to the scene. Cousins, crab apples and hawthorns, sport reds too. Interesting to note that some hawthorns (there are many kinds) are the first trees to drop leaves in the region; therefore, revealing the clusters of red fruits, looking like miniature apples. Highbush cranberry (not a cranberry) has groups of juicy red berries while winterberry holly, in the swamps, has smaller ones.

Red leaves and fruits appear to be a way of advertising them to hungry birds and mammals. Nearly all have seeds within and the consumed berries will be carried off. Such dispersal is what the plant wants. Earlier this season, red elderberry and pin cherry did the same.

Among the lower plants in the forest, a few also produce red berries. Back in May, we noted the flowers of trillium, baneberry and false Solomon-seal. Since then, all have formed bright berries. Another one; jack-in-the-pulpit ,does so too and may be quite a surprise.

When we saw this plant with its unique flower in May, it did not look anything like what we see now. The unusual floral in the vernal woods held a structure appearing as a green-purple cylindrical shape. Sticking up was a finger-like growth called a spadix (jack) and over it a folding leaf-like spathe; appearing like jack was in a pulpit. Insects attracted to the lower part were able to pollinate it.

In the midst of all the greening in the forest, we forgot it. During the following weeks, the pollinated plant grew green berries to help with reproduction. Now in late summer or fall, with flowers gone, we see the berry cluster that has matured to red. When first seeing them, it is hard to make a connection with the flower that we saw in May. But looking higher on the plant we see the large three-part leaves similar to the spring. Jack was a delight to see in spring and though quite changed now, still a delight. Jack-in-the-pulpit is another plant holding red in this colorful botanical time of late September.

Fourth Quarter

October 1, 2022

Insect Mimicry on Goldenrods

The wild flowers of September were fading. Roadsides and fields glowed with asters of several species and colors of whites and purples. Nearby, mixed with these late-flowering plants, were sunflowers of varying heights and kinds. And there were the goldenrods. With ample sunlight and moisture, these delightful yellows of late summer lingered through the weeks. Some began blooming earlier in summer and for them, these September days were the time of waning blossoms and formation of seeds. This continued to happen through this month of the autumnal equinox and as the days exited, most goldenrods have now gone to seed. Producing the fluffy growths where flowers were, they allow seeds to drift in the breeze. But not all have made seeds.

Recently, as the second half of the month unfolded, I went for a walk in the roadsides and fields. Many of the goldenrods were past flowering, but other were still well in bloom. I went into these flowering patches and I quickly discovered that I was not the only one to find these fascinating flowers still in bloom. The plants were buzzing with activity of myriads of insects. I paused to observe these six-legged critters.

Large and numerous, easy to see (and hear), were the bumbles bees. A couple of different species were here wearing various colors. They appeared to be totally oblivious to my presence and went about their business gathering pollen and nectar from the abundant tiny yellow florets of the goldenrods. But they were not the only bees. I also saw honey bees and sweat bees along with a couple of distant cousins; hornets, yellowjackets, paper and spider wasps (black wasps that specialize on catching spiders). We often associate these insects with stinging and so, it would be beneficial for other insects to look like bees and wasps; and get left alone. As I walked, I found these mimics. Among the bees were the look-alike flower flies. Again, there were several species and they ranged in shape and sizes. Some of the smaller flower flies (syrphid flies) are also known as hover flies since they can hold still at one spot in their flights. This bee mimicry is superficial and when we look more carefully, we can discern the bees from the flies. Bees have four wings while flies have only two wings; held out away from the body. The mimicry comes from the stripes of brown and black mixed with yellow to somewhat resemble bees. Mimics or trues, they were all active here and no doubt doing much pollinating.

But this site gathered more and I saw the predaceous ambush bugs, stink bugs, ladybugs, damselflies and two kinds of dragonflies; large darners and small meadowhawks. Some crab spiders were also taking advantage of the possible prey. Black and yellow goldenrod soldier beetles climbed over the stalks while crickets, grasshoppers and locusts hopped and moved along the ground. A day-flying moth came by for a rest. A couple of south-bound monarchs paused for a snack and two other butterflies; a white cabbage and a yellow sulphur were here too.

As we proceed further into autumn, the insects (and goldenrods) will be fading. While the monarchs migrate, most of the remaining insects will succumb to chilly temperatures and frosts; but not before laying eggs. A few, like the ladybugs, will hibernate. But for a time during these clear and pleasant days of late September and early October, the lingering blooming yellow flowers continue their hosting of predators, herbivores and mimicry; all in a single patch of goldenrods.

October 8, 2022

Ash Time in the Local Swamps

Late September and early October is when trees of the northland put on quite a show of colors. Even though we've seen the autumn arboreal attire before, we want a repeat performance. We are seldom disappointed. With the shorter daylight at this time, trees have a breakdown of the green substance; chlorophyll. It will no longer be needed to produce food that had been going on all summer. With the disappearance of this food-making material, yellow color (xanthophyll) that was present all summer, but overshadowed by green, is able to show just how common it is. Yellow leaf colors may appear on many species of trees during these weeks. Despite the abundance of yellows, we often seek out the more vibrant reds.

Red substance (anthocyanin) is different from yellow. It was not present in leaves all summer, but was recently formed from excess sugars in leaves. Since trees that have these brightest colors are often small, they tend to grow along the edges of woods or roadsides where they get plenty of sunlight. This pigment, a delight to see for us, is also useful to the tree as a form of "sun screen" helping protect other cells within the leaves.

We tend to look for the reds, and they do stand out. Though yellows are much more common than the reds, we see scarlet colors on quite a variety of trees: red maples, red oaks (usually smaller ones), dogwoods, cherries, highbush cranberries, American hazels and the vines of Virginia creeper (woodbine) and poison ivy. Bushes and shrubs hold this color as well: raspberries, blackberries, blueberries, roses and bush-honeysuckles. But I find that it is the small tree: sumacs, that glow the most with their bright reds. Often these little trees grow in rather large numbers along roadsides. It is not unusual that an entire growth, not just a few trees, show their red compound leaves. Indeed, it may be hard to keep our eyes on the road as we drive by.

Reds are a bright delight, but they fade earlier than yellows that linger into October until the big leaf drop of mid-month. Birches, poplars, willows, sugar maples, mountain-maples, basswoods, oaks, ironwoods, big-tooth aspens, beaked hazels and elms all give this glow show as we exit the month of September. The abundant quaking aspens are a bit later to take on this hue. Aspen time is usually early in October. At this time, we see how numerous the trees are. Even pines often hold yellow needles now, while swamp tamaracks glow gold a bit later in October.

But of all the yellows in the region of late September, it is the black ashes that dominate. These ashes are not particularly large and grow in wet swampy sites. They normally do not even get our attention. But now, in the northland where swamps are common, we note a dramatic glow of yellow in the wetlands. Unlike most local trees, ash leaves are compound; leaves and leaflets are yellow at the same time. Growing in groups in these locations, it is hard to not notice them even if black ashes are not as big as other trees of forests, parks and yards. This wetland show does not last too long; usually only a week or two; and just as quickly, this foliage show ends. But for a couple of weeks, it is ash time in the swamps.

Entering October, we start with foliated forests. Within weeks, we will experience the leaf drop as most get defoliated, but for now, we can enjoy the annual autumn attires of reds and yellows.

October 15, 2022

Shelf Fungus on the Ground

Trees demand our attention during this outstanding month of October. Beginning these thirty-one days as fully-foliated plants, they undergo quite a change when dropping all their foliage that has been on the branches for five months. This leaf drop takes place during this month. Leaves are falling every day, but the big amount of defoliation is a phenomenon of about mid-month. But it is not just leaves falling that we note. Before they depart to join the litter of the forest floor, they light up the surroundings with bright delightful colors. Indeed, early October may be considered the most colorful time of the year in the northland. The reds of earlier times persist for a while, but then are replaced by the abundant yellows; during the first half of the month. Tamaracks in swamps and a few others will hold colors, almost until the end. Walking at this time is an amazing experience. But it is possible to "not see the forest because of the trees".

Much more is happening in the autumn woods. This is also the time of migration. Probably the biggest variety of sparrows to be seen during whole year is early October. Blue jays, thrushes, blackbirds, kinglets and lingering warblers are here too. At night saw whet owls come by as well. But I find that October days are often good times to see forest fungi. Mushrooms are most prolific earlier in the season when they grow quickly in ample moisture and temperature But there are those that remain until now. I have often walked in October and found Pholiota (scaly cap), Armillaria (honey mushroom), Entoloma, Hygrocybe (waxy cap), Russula and Mycena on or near the forest floor.

Nearby yards may have Coprinus (shaggy mane), Agaricus (meadow mushroom), Amanita and maybe rings of Marasmius and Lepista. The woods is also where we can find a plethora of puffballs. And with the leaf drop, fungi on tree trunks are easier to see. Shelf fungi or brackets of turkeytails, artist fungus and horse' hoofs can be found now. Such fungi differs from mushrooms by being tougher flesh and lasting longer (often for years). Though we expect to find these shelf fungi sticking out from the sides of trees and logs, I recently found one among the grasses in the yard.

Right there on the lawn under a white pine tree was the growth appearing much like that of a shelf or bracket. With a light outline and concentric circles that darkened towards the center, this tough fungus was about a foot and a half in diameter. Though not on the tree trunk, it was part of the tree. Most likely this "shelf fungus on the ground" was getting nutrition from roots of the nearby pine. Soft material on the surface accounted for the name of velvet-top fungus (Phaeolus schweinitzii). It is one of many kinds of brackets that are known as polypores; a reference to the many tiny holes on the underside where the spores are produced and released.

The flesh is very tough and persistent. When most mushrooms fade in days, this polypore will linger for weeks. The flesh is too hard to be consumed, but the fungus is gathered by some as a source of a natural dye. With proper treatment, green, brown and yellow dyes can be formed. That is why this ground-growing fungus is also called dyer's polypore or dye-maker polypore.

October gives us much to see in the trees, but beneath them, there is also growth happening as seen in this polypore. Soon much of the ground will be covered by the fallen leaves.

October 22, 2022

Snakes Moving to Winter Sites

By the time we reach this date in October, local wildlife are preparing for the impending winter. Those that have been living here will need to deal with the cold season. There are basically four ways to cope with winter: migrate, hibernate, die or stay active. And we can see examples of all of these happening now.

Those that choose to migrate are taking the route of going somewhere else, some place where this difficult season is not as severe; mostly further to the south. The most obvious ones to use this method of wintering are birds. Many avian species that nested here in the warm months, now go other places; some quite far. Mostly, it is those that have a diet of insects; not available in the cold. For some northern birds, their wintering site will be here. We see this with various finches that may be at our feeders or perhaps owls that leave their boreal world to winter nearby. Now, in October, we may be noting some birds as they pass through the region from further north to further south; such as kinds of sparrows. A few mammals, mainly bats, will migrate as do a couple of kinds of insects. Best known insect migrant is the monarch butterfly, but they are not alone. The large green darner dragonflies have a fall flight as well. More limited in their migration is that of snakes.

Snakes use hibernation to cope with winter as do many other cold-blooded animals; such as frogs (most of our local frogs hibernate on land), insects (including some butterflies) and a few warm-blooded mammals. But before the snakes can hibernate, they need to travel to get to the proper sites for wintering. Such places are known as hibernacula and when there, snakes will form a conglomeration, curling below the frost line. (We have only two kinds of snakes common in the region; garter snake and red-bellied snake. A third one, ring-necked snake, is seen occasionally.) During these autumn days, snakes will travel to their hibernacula that they left last spring. This trekking route, a form of migration, may take them over roads and trails; exposing themselves to a danger, but also allowing us to see them and just how common they are at this time. Autumn sunshine on a paved road must feel good to a passing snake and some will want to bask a while; even though it can be hazardous. Roadkill snakes tell of this situation. When walking or biking in much of October, I expect to see some of these reptiles.

The critters that die in the as cold and daylight lessens, do so after laying eggs to assure a population next spring. We see this mostly with insects. I note many grasshoppers, locusts, moths, meadowhawk dragonflies and hornets all active as the days get chilly and they succumb to the cold.

Those that remain active all winter often need to make changes in how they live and what they eat to survive. Mostly, these are birds and mammals; many of which spent summer with us. Food and shelter are very important in this season, but they can make adaptations to handle the northland winter. We might be seeing this preparation now. We can watch squirrels gathering nuts and acorns or beavers caching food near their lodges. Others are growing thicker coats or changing colors. Birds that ate insects last summer, are switching to a diet of seeds. All of these wintering techniques are now seen in the local wildlife.

Oct. 29, 2022

Grackle Flocks Add to Fall Migrants

The bird migration of October has been very active. I doubt that I can take a walk during this whole month and not see this movement of birds. They range in size from tiny to quite large. Many are seen in our yards and woods. Others are in wetlands. Diurnal migrants are common, but maybe more take their trips at night.

In the northland, probably the best-known site to observe these southbound flights is Hawk Ridge. Any time spent there in fall is seldom a disappointment. Huge numbers of broad-winged hawks come by in September. Kettles of hundreds often rise on thermals above the edge of Lake Superior. With a winter in Central and South America, they were early migrants. Skies in October often hold good amounts of sharp-shinned hawks, red-tailed hawks, bald eagles, turkey vultures and American kestrels. Though not seen by most of us, small saw-whet owls were also very common this month. Flying low at night, they were caught and banded by the dozens at Hawk Ridge.

Maybe the loudest of avian migrants were the Canada geese. During many chilly early mornings and nights, I heard these birds; perhaps miles away. V-flocks may number fifty to a hundred, but usually less. Also loud were the groups of trumpeter swans and sandhill cranes. (These two are maybe the noisiest birds in the area.) Sandpipers, snipes and plovers came by too. Among woodpeckers, flickers and sapsuckers were September migrants, but I did see both in October.

Songbird migrants are probably more visible and numerous in September, but some kinds are plentiful in October as well. Not considered a songster, blue jays came across in the hundreds. Hard to find a day when I did not see or hear them; along with crows. Warblers that were diverse last month have some lingering now; mostly yellow-rumped and palm warblers. Thrushes silently moved in the woods. Tiny kinglets fluttered among the branches. And sparrow-like pipits were seen with tail movement up and down as they walked in the open sites. But two groups of songbirds that I find quite abundant this month are the sparrows and blackbirds.

There may not be a better time of the whole year to observe kinds of sparrows than the first half of October. To many people, sparrows all look alike; little brown birds. Superficially, they may appear that way, but a closer look reveals different markings of their heads, undersides or tails. Juncos, a kind of sparrow, are gray-black and stand out from the rest, but they often are with other sparrows; white-throated and white-crowned, when in our yards. Fox, song and Lincoln sparrows are spotted below while Harris has black markings on the head. Migrant sparrows do not sing much when feeding and resting in our yards and roadsides. Sounds are provided by the flocks of blackbirds.

A few days ago, the backyard became a jumble of creaks and calls as a migrating flock of grackles settled while southbound. Finding food of various seeds, they gobbled as they crackled. The sound of such a flock; often mixed with various blackbirds; red-winged, Brewers and rusty, is a delightful sound of migration in both spring and fall. They may not always be appreciated. One October day, I watched as these dark foot-long birds descended on a newly-stocked bird feeder and remained until every seed was devoured. Flocks may be in the hundreds as they restlessly move through the region. Southern grackle wintering flocks can be even larger than what we see now in late October.

November 5, 2022

Giant Puffballs in a Yard

With the leaf drop that occurred mostly on schedule between October 13 and 20, the landscape took on a different appearance. The green-leaf trees that had been with us since mid-May had spent the previous couple of weeks in their autumn attire. During the early days of October, this arboreal show was hard to not notice. Reds were far outnumbered by trees that had yellows, but their presence was searched for by many nature watchers before waning. (I find that the red-leaf plants that last the longest are some of the smaller ones, such as raspberry, blackberry, blueberry, rose and bush honeysuckle.) But the abscission layers of the yellow leaves also formed and they fell in huge numbers near the middle of October. Here they joined the others on the forest floor. Before they decay here, they provide for a colorful substrate for us when taking woods walks.

Not all the colors have gone from the trees and with some searching, we may see willows (especially, weeping willows) and silver maples still holding yellows. These will often last into November. And out in the swamps, the patient tamaracks have waited until the broad-leaf trees have mostly dropped foliage before they light up with yellow-gold glows of conifer needles. Such a show can cause us to forget all the leaf looking that we did earlier in autumn.

After the leaf drop and before the lasting snow cover, we have a period of time that I like to refer to as AutWin. (The interlude between autumn and winter; some call it "Finter".) This is a remarkable time that allows us to see much of the forest landscape that was kept from us during the summer. It may last for only a couple of weeks some years or it may persist all the way into December during other years. We now see the lower green plants of the forests; mostly mosses and clubmosses, but also some ferns and leafy flowering plants that were not seen during green-leaf days of warm months. Also, we can find late-season fungi.

During a recent AutWin walk, I noted in the woods shelf fungi growing out from trunks of trees and a thick growth of Pholiota at the base. Out at the edge of the woods were Agaricus and Amanita with a circle of brown Marasmius. Rising above these was another mushroom, a type of Coprinus (shaggy mane). Such fall fungi are typical but what I saw next out on a lawn, made me stop and take a closer look.

Out here, appearing a lot like a large white rock, was a giant puffball. Living up to its name, this growth was circular, about twelve inches in diameter and nearly five inches tall; maybe as big as a water melon. We see plenty of puffballs in our woods and I expect more as we go through the days of fall, but usually not this big.

Giant puffballs (Calvatia gigantea) are a regular, though never abundant part of the fall happenings. I see them nearly every year, but still marvel at them. Like smaller puffballs, they begin as a light-colored growth that dries to pale brown in maturity. And like the other puffballs, numerous tiny spores are formed within; getting released only when disturbed from above. Near this young white giant was mature brown one. Some researchers claim that they can hold trillions of spores. Rather than disturbing them to find out, I was content with just seeing the giant puffballs; another sight of AutWin.

November 12, 2022

Green Wood Ferns in Forests

Walking the woods of November is always a delight. On these AutWin days, there are no leaves on the trees and the snow has not yet coated the ground. And insect companions of the summer are no longer with us. The trek is easy. Despite the gray and bland appearance that is often associated with this month, I find that time here is very interesting.

Green and more-recently colorful leaves of the deciduous trees have fallen and now their foliage covers the forest floor. Most tree trunks look gray-brown; almost black. This monotonous pattern does not extend throughout my walk. There is plenty more to see. It seems like on nearly all of the trees, there are patches of gray, bluish and green; even some yellow as lichens thrive is such a setting. Growing for many years, these growths of various kinds and colors will survive the coming winter; right out in the weather. Also, on lots of the tree trunks, stumps and downed logs are growths of shelf fungi. Unlike the related mushrooms, they are perennials and I expect to see them in these sites all winter. But there is much green here too.

Scattered among the deciduous trees are conifers. With the exception of tamaracks, they still hold their green leaves (needles). Looking beneath the trees, I note the abundance of another ever green plant. Much smaller, but more common, are the growths of mosses. They seem to cover the base of nearly every tree and more. Logs, rocks and even on the ground itself, these tiny leafy plants show their greening. To many of us, all mosses look the same; little green stuff. A closer look shows variety in size, shape and branching leafy stems. Several (maybe even many) different species are in this woods.

Nearby are some clubmosses. Also called princess pine, ground pine, ground cedar or lycopodium, they are not mosses, but growing taller; maybe six inches, and covering vast areas. They are cousins of ferns.

Some of the wild flowers of earlier this year have kept their green leaves. I'm reminded of spring when I see hepatica still with green leaves. Two summer blooming flowers are here too; pyrola and wintergreen. The latter is also holding red berries. But it is some ferns that stand out now.

During the summer, the woods held a variety of these leafy feathery green plants; many up to five feet tall. I had to walk through growths of ostrich, interrupted and lady ferns. Smaller, but also abundant, are the bracken and sensitive ferns. Cinnamon ferns were in wet sites. And at a few locations, I noted the presence of the delightful maidenhair ferns. With the onset of shorter cool days, their green fronds faded and now most appear as just brown or dark stalks; except for wood ferns.

Wood ferns (Dryopteris) were here all summer. Fronds may be two feet tall, but with the presence of many ferns, they got overlooked. However, when the fronds of the others faded, those of wood ferns kept their green colors. And now as we walk through these AutWin woods, we see many of these green ferns; standing out among the faded ones. Plants continue to be green as we enter the snow season. Even when covered with snow, they will keep this color, but they are not true evergreens and when snow melts in spring, we'll note that fronds wood ferns will also fade. Now, as the month of November unfolds, green wood ferns are appreciated and add to the scene.

November 19, 2022

Flowers in Fields of November

November is a month when we see plenty of seasonal happenings. The forest with the leaf drop so apparent, now reveals the green plants of mosses, clubmosses and ferns under the trees; still green and remaining so. Out in the wetlands, we note the formation of ice during early morning walks. Soon the ice covers the whole surface of the small bodies of water; ponds and swamps. By the end of the month, this trend continues and we'll see ice on nearby lakes. And often by this time, the whole landscape is wearing its white winter attire. But besides the woods and wetlands, I think there is much to see while wandering in the fields of November.

It wasn't that long ago when I walked out here, I was surrounded by yellow of goldenrods and sunflowers with a mixture of white and purple asters. With these native plants in bloom, they buzzed with the movements of a variety of bugs that came by for nectar and pollinating. This insect activity proved to be successful and the pollinated plants proceeded to develop their seeds. With the onset of shorter and cooler days, the insect flights waned and without their presence, the floral bouquets of these open sites changed into the next phase. Now, when I walk here, I see the results of this plant-insect interaction.

Instead of colorful petals and rays among the green stems and leaves, the whole field appears to be a monotone of gray-brown; but the late summer wild flowers are still here. Perhaps the most obvious ones seen today are the ones that were so bright and abundant weeks ago; the goldenrods. Instead of flower heads of numerous yellow rays and discs, these same plants hold fluffy growths. This grayish fluff appearing on nearly every goldenrod is an adaptation to their next phase. The plants have produced seeds and now disperse them. Taking advantage of the breezes out in this open site, the fluffy pappus attached to the seeds will carry them off. We may be in November, but plants are preparing for next summer by sending off the seeds. Most will not grow, but enough will so that I look forward to fields of yellow in the future.

Other plants out here also disperse their seeds in several ways. Asters, pearly everlastings, fireweeds, milkweeds and thistles also drift in the winds of fall. Others, such as clovers, sweetclovers, sunflowers and the ubiquitous tansy merely drop their seeds; often relying on animals, such as birds to eat them and so carry them off. Burdock, sticktights and agrimony will attach their products to passing animals; including us. This "dead" looking field is one of plenty of life and preparation is done for the coming winter and the following warming times. What appears to be dead is only partially so. The leaves, stems and flowers of the plants have succumbed to the cold, but above the floral sites, the seeds in their new attire survive. Fields and roadsides will continue to look like this for the coming winter.

Also, underground, the rootstock of these perennial plants will cope with and live through the coming cold. Even if they were not to form seeds, the plants here will prevail.

There are a few other colors here too. Yellows of reed canary grass and asparagus may still be seen and at the field's edges, I find some blackberry plants with bright red leaves. But the grays and browns have much happening as we go through late fall and into winter.

November 26, 2022

The Rainy Woods of November

October and early November were warmer than normal and much drier. According to the National Weather Service in Duluth, October had less than one-third the usual precipitation; despite the five inches of snow. And so, when a system moved in that brought fog followed by thunder-showers, rain and strong winds, I was glad that we were getting the needed moisture. I recorded three inches in our gauge. It had been nearly empty for the previous weeks. Temperatures were about 40 degrees; too warm for ice and snow, good conditions to take an autumn woods walk.

Each November, I like to visit several ponds that serve as frog breeding sites in spring. The ponds at this time will give an indication of how they are as we enter winter. Today's rains help with this. The last time that I checked these ponds, several were devoid of water; thanks to the earlier arid days. I wandered through the light rain and looked again. As a result of this rainy time, they now held water. With the forecasts of temperatures to drop, I expect these ponds would soon be covered with ice. The ponds returning to water was a welcome site, but as I walked in this chilly rainy day of November, I saw more that were taking advantage of this newly falling rain; despite the chill.

We have lichens on trees all year long. They are mostly on tree trunks, but often on branches as well. These strange growths of algae and fungi are very hardy and remain here throughout the year; hot or cold, dry or wet, and they have a lifetime of many years. Those on tree trunks look like patches of paint. During recent dry times, they almost went dormant and shriveled up for protection. But, being the opportunists that they are, the lichens were quick to absorb available moisture and swelled to a larger size. The patches of green, blue-green, gray and yellow now were looking much better and more pronounced than they had been for weeks. They appeared glad to get this November rain.

But as I walked through the wet woods; dripping branches and wet leaves, soaked on the forest floor, I saw that there were others taking advantage of this new-found moisture. Fungi this fall had been hard to find. Such growths need available precipitation, and there was little; until today. Stopping to look more carefully at dead tree branches, I noted wet lichens, but nearby, I also saw some swelling of jelly fungi.

One of many fungi that use dead wood as a substrate, jelly fungi is here in the wood all year, but highly dependent on moisture. It is called jelly fungi due to its texture of growth; feels like jelly, if it is wet; as today. What I found was black jelly fungi coating a small dead branch. This jelly slimy looking material was very much alive and swelled up from its bland and flat dry phase. Also known as black witch's butter (Exidia). (A closely related one is yellow; called yellow witch's butter.) As I looked over the branch, I saw more jelly. This was brown, standing up a bit; it is called leafy jelly fungus (Tremella). This rainy November day proved to be fine for locating some late-season fungi. But conditions were quick to change and with the cold and dryness in subsequent days, the jelly returned to its phase of surviving cold and dry, but I was glad to see the jelly fungi and lichens taking advantage of the chilly rain of November.

December 3, 2022

Winterberry Holly in Swamps

It came on rather quickly. The month of November began warm. Both the first and second days had high temperatures that tied records for those dates. Though the record setting was over, the first week of the month continued to be warmer than normal. And then the weather started to change.

November 9 gave us a day of thick fog. With temperatures in the low 40's, we got some rain; but it was the fog that prevailed. Overnight; shortly after midnight, we received thunder showers that passed over; pausing for a couple of hours and along with the lightning that brought back memories of summer, we also received a few inches of rain. Wind, cooling temperatures and periods of showers that lasted on and off for the whole day; revived the gales of November.

Thanks to the very dry month of October, some of the ponds that I walked by two days ago were dry. But with the influx of rains, they now held water. The weather continued to make news and the next day, as I walked in temperatures in the low 30's I saw ice on ponds and swamps that had none yesterday. Over the next couple of days, every pond that I visited was holding this cold cover. Larger bodies of water, the nearby lakes, followed this coating a few days later.

Not only did these wetlands have an ice cover, but subsequent snows blanketed this too; making it easy to see the ice extent. Within a week, we transitioned from ponds with no water to icy snow-covered ones. With persistent chilly temperatures, this snow cover may be the one that will continue through the coming cold months.

The new arrival of snow changes the landscape greatly. Most of the snow was dry, but with some rising to the 30's, I found a few sites where the fallen snow on tree branches was sagging off and forming phenomena; often called "snow ropes". I also saw that the active local wildlife left their tracks and marks in the new cover. Deer, squirrels, mice and shrews moved about telling tales of usually unseen activities.

Driving by a swamp during the following days as November was waning, I looked out among the plants of this wetland and noted that besides snow-covered alders, willows, ashes and tamaracks there was some red. Stopping for a closer look, I could see that these bright colors were due to numerous small red berries. These were the fruits of a small tree or shrub known as winterberry holly. (Ilex verticiliata)

Though related to the well-known American holly (Ilex opaxa) of the south, often seen during the holidays, this holly does not have evergreen leaves. Plants grew at the edges of swamps in summer, but with the greens of nearby other small trees, they were not likely noticed. Flowers were tiny and also overlooked. The surrounding yellow-golds of tamaracks in late October also kept us from seeing this plant. But now the abundant spherical berries, only about one-fourth inch in diameter, cover branches and stand out in this snowy scene.

Years will vary, but this year, the plants are quite common. We are not the only ones to notice this red-berried plant at the swamps, birds also find and devour the berries. Unlike the Christmas holly, I find that the berries of winterberry holly are usually gone by the holiday. But now, they add a touch of red to the white snowy wetlands; as we enter this solstice month of December.

Dec. 10, 2022

Pileated Woodpecker in Crab Apples

As we reach the second week of December, we enter an interesting time in the cycle of the year. We are at the time of the earliest sunsets. It appears to be still afternoon, not dusk, when the sun sets at 4:20 PM. Sunrises also get later each day. After about ten days of pausing with this early exit time for Sol, by mid-month the sunsets start getting later again.

Sunrises continue to be late until the end of the month. And when we get to the winter solstice on December 21, we are at the shortest period of daylight for the whole year (about eight and a half hours). Some refer to this time as the "dark week".

Along with the lessening amount of sunlight, temperatures are also quite chilly. Short daylight along with cold can make this a tough time for local wildlife that stay active all winter. Food finding can be difficult. We do not usually see what many of the wild mammals do as they search for food; often nocturnal, but we do see what some birds do.

I have noticed that during mild temperatures; especially on clear days, the bird feeders will often remain inactive. Local birds do not use these meals as much as they do in cold and snowy times. This is a little lesson they give us to let us know that they really do not need our handouts. But typically, I have six kinds of birds that choose to dine at the feeders. All of these avians will remain for the duration of the cold season. The regulars are: black-capped chickadee, blue jay, white and red-breasted nuthatches and threes kinds of woodpeckers; downy, hairy and red-bellied. (This last one was not here twenty-some years ago, but now is a regular winter resident.) Often others, such as turkeys, wander in from the surrounding woods. As the season moves on, I expect to see small wintering finches. And there may also be a pileated woodpecker.

When in the forests, woodpeckers use their powerful bills to break into the tree trunks. Here, within the wood, under the bark, they find insects; larvae and adults, that they feed on. When coming to the feeders, they devour suet. While the three smaller kinds of woodpeckers are frequent arrivals, the pileated woodpeckers are sporadic. Mostly, these large woodpeckers; about seventeen inches long, with mostly black feathers, white undersides of the wings and red crests, spend the winter excavating sites on tree trunks for their insect meals. Being as powerful as they are (more of a wood pounder than a wood pecker), they get deep into the wood and often leave large piles of wood chips at the base of trees. But I have noticed now as we move towards winter, they appear to tire from their diet and come to tree fruits as a change of pace. Their arrival at the trees is usually quite loud.

It seem like for the last couple of weeks, each afternoon, I will hear the repeated "wuck…wuck…wuck" calls as these big birds fly into a nearby crab apple tree. Here, they take on some strange acrobatics while hanging onto small stems to grasp and eat the frozen fruits. They appear to have a desire or need of fruit sugar to supplement their insect diet. Such feeding continues until they have completely depleted the crab apples. Then deeper in winter, we may see them at the feeders. But now, I enjoy seeing and hearing their afternoon arrivals and antics in the crab apple tree.

December 17, 2022

The Turkey Feast

As we move deeper into December; we have passed the time of the earliest sunsets of the year (December 7 – 14), and sunsets now will start to slowly get later. Soon we reach the day of shortest daylight; winter solstice, first day of winter. Along with light and dark conditions, we regularly look out on a landscape covered with snow. And subzero readings are a regular part of our days.

Though some northlanders become migrants; spending time in the south, many of us will be here for the duration of winter. We are not alone. A large number of mammals with thick fur coats are able to remain in the region as well. They stay active and even if we do not see them during these weeks, we can read of their activities by seeing tracks in the persistent snow. I have not seen deer, fox, coyote, mice or hare in the yard lately, but tracks tell of their presence; often at night.

Also wintering with us are a variety of birds. Being active in the day time, we are more likely to see the activities of these avians. Often, they come to us. We may enjoy watching chickadees, nuthatches and jays feeding on sunflower seeds on a nearby feeder, while finches go for thistle seeds and woodpeckers dine on suet. But there are other birds that remain here during the cold that do not make use of our feeders. Raptors, such as hawks, eagles, owls and shrikes continue their searches for small bird and mammal meals. The opportunistic crows and ravens seem always to be able to find food despite winter weather conditions. Also present at this time are a couple of gallinaceous (chicken-like) birds; grouse and turkeys. Seeds of several kinds can serve as food for these foraging birds and unless the snow is very deep or hard, or the season is very limited in its productivity, they will survive. And sometimes, they thrive.

I have noted a group of about fifteen wild turkeys that are wintering in the woods near me. Quite often, I find their large-toed tracks in the snow. Occasionally, I'll disturb them in their cold-weather pine tree roosting sites. Usually, they find various seeds in the woods. But there are some cold and snowy days that they join smaller birds at the feeders to gather fallen sunflower seeds on the ground. Recently, as I was going through the woods a couple of days after a new snow, I found much more evidence of their feeding activities.

The snow cover of three to four inches was easy for me to move through and the abundance of turkey tracks and foraging along with deer and squirrels near the trail told of their movements too. Wild turkeys are large and strong enough to dig through the snow cover and the leaves below to find meals. We had a good crop of acorns this fall and now the turkeys locate them. And I found where they had a feast. I went by a south-facing hillside in which the snow and leaves of the forest floor were rummaged in an area of a couple hundred square feet. Obviously, a group of turkeys found conditions were fine for feeding and so they proceeded to leave no leaf unturned in the searching for acorn meals. With this big of an area fed upon, they must have devoured many. The turkeys fed well here. There is much more of winter to go, I hope they will continue to find acorn meals on cold days; and maybe even more feasts.

Dec. 24, 2022

Snow Garland on Deciduous Trees

Now, that we have passed the solstice, we are officially in early winter. Living in the northland, we see plenty of snow for about five months of the year. Though we may have a landscape covered with the cold white (it looks white, snow is actually clear) material, it is not a static situation. The snow that we get during the time from November through April varies much. Temperatures, winds and water content causes variations and though we have a snow coat, it is constantly changing. Not only does the snow fall under different conditions, it changes after it has fallen on the ground. Anyone doing snow removal is aware of the differences in snow under varying temperatures and how long it has stayed on the ground.

I find that having snowfall once or twice a week is a delight; even if we get buried for a few hours. The snow acts as a substrate for holding tracks of critters still active with us. We can go out within a day after new snow has fallen and we can see what the local wildlife has been doing. Whether it is squirrels, rabbits and mice hopping in the yard or deer, foxes and coyotes walking across the road, they leave their marks that tell stories. A few days later, after these new tracks have become old, another snow has covered all of this; allowing for new track news.

Walking each day and looking at the snow cover has become something like reading the local newspaper. There is always something going on. And the snow continues to give more to see.

Recently, we had three snowfalls over a period of about ten days. Each time, I was able to get out within a day and catch up on the news with local wildlife. Squirrels dug into their caches while deer and turkeys rummaged through snow and leaves for acorns. Mice scampered to shelter under logs and coyotes made the rounds in pre-mating time; even leaving some scent markings. And I found where a confused (desperate) muskrat left a swamp and passed through a woods to seek shelter under the ice of a nearby lake.

But besides all of this critter news, the snow gives news of its own. Some of the recent snows fell on calm days. And whether the snow was wet or dry, it stayed on trees; settling on horizontal branches. A dark branch with a light-colored topping is interesting to see, but it does not remain that way. Winds following the snow will often take the snow from the branch or it could stay and change.

Snow goes through a metamorphosis as it lies on the branches. The water content of the snow becomes more apparent and causes the snow to adhere; sticking to the branch. If the temperature rises to about freezing, this sticky snow may sag from the branch; but remains stuck together. The result is a phenomenon that is called snow garland (snow rope or snow snakes). And finding them is a marvel to behold. Though this decorative snow garland can hang from the tree branches reaching a foot long, I usually see just a few inches. It is delicate and wind, bumping or warming can cause it to fall. But being at the right place at the right time, we can see this snow garland. Not quite like the green garland that we might see indoors, but still a great winter sight. It may be here much of the season, but more common in early winter.

December 31, 2022

A Year's End Woods Walk

It's a pleasant winter day for a walk in the woods; chilly, but dry. Traveling in the deep snow is a bit of a challenge, but thanks to the plethora of deer paths, I'm able to negotiate a route. Besides deer, the new snow holds lots of squirrel tracks; grays going over the snow, reds moving over or under. At a couple of sites, I see where white-footed mice (deer mice) have hopped on the surface; leaving tail marks. And a few members of the weasel family have been active as well. Ermine, are small enough to go above or through the snowpack, while their larger cousin, the fisher, jumps right into the deep cover. Snowshoe hare tracks are on a well-used route. Snow and cold has not slowed these white boreal residents. The brown cottontail rabbits remain more in the yard. Other critters are active under the snow in the safety and relative warmth of the sub-nivean space. Here mice, voles and shrews move about. I do not see them; only an occasional opening to the surface (vole holes). Turkeys have been working their way in the forest too. They roost in trees while their gallinaceous cousins, the grouse, take shelter beneath the snow.

Winds are mostly calm and the day is quiet. I hear crows caw and ravens croak as they fly by. An adult bald eagle goes over. A pileated woodpecker calls loudly as it visits a crab apple tree for a meal. Other woodpeckers; hairy, downy and red-bellied, are tapping on bark to get the larvae within to add to their winter diets.

The coniferous trees still hold plenty of the recent record-setting snow. I pass many spruces that are bent from its weight. Not likely to break these branches, once the snow is gone, they will recover. Dozens of horizontal limbs on deciduous trees also have snow piled up and remained for a couple of weeks; often several inches deep. Birches appear to be most laden with now; bent to the ground. At a few locations, I see where snow has sagged from its horizontal site and changed to form "snow rope".

And then I pause in my winter woods walk. I look around at the arboreal snowy landscape and I realize how pleasant is this forested scene. This is mostly the way we want our winter woods to be; cold, deep snow on the ground and trees with tracks and signs that tell of active residents. Enough of each of these makes for a very tranquil setting. What a pleasant day for wandering in the cold season.

I'm reminded of other walks that I have had this year where I was in the midst of seasonal happenings. I remember in May stopping and looking at surrounding spring wild flowers; and being captivated by the sight of sixteen kinds of warblers without moving. There was the June day that I observed a seemingly never-ending flight of newly-emerged dragonflies. And after dark in July, I paused to marvel at the antics of fireflies. An August morning stopped me as I wandered through a dew-covered field filled with dozens of dew-draped spider webs among the goldenrods. On an October day, I happened to be at the right place to be surrounded by peak fall foliage and some late-season mushrooms.

A winter walk in the northland at year's end does not give us these views, but I'm satisfied with what I see in this woods. The Winter Solstice has passed. Soon we will be at Perihelion, the season is moving on. I expect to do more wandering through snowy arboreal scenes.

About the Author

Larry Weber was a science teacher for 40 years, mostly middle school. His classroom was often outdoors. He received the Minnesota Secondary Science Teacher of the Year Award and the National Biology Teacher Association's Middle School Science Teacher of the Year Award. In 2020, he received the Minnesota Association for Environmental Education Lifetime Achievement Award. For more than 20 years, he has had two nature radio programs and has written a weekly column for a Duluth Newspaper.

He is author of more than ten books including: *Minnesota Phenology, Webwood, Butterflies of the North Woods, Spiders of the North Woods, Fascinating Fungi of the North Woods, Teaching Phenology-Based Science, A Guide to Web-Watching, Awesome AutWin, In a Patch of Goldenrods, Backyard Almanac, 365 Days of Northern Nature,* and *Through the Year with Northland Nature.* He has written several articles for the Minnesota Conservation Volunteer. He is a frequent speaker on a variety of phenology topics, especially spiders. He has taught numerous classes for the Minnesota Master Naturalists, Road Scholars, and University for Seniors at UMD. He is also co-founder of the Minnesota Phenology Association. Daily walks on his land keeps Larry in tune with phenology of our northern flora and fauna. There is a new story here every day. Phenology is a never-ending story.